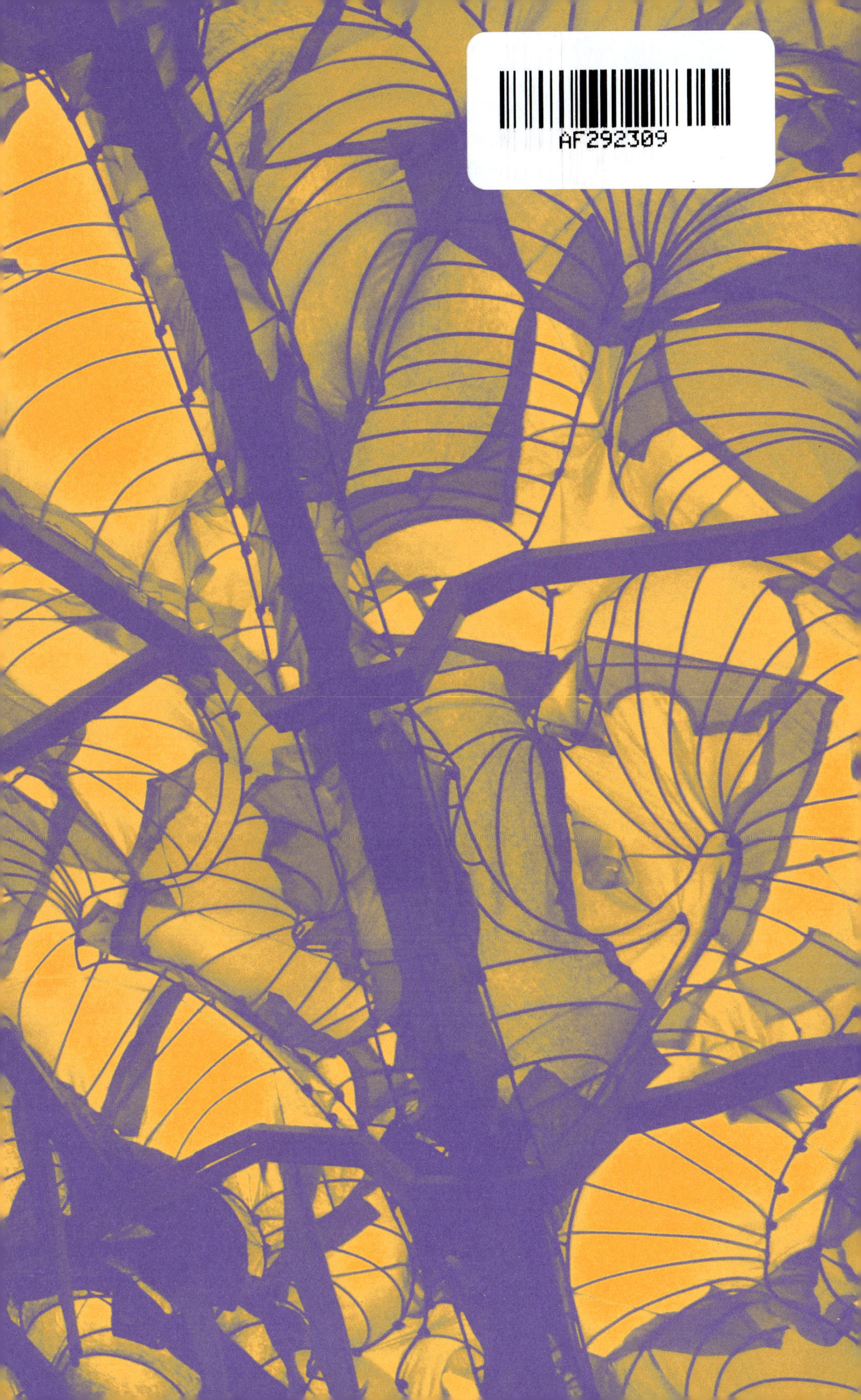

AF292309

YIN

Heart to Heart

XIUZHEN

HAYWARD GALLERY PUBLISHING

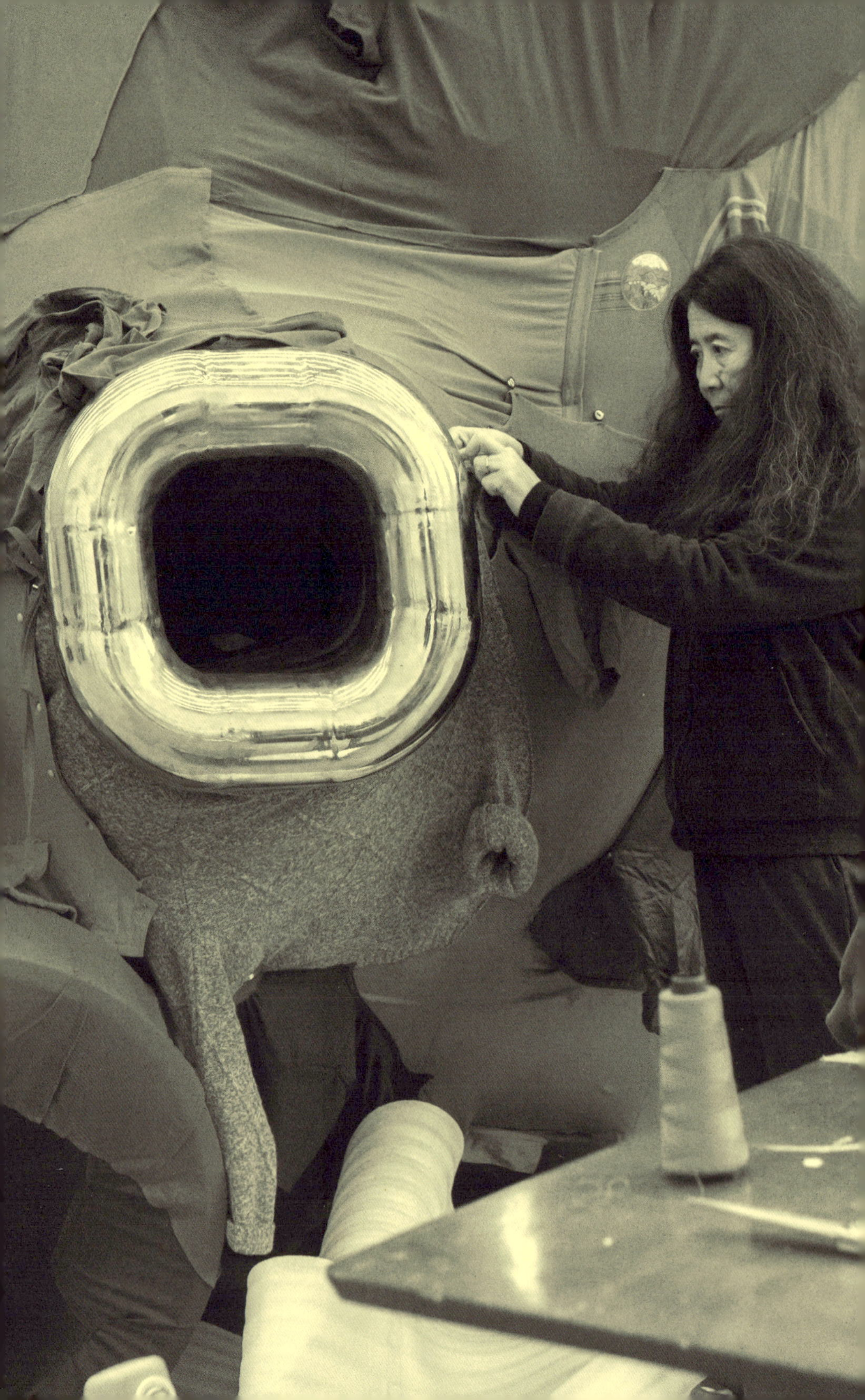

FOREWORD
Ralph Rugoff
4

YIN XIUZHEN:
DEPARTURES
AND ARRIVALS
Lydia Yee
6

THE KEEPER
OF MEMORIES:
INTERVIEW
WITH YIN XIUZHEN
Yung Ma
15

WORKS
33

CHRONOLOGY
130

LIST OF WORKS
136

ACKNOWLEDGEMENTS
141

3

Yin Xiuzhen's art emerges from the intimate spaces of everyday life, yet speaks to the vast transformations reshaping our world. For over three decades she has drawn on the materials of daily existence – worn clothing, discarded suitcases, domestic ephemera – to create works that are at once deeply personal and profoundly social, referencing subjects from environmental degradation to economic migration. Her practice is rooted in a belief that objects carry memory, that the fabrics that touch our bodies and shelter our lives absorb something essential about who we are and where we have been. In an era of accelerated urbanisation and displacement, particularly in her native China, Yin has developed a visual language that honours what is lost even as it conjures far-reaching societal change.

The materiality of Yin's work demands attention. From the unexpected tenderness of miniature cities sewn from second-hand garments to the delicacy of a giant heart-shaped fabric sculpture that you can enter into, her objects and installations possess a deeply engaging and tactile presence. These are not works that maintain a cool distance from their subjects; indeed, to encounter Yin's art is to be reminded that globalisation and modernisation are not abstract forces but lived realities that reshape communities, families and individual lives. As it explores some of the most trenchant questions of our time, her art invites us to reimagine what happens to our sense of belonging in an age of constant motion. How do we preserve memory in the face of its continual erasure? Can art itself become a vessel for collective recollection? In her inventive transformations

of quotidian objects and garments into artworks layered with resonant
cultural and emotional import, Yin powerfully affirms a vision of
art as a means of connecting people as well as sparking fresh ideas.

This book is an overdue exploration of an artist who has been
one of the leading luminaries of Chinese contemporary art for
the past 30 years. Lydia Yee's thoughtful essay on Yin's work provides
crucial insight and contextual perspective, while Hayward Senior
Curator Yung Ma's revealing interview with the artist is truly compre-
hensive. Elegantly designed by In the shade of a tree, this book has
been expertly produced by Hayward Publisher Mary Richards.

Yin Xiuzhen: Heart to Heart was realised with generous support
provided by the Huo Family Foundation. We are also grateful for
key support from Beijing Commune, Eleanor and Francis Shen, and
Max and Monique Burger and the TOY family.

The exhibition reflects the deft curatorial touch of Hayward Senior
Curator Yung Ma, who has been in close dialogue with Yin Xiuzhen
for several years. Assistant Curator Hannah Martin and Curatorial
Assistant Felix Choong played indispensable roles in realising
many aspects of the exhibition with the skilful help from Assistant
Curator Thomas Sutton who carried out important early organisation
and research. Senior Installation Manager Archie Bell planned
and expertly oversaw the installation, whilst Registrar Sophie
Ridsdale-Smith adroitly supervised the transport and conservation
arrangements for the artworks in the exhibition. Finally, we
are all deeply grateful to Yin Xiuzhen for the great amount of thought
and energy she has put into making this exhibition, including the
fabrication of major new commissions.

Finally, it would not have been possible to produce this exhibition without the ongoing support of Arts Council England, and,
as always, the support of Southbank Centre Chief Executive Elaine
Bedell, Artistic Director Mark Ball and Southbank Centre's Board
of Governors is greatly appreciated.

Ralph Rugoff
Director, Hayward Gallery

YIN XIUZHEN:
DEPARTURES AND ARRIVALS

A few years after graduating from Capital Normal University in 1989
with a degree in oil painting, Yin Xiuzhen began taking a camera
on her daily walks in Beijing, snapping a city she had known for
nearly three decades but which was now transforming before her eyes.
Her hometown was undergoing rapid economic and population
growth, accompanied by accelerating urbanisation. Low-rise *siheyuan*
– residential compounds organised around courtyards that had
stood for hundreds of years – were replaced almost overnight,
by piles of rubble; entire neighbourhoods were razed in the name
of modernisation and infrastructure development.

The slow-drying medium of oil paint was ill-suited to capturing
the rapid changes taking place in the urban landscape. By the early
1990s, Yin began to distance herself from the medium, leaving behind
the socialist realist tradition in which she had been trained and
adopting a more conceptual approach before abandoning oil painting
altogether. Photography – an indexical and diaristic medium –
offered a counterpoint to realist painting for Yin and other artists
of her generation, including Song Dong, whom she met at art
school and married in 1992.

For these artists, the camera, whether still or video, became
a particularly valuable tool for directly recording the rituals of
daily life. Marking a decisive break from the limits of socialist realism,
Wang Zhiping, who co-organised the 1979 April Photo Society
exhibition *Nature, Society and Man* in Beijing, redefined the role
of photography after the end of the Cultural Revolution: 'The beauty

6

of photography lies not necessarily in "important subject matter"
or in official ideology, but should be found in nature's rhythms,
in social reality, and in emotions and ideas.'[1]

While observing Beijing's shifting urban fabric, Yin photographed the doors and gates that she had routinely passed by
or through during the three decades she had lived in Beijing. Each
passageway was shot from the exterior and the interior. For her
work *The Doors* (1995, p. 11), she selected 36 pairs of images, ranging
from the grand ceremonial Tiananmen Gate of Heaven's Peace
– representing imperial power and central authority, and dominated
by a monumental portrait of Mao Zedong painted by Ge Xiaoguang
(who coincidentally had graduated from Yin's alma mater) –
to the entrances of modest homes, shops and even the local bus.
Yin printed and mounted each pair on both sides of 36 rectangular
blocks of wood, roughly the size of a passport, which she fixed
perpendicularly to the wall.

The small scale and repetition of these photographs underscored
the daily rhythms of urban life. As Yin explained: 'I've been walking
through doors into different spaces, including my home, my friends'
homes, or other places we are familiar with. Doors are everywhere
in our life. They either join in or separate our life.'[2] Beyond their
practical function as providing privacy, protection and boundaries,
doors in China are potent symbols of family status as well as of
spiritual passage. The entrances to imperial tombs were designed
to both ward away evil and serve as a portal to heaven, while in the
domestic practice of feng shui, a door must be strong and properly
aligned in order to bring energy, peace and prosperity into a home.
By presenting all the doors and gates she photographed at the same
scale, Yin levels the traditional hierarchy between the grandeur
of imperial gates and the entrance to the humble apartment block.

During this period, Yin also rescued objects from the rubble
of Beijing's old low-rise neighbourhoods, assembling them into the
large-scale installation *Ruined City* (1996, pp. 65–69), also known
as *Ruined Capital*. Domestic furnishings and the grey clay roof tiles
typical of the city's courtyard houses were covered with piles of dry
cement powder for the work, initially shown at Yin's solo exhibition
at Capital Normal University and later in several venues of the
international touring exhibition *Cities on the Move*, curated by Hou
Hanru and Hans Ulrich Obrist.[3]

When *Cities on the Move* arrived at the Hayward Gallery in
London in May 1999, *Ruined City* was replaced by the more modestly
scaled *The Doors*. The Hayward presentation was subtitled *Urban
Chaos and Global Change – East Asian Art, Architecture and Film Now*,
highlighting the rapid economic, urban and cultural development
transforming East Asian cities, and the contradictions that arose
from such accelerated change. It was the largest and loudest works
– mostly installations, sculptures and videos – that dominated
both the physical space in the Hayward's galleries and the critical

discourse surrounding the exhibition: as critic Adrian Searle observed,
'Like real cities, the exhibition is all about expansion and congestion,
chaos, speed and inertia, big plans and small, incidental, fragile
attempts to humanise the alienating psycho-geography of the modern
city.'[4] Quieter and more subtle, Yin's *The Doors* was assimilated into
the exhibition design and went largely unremarked in the press – yet,
in many ways, this work more accurately reflected the lived reality
of the region at a time when many countries were still recovering from
the 1997 Asian financial crisis.

A pivotal and metaphorically rich work, *The Doors* opens in two
directions – one outward, addressing broader social and environmental
concerns, and the other inward, reflecting on intimate personal
experiences – that Yin has continued to explore throughout her oeuvre.
The outward path is exemplified by *Washing River* (1995, pp. 56–57),
an important early project she made in Chengdu, Sichuan Province.
Yin had been invited by the American ecofeminist activist and artist
Betsy Damon to participate in *Keepers of the Waters*, a series of temporary public artworks and performances along the polluted Fu and
Nan Rivers. For this project, Yin removed ten cubic metres of industri-
ally contaminated river water and had it frozen into blocks of ice
at a factory. These murky slabs, yellow and brown in appearance, were
stacked to form a large plinth-like structure on the riverbank.
Over two days, Yin invited passersby to scrub the dirty ice with brushes
and buckets of clean water, symbolically cleansing the river, until
the ice melted away and returned to the waterway. Although Yin had
previously created other temporary outdoor works, documented
in photographs – among them *Silenced Voice* (1994), *The Tree of Parting*
(1994) and *Tree Harp* (1995, p. 11), in which she fastened hemp
ropes to trees, modifying them temporarily through quiet, poetic
gestures – these works, which share affinities with American and British
land art of the 1960s and '70s as well as the Chinese 'Apartment Art'
movement of the 1980s and '90s, were made primarily for a small circle
of artist friends.[5] Significantly, in *Washing River* Yin directly engaged
the broader public in dialogue about ecological concerns, making
it one of the earliest environmentally conscious artworks in China.

Yin was subsequently invited to participate in a follow-up
to *Keepers of the Waters*, this time along the Lhasa River in Tibet.
For this new work, *Living Water* (1996, pp. 58–59), Yin filled dozens
of plastic bags with river water and propped them casually on
chopsticks, evoking a sense of ecological fragility and human impact.
A photograph capturing the ephemeral installation shows transpar-
ent sacs of water that appear to hover along the riverbank, mirroring
the clouds overhead and blending with their billowing reflections
in the water. 'Tibet was always a "pure land" in my mind,' Yin recalls,
'but when I got there, I discovered they were also facing the issue
of pollution, and so environmental issues came to seem all the more
pressing.'[6] While in Lhasa, Yin also created *Shoes with Butter* (1996,
pp. 60–63), filling dozens of shoes donated by local residents with yak

butter and inserting wicks before placing them in and around
a shallow stream. In Tibet, yak butter serves many purposes:
as a cooking fat, for making creamy butter tea, as a modelling material
for monastery sculptures and in butter lamps used for Buddhist
rituals. In a place revered for its traditional culture, Yin was struck
by the ubiquity of mass-produced footwear identical to that
worn in mainland China, whose government policies have threatened
Tibetan culture with assimilation for decades. For Yin, shoes are
akin to boats – vessels that carry their wearers through the journey
of life. By lighting the wicks at night, Yin transformed the shoes
into glowing lanterns, honouring ancestors and symbolically guiding
the spirits of the deceased through the afterlife.

Back in Beijing, Yin turned her attention once again to her
immediate surroundings. *Beijing Opera* (2001, pp. 70–75) – a
multimedia installation combining large photographic prints, sound
recordings and a group of small stools – captures the informal
interactions of elderly residents who gather in the scenic area around
Houhai lake where they sing, listen to songbirds, make music, play
cards, exercise, and drink tea in the open air. These activities stand
in contrast to the highly codified world of formal Beijing opera,
where meaning is conveyed through elaborate costumes, makeup,
gestures and symbolic movement rooted in historical narratives.
Yet, through Yin's photographic and sound recordings, these daily
rituals of the elderly reveal their own form of choreography –
social, intimate and deeply attuned to the rhythms of communal life.
Visitors to the installation are invited to sit, look and listen,
becoming participants in this quiet act of observation and reflection.

As China's economy grew throughout the 1990s, the narrow
hutongs of old Beijing gave way to skyscrapers and multi-storey
apartment blocks, the human-scale grid of its alleyways was replaced
by a web of wide multi-lane roads, encircling and radiating outwards
from the city centre. This process of expansion was a source of
both imagery and materials, including discarded furnishing and
architectural remnants from the old houses, for artists such as
Yin, whose work continued engaging with the urban public. At the
same time, she began to look inward, reflecting more deeply on
memory and personal history. In preparation for her first solo exhibition, held in Beijing at the Central Academy of Fine Arts' affiliated
High School of Fine Art (also known as Beijing Contemporary
Art Museum) in 1995, Yin carried out a private ritual in an empty
classroom at the Beijing No. 41 Middle School. Filmed by
Song who taught at the school, the work marked a deeply personal
shift in her practice. Beginning with a pile of her clothing –
garments that had been worn, altered and repaired many times
– she carefully folded and stitched them together. She then placed
the garments into an old wooden trunk made by her father, poured
wet cement over them, and allowed it to harden, entombing her
past. For Yin, 'clothes are like a second skin; they have their own

expressive language and are connected with their times and therefore with history'.[7]

This piece gave rise to two related works: *Dress Box* (1995, p. 95) and *My Clothes* (1995, pp. 96–97). In *Dress Box*, Yin affixed to the inside of the trunk's lid a small metal plaque inscribed in Chinese with the following epitaph: 'The clothes sealed in cement inside this dress box are those I wore over thirty years, bearing my experiences, your memories, and the imprints of time.' The trunk is accompanied by a 20-minute video. *My Clothes* is a photographic record of the 32 garments enclosed within the box. While it seems hard to imagine that this represents the totality of Yin's wardrobe from birth to adulthood, it should be remembered that her childhood coincided with the economic hardship and social upheaval of the Cultural Revolution, when fabric was scarce, and her mother had to save ration coupons and money throughout the year to buy enough material to make each child one new garment annually. Continually mended, altered and passed down, each piece of clothing embodied a history of labour and care. With *Dress Box* and *My Clothes*, Yin metaphorically sheds her old skin, closing one chapter of her life while embarking on a new artistic and personal phase.

If Yin's early works followed two distinct paths – one focused outwardly, on public and environmental concerns, the other inwardly, on memory and identity – after the year 2000 these paths began to converge. *Collective Subconscious (Blue)* (2007, pp. 52–55) is emblematic of this synthesis. First exhibited in her 2007 solo show at Beijing Commune, the large-scale installation takes the form of a small van, affectionately known in China as a *miàn bāo chē*, *xiǎo miàn* or *miàn di* (little bread loaf van). Introduced in the 1980s as an affordable commercial vehicle when there were few private cars in China, these vans were commonly used as shared taxis or to transport goods. By extending the mid-section of a Hafei Songhuajiang vehicle by means of a structure made from wheels, steel and a patchwork of clothing collected from family and friends and arranged in long coloured strips resembling the segments of a caterpillar or an articulated bus, Yin transforms the bread van from a boxy little loaf into an elongated baguette. Visitors are invited to climb aboard, sit on small stools, chat with fellow passengers, and listen to the popular rock ballad 'Beijing Beijing' by Wang Feng, which laments the city's hardships and disappointments. Together, the van, the clothing and the music form a collective portrait of a generation navigating the emotional and physical transformations of the capital.

While the bread van symbolised a quintessential form of urban transport in the China of the late 1980s and early '90s, the following decades brought new modes of mobility. Private car ownership and long-distance air travel became increasingly accessible, and these experiences soon entered Yin's work. After taking her first flight (to Chengdu in 1995), she began to travel more widely within Asia

Tree Harp
1995

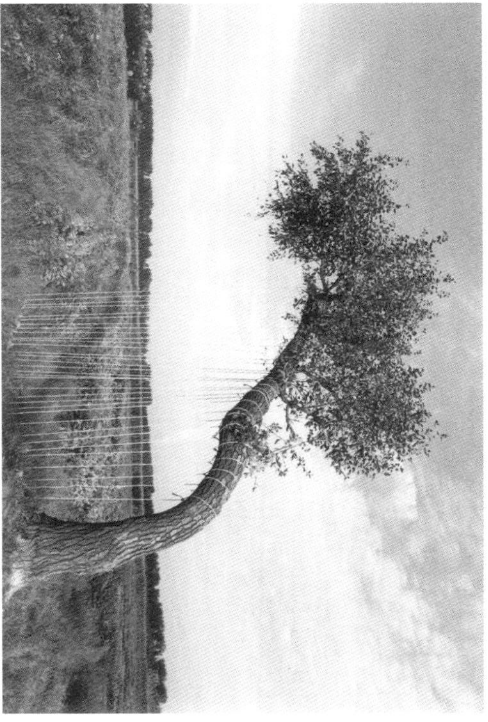

The Doors
1995 (detail)

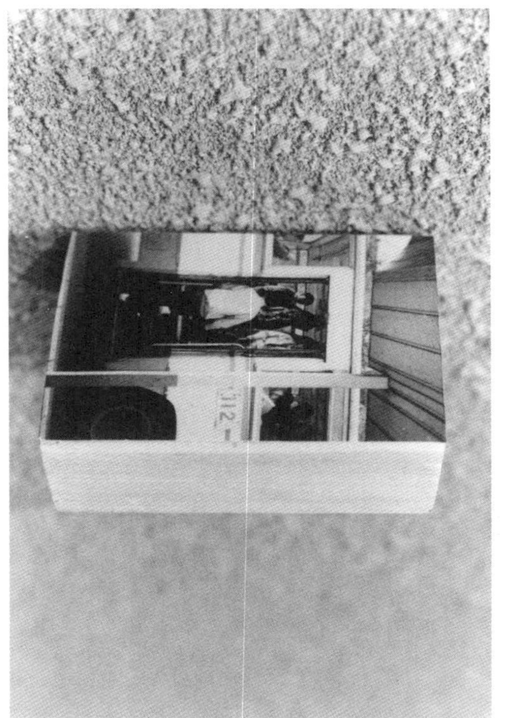

The Doors
1995

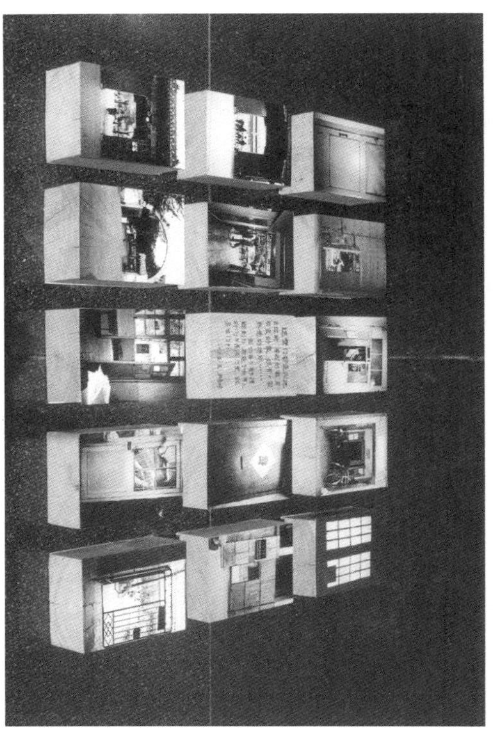

as well as to Europe and the United States, leading to works such
as *International Airline* (2002, pp. 50–51) and her ongoing series
Portable City (2001–, pp. 32–47). The latter drew inspiration from her
Dress Box and from Yin's habit of watching luggage circulate on
airport conveyor belts and imagining the hidden contents of each
suitcase. 'A suitcase is like a home', Yin explains. 'You carry your
home with you when you travel.'[8] Each *Portable City* comprises
a suitcase that opens to reveal a miniature pop-up cityscape made
from used clothing donated by local residents, accompanied by
a sound recording from the featured city. Some cities are represented
by distinctive landmarks, the works resembling souvenirs travellers
might bring home as mementos: created two years after the September
11 attacks, *Portable City: New York* (2003, pp. 44–45) features a golden
Empire State Building at one end and ghostly twin towers at the
other. In contrast, the first work in the series, *Portable City: Beijing*
(2001, p. 14), is more abstract and conceptual, reflecting Yin's
intimate familiarity with her hometown. Instead of iconic structures
such as the Forbidden City, Temple of Heaven, CCTV Headquarters
or the Bird's Nest Stadium, Yin depicts Beijing through its defining
infrastructure: the ring road. Generic buildings line the perimeter
of the suitcase, encircling an empty central space. Viewed through
a magnifying glass, a hidden map of the vanished old city appears
beneath. Made for her Hayward exhibition, *Portable City: London*
(2025, pp. 38–39) is pieced together from articles of clothing collected
from Southbank Centre staff, including men's shirts, sportswear
and even employee uniforms. Yin approaches London like a tourist,
fashioning a collection of the city's landmarks in miniature.
She arranges Big Ben, the Houses of Parliament, BT Tower, St Paul's
and the Gherkin along one side of an imaginary Thames with
the Shard, Tate Modern, the London Eye and Hayward Gallery
on the other. Low rise buildings fill out the dense cityscape packed
within a grey suitcase.

For her installation at the Hayward, Yin is displaying the
Portable City series as an airport-inspired environment, complete with
a luggage carousel and trolleys. The Brutalist architecture of
the Southbank Centre, which evokes the aesthetic of a 1960s airport,
makes it a fitting setting for such a project. Suspended overhead,
International Airline, a seven-metre soft sculpture of a commercial
airplane made from used clothing wrapped around a steel armature,
appears to take off or land within the gallery space.

In Yin's world, used clothing serves a vital, protective function.
As she explains her fascination:

> Why do people abandon their old clothes? And why am
> I so interested in them? Because they bear special traces of
> people's lived experiences … I've gathered together such
> 'experiences' from numerous people in many countries, includ-
> ing my family, friends and strangers, forming a new 'collective'

with a hidden subconscious. Experiences can't be duplicated.
What I've done is to 'stitch' these fragmentary experiences
together so they can start a new life.[9]

Clothing can be discarded, shed like skin, or it can reconstituted into
new forms, standing in for both the rigid aluminium alloy of an
aircraft's fuselage and the thin membranes protecting the body's
organs. This metaphor is extended in other sculptures such as
Thought (2009, pp. 120–23), a bright blue fabric work shaped like
a human brain, and culminates in *A Heart to Heart* (2025, pp. 124–28),
the centrepiece of her eponymous exhibition. The new sculpture
is assembled from used clothing in shades of red, purple, pink
and orange, stretched over a metal frame to form the chambers
of a heart, which visitors can enter. Yin's title contains a significant
play on words: as linguist Ning Yu explains, 'In traditional
Chinese culture, the heart is believed to be the home of the inner self,
the residence of personal disposition, the abode of moral character,
the center of thought, the seat of emotions, and so forth. The
heart is, therefore, the organ holding or possessing all these cognitive
and affective faculties.'[10] The Chinese concept of *xin* (heart)
thus encompasses both heart and mind – emotion and intellect –
in contrast to the Western heart-mind dichotomy. Yin's *A Heart
to Heart* synthesises these ideas, bringing together themes of
body, emotion, memory and home.

Although Yin has travelled extensively over the past three
decades, she always returns to Beijing, where her practice remains
deeply rooted in her home and studio, which she shares with her
husband, artist Song Dong. While each works independently, they also
collaborate on the long-running project *The Way of Chopsticks* (2003–),
in which they each create a chopstick sculpture according to agreed
parameters but without discussing their plans beforehand. The
two halves are combined into a single work. In truth, their dialogue
and collaboration stretch back to the early 1990s, since when they
have been sharing ideas, offering feedback and assisting one another
in making, installing and documenting their works. The couple's
conversations – about art, family, water, food, doors and cities –
embody the spirit of the title *A Heart to Heart*: a lifelong exchange
of ideas, emotions and mutual respect and understanding.

1   Wang Zhiping quoted in Wu Hung, 'Between Past and Future: A Brief History of Contemporary Chinese Photography', in Wu Hung and Christopher Phillips, *Between Past and Future: New Photography and Video from China*, exh. cat., Smart Museum of Art, Chicago, 2004, p. 16

2   Quoted in Jingjing Lu and Xiyuan Zhang (eds.), *Yin Xiuzhen* (Hong Kong: Blue Kingfisher, 2012), p. 22

3   *Cities on the Move* originated at the Secession in Vienna and toured to Musée d'Art Contemporain de Bordeaux; P.S.1 Contemporary Arts Center, New York; Louisiana Museum of Modern Art, Humlebaek, Denmark; Hayward Gallery, London; Rama IX Art Museum, Bangkok; Kiasma Museum of Contemporary Art, Helsinki

4   Adrian Searle, 'Take a left at Hong Kong, a right at Kuala Lumpur and there you are… London', *Guardian*, 18 May 1999, https://www.theguardian.com/culture/1999/may/18/artsfeatures5 (accessed 10 November 2025)

5   Yin and Song are associated with 'Apartment Art', a term coined by Gao Minglu to describe the practice of artists presenting their work in private spaces for their peers in response to both the repressive bureaucracies of official art institutions and the burgeoning commercial art market. See Gao Minglu (ed.), *Inside Out: New Chinese Art* (Berkeley, Los Angeles, and London: University of California Press, 1998)

6   'Hou Hanru in Conversation with Yin Xiuzhen', in *Yin Xiuzhen* (London: Phaidon Press, 2015), p. 19

7   Yin Xiuzhen, 'Guanyu yifu' (About Clothes), unpublished manuscript, quoted in 'Yin Xiuzhen: Dress Box', *M+ Magazine* (30 November 2021), https://www.mplus.org.hk/en/magazine/yin-xiuzhen-dress-box (accessed 10 November 2025)

8   'Yin Xiuzhen, 'Artist's Writings: Portable Cities, 2009', in *Yin Xiuzhen* (London: Phaidon, 2015), p. 134

9   Yin Xiuzhen, 'Artist's Writings: About Clothes, 2000–02', in *Yin Xiuzhen* (London: Phaidon, 2015), p. 126

10 Ning Yu, *The Chinese Heart in a Cognitive Perspective: Culture, Body, and Language* (Berlin: De Gruyter Mouton, 2009), p. 275

14

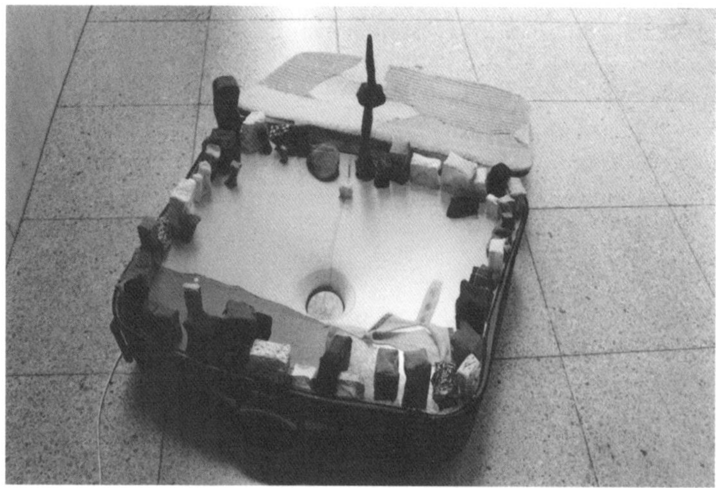

Portable City: Beijing, 2001

YUNG MA
WITH CONTRIBUTIONS BY SONG DONG

THE KEEPER
OF MEMORIES:
INTERVIEW
WITH YIN XIUZHEN

15

YUNG MA   *I wonder if you could start by talking a bit about your
artistic journey.*

YIN XIUZHEN When I first started studying at what was then
Beijing Normal Academy (now Capital Normal University) in 1985,
I learned oil painting. At that time, China wasn't very open yet, and
because my teacher had studied in the Soviet Union we were learning
the Soviet style. Realism – socialist realism. As young people we
always wanted to do something innovative, and so, after painting a bit,
we started to go off in different directions.

That's where [my partner] Song Dong and I met – we were
in the same class from the beginning. Contemporary art in China
was just beginning to emerge, and there were hardly any exhibitions.
Back then, if we heard of one, we'd rush to see it – but it was
all underground.

YM   *Did you know at the time about things like the '85
New Wave movement?*

YX   Yes. We had *China Art News*, which covered topics on the
arts. There were publications like *Art Trends*, too, which was pretty
active at that time. It wasn't like now, where the internet provides
so much information. But we knew there was a previous generation
of artists born in the 1950s, such as Wang Luyan, who was in the
Stars Art Group.

YM   *I know that you saw the Robert Rauschenberg exhibition at
the National Art Gallery, Beijing in 1985. That show had a huge
impact on many Chinese artists at that time.*

YX   Yes, that was especially huge. The impact and shock
on everyone was enormous.

YM   *What impact did it have on you personally?*

YX   The impact was like, 'Is this really art?' It was exhibited
in a museum, so we knew it had to be art, but we didn't understand
why it was done this way. Still, it felt really interesting, and we
returned to university restless and wanting to do something ourselves.
Our teacher said: 'If you guys do this, I can't teach you anymore.'
But he didn't oppose it, or tell us we had to follow his lessons strictly.
After class, you could learn however you wanted. So we were quite
free, and that's how our generation started.
    Also during that time, our department imported some foreign
art catalogues. The library became our window to understand
people like Cézanne, Picasso – nothing very contemporary. Still,
as we looked, we felt we had to change ourselves.
    Later, there was the China National Publications Import
& Export Corporation (CNPIEC), and we would go there to look
at art catalogues from abroad. The Goethe-Institut in Beijing
also influenced us – from there we could borrow videos of exhibitions
like the Venice Biennale, Documenta, and others.

YM   *The Goethe-Institut was really interesting. Because in many
countries – not only China, but also Vietnam, Myanmar –
it actually played an important role in the local art scene.*

YX   Definitely. They were very important to us in that period.

SONG DONG   I definitely learned about Nam June Paik from
the Goethe-Institut. Before that, China had already translated
some Western modern art history books, but they translated Paik's
name as '纳姆准派克' (Nàmǔ Zhǔn Pàikè). I thought, 'How
could this person be Asian?' Later, at the Goethe-Institut, there was
more detailed information. That's how I learned about the Fluxus
movement.

YM   *But back then it was still mainly painting you were both doing.*

YX   During school, I was still mainly painting. [To Song Dong]
Did you try other things?

SD   Yes, I tried other things. Capital Normal University was relatively conservative. In my first year, we had to paint plaster casts or ancient Roman or Greek statues. I wasn't satisfied with that. I wanted to create.

YX   Capital Normal University trained teachers, so we became teachers. After graduating, I went to teach at the secondary school affiliated with the Central Academy of Arts and Design. At first, I thought it was pretty boring because the courses were very basic. The school didn't have much information, but since I knew a bit, I brought in some films and even invited Song Dong to our school to help, giving talks and showing slides to students, explaining what installation art and performance art were. Later, the school confronted me and said: 'This course is for exam preparation. You can't give them these things.'

SD   Oh no, teaching ideas outside the school system, you can't have that.

YX   Later, when I started having some overseas exhibitions, I asked for leave. My supervisor said: 'If you want to be a good teacher, stop being an artist.' I thought about it and said, 'I'll be an artist', and resigned. That was in 1998 and I graduated in 1989, so I'd been teaching for about ten years.

YM   *During the 1980s, China was undergoing great changes. The reform and opening-up policy had been implemented by the government in the late '70s, and the atmosphere in the country at that time was also somewhat more open, especially economically. Where do you think the influence of that openness showed up for you?*

YX   At the very beginning, the outside world had a huge influence on both Song and me. People returning from abroad would bring some new information with them. In terms of openness and control, I felt that the tighter the restrictions, the more you wanted to break free and do those things they told you not to do. Was it the 1989 exhibition where Xiao Lu fired a gun into her own artwork?

YM   *Yes, the big '89 China/Avant Garde Exhibition.*

YX   After that, things got tighter. There were more restrictions on everyone.

YM   *With economic reform and opening-up, interactions with foreign
      countries increased. Things didn't move so quickly for artists,
      but by the '90s there were opportunities to go abroad for exhibi-
      tions. Can you talk a little about those opportunities, and the
      influence of transportation and tools?*

YX   Our first exhibitions after the opening up were in Korea
and Japan in 1996, '97. I started going abroad then, and more
opportunities came along. Every time I went overseas, it really
broadened my horizons. Some of my works were even created during
my travels. So I do think transportation – planes, trucks, whatever
– can really change people. You could even say that transportation
is actually a tool of communication. For example, the idea for
Portable City (pp. 32–47) first came to me while I was waiting for my
luggage at Melbourne airport in 2000. I thought it was really
interesting to watch the conveyor belt with suitcase after suitcase
going by, because sometimes the wait is long, and you start to
wonder, 'What's inside that suitcase?' Each suitcase belongs to one
person, holding their personal items. Different countries, different
people. On their short journey, they might have packed their
most important and needed things. So after initially working on
suitcase pieces, *Portable City* emerged. And so transportation
came into my work through travel.

18

YM   *I wonder if you had already been thinking about it even earlier.
      There's an early unrealised piece you made at university –
      the work combining two bicycles together, combining two families
      – that makes me think you had been considering this idea
      about transportation quite early on.*

YX   Remember, when we first started, we didn't have any
concept of what installation art was, or performance art. We were
just doing things beyond painting, and the concepts came later.
      There's a sketch of that work you're talking about, which
I drew in the 1980s or '90s, though I don't know where it is
now. Back then, Song and I both rode bicycles. Mine was smaller,
with a 20-inch wheel, and Song's was bigger, with a 28-inch
wheel, so although we rode together, we weren't in sync. Then we
wondered if we could modify our bicycles and combine two into
one – so we combined our bikes together and designed a canopy
to go around it, because we thought it would be good to have
protection from wind and rain, as well as some privacy. From the
outside, it looked like one single vehicle, but inside, there were
two people pedalling away.
      We kept wanting to find a way to weld it, but it cost a lot of
money, so the project was never realised. When we talk about it now,
we still think it's really interesting and fun.

YM   *Let me briefly mention that back then, most people in China only had bicycles, not cars.*

YX   The first privately owned car in China – before that, all cars were state-owned – was the Santana sedan from Shanghai, which came out in the '80s. That type of car also appeared in my artwork – the white one you saw as part of *Piercing the Sky* at Shanghai's Power Station of Art last year. That was a high-end one. Later there was the bread van, also a private car, which later became what we called *miàn di* vans.

SD   Yin has a piece where the van is sawed open – that was the bread van. It was very popular with Chinese families, because it could carry both goods and people – it did everything.

YM   *Bread vans came a bit later, in the 1990s?*

SD   Yes. In the 1990s, we never took taxis – we were very poor and they were too expensive. The Xiali was the most expensive taxi, but even a bread van taxi cost ten yuan minimum. That was the *miàn di* taxi – a play on words, combining the Hong Kong word for taxi, *di shi* (taxi) with *miàn bāo chē*, meaning bread van, so it became *miàn di*.

YX   It also looked like a small loaf of bread! People said the *miàn di* could carry more passengers, so I made a piece called *Collective Subconscious (Blue)* (see pp. 52–55) where I cut it and stretched it out.

YM   *Can you talk about why you wanted to use the bread van? For me, it's a vehicle that represents an important phase of China's economic development.*

YX   Back then, everyone dreamed of owning a car. The first car many families bought was a bread van – it was Song's family's first car, and it belonged to his sister. She originally had a minivan, but it got stolen, so she bought another car. Then, months later, the original van was found and brought back from somewhere far away. But by then it was messed up – I think the engine had sand poured into it.

SD   Funnily enough, the man who ended up buying this stolen minivan was the head of the traffic police squad in Hebei. He bought it and drove it himself. Later, when the case was solved and the thief was charged, and the police captain found out it was a stolen vehicle, he was so angry that when he returned the car, he filled the gas tank with sand. Later, I wanted to make this into an artwork.

YX   That bread van ended up having a lot of stories of its own,
but the minivan was the first car we ever owned. So later, when I
made *Collective Subconscious*, I found it really interesting – putting
people's dreams, the dream of an entire era, onto that car. We cut
it open and connected the two halves with clothing from around
400 people. Inside, we placed some small stools so people could sit
down, and we played music. At the time, Wang Feng's song 'Beijing
Beijing' was number one in the charts, so we used that. I didn't
want it to be a song I personally chose. It had to be everyone's choice
– something from the collective subconscious.

YM   *It's interesting you describe that as subconscious. The
subconsciousness, in my view, means something that is not only
unexpressed, but also an involuntary choice. It's a potential
possibility, and with the collective aspect added, everyone
is influenced by this.*

YX   Many people's subconscious dreams are presented in that
work. When the audience goes in, you actually become part of it.
Or rather, it's hard for you to be completely outside of it.
    Interestingly, another characteristic of that era is that everyone
had ideals and hopes and dreams, and they thought that if you
worked a little, you could get something back. Even though the tools
you had were poor, and your starting point was low, you always
wanted a better life, wanting to move forward, keep moving forward
– that's the feeling. For example, everyone was trading stocks,
feeling like if you just traded, you'd win and make money. It was
a very lively, passionate era, full of confidence. That's why we
have a Chinese saying 'A little horse pulls a big cart', because the
whole progress of China is like a huge train or a giant ship.

SD   Nowadays, many people are just 'lying flat' – giving up.

YM   *If we look a bit further back in the '90s, you did a lot of perfor-
mance-like works, or something quite close to land art –
'outdoor things'.* Washing River *(pp. 56–57), in particular, relates
to pollution, and you made it in the '90s when not many
people talked about that. Why did you head in that direction?*

YX   When we first started, there wasn't any space to exhibit art
– no museums or galleries – and not much money, either. But we
wanted to create, and we had just enough money for some materials,
so we decided to find a place outdoors to work. A few of us would
agree to go to a park or out of town, where we'd make something.
For example, *Tree Harp* (1995, p. 11) was made and left there, and
The Tree of Parting (1994) was also done outdoors. Friends would
come to see it, and that was it. After finishing, we'd just leave it there

and go home. The artwork stayed there, on the land, living and dying
on its own.

> YM   *So those works weren't really for exhibitions. They were completely
> spontaneous, casual and informal?*

YX   That's right. It felt very fulfilling and interesting. We never
thought about selling the work – we really didn't think one day our
works *could* be sold – so there wasn't a strong desire or plan to create
something for sale.

> YM   *But* Washing River *was different? It was a part of an arts
> festival.*

YX   *Washing River* was in 1995. An American ecofeminist artist
named Betsy Damon came to China to do something related to
environmental protection, at the Funan river in Chengdu. It became
the *Keepers of the Waters Initiative*. She communicated with the local
government to make this happen. So she invited artists from different
Chinese cities – mainly Beijing and Chengdu – as well as other
countries, maybe Denmark or Sweden, but not many, it was mostly
artists from Beijing and Chengdu. [Artist] Wang Peng and I went
in 1995.

Damon was interested in environmental protection, especially
river water. The Jin River (Fu and Nan Rivers) used to be very
clean in ancient times – clean enough for silk to be washed in it. Later
it became a heavily polluted river, where many people went to
the bathroom, so it was dirty and messy and smelled bad in summer.
Damon wanted to transform it into a living water park, but before
that, she invited some artists to make work with the river water.

At that time, I didn't know what performance art was. My idea
was to collect river water, turn the liquid into solid, and have everyone help clean the whole process. The team and I transported
the river water to an ice rink, a freezing factory, and turned it into ice
blocks, which were then placed on the riverbank. Many participants
in this work were passers-by, and we talked with them.

I actually made three works at the time, but this was the one
that became more publicised later and most people know. Now
the video of it is at Hong Kong's Asia Art Archive. I barely recognise
myself in it when I see it now!

> YM   *You said you didn't know what performance art was back then.
> How did you have the courage to do it? In Chinese contemporary
> art, this was still pretty rare – not just a performance, but
> a collective one, since you invited local residents to participate.
> That was uncommon at the time, right?*

YX   Very rare. It's not like I knew what it was, researched its
history, then planned it out. Sometimes, you start doing something
before you really know what it is. Even though I had no concrete
ideas or plans, I just wanted to do it.

YM   *A very intuitive reaction.*

YX   Yes, very intuitive. Including art movements – many artists
just create, and only later does a theory or label emerge, like
Impressionism or whatever. It's not like a theorist comes first and
then artists practice it. Later, when I did a performance, other
people called it performance art – that's when I realised that many
things are defined after the fact.

In the '90s, performance art was considered a new thing in
China – and you couldn't make money from it – there was nothing
but passion and love for it. Back then I was just feeling my way,
taking it step by step.

That was my first time on a plane, flying to Chengdu, and
once the plane took off, I immediately regretted it – it was scarier
than riding a train. But that trip was very special for me. Flying
became a big thing in my life, and I have many thoughts about planes.

YM   *Things developed, and, by the late '90s and early 2000s,
      works like* Portable City *– as you mentioned – felt more
      professional, right?*

YX   By then I had seen more varied artworks in person, and
had begun engaging more with the outside world. In 1999, I went
to Germany for a year, to a foundation in Bad Ems, near Koblenz.
That year changed me a lot. The foundation didn't ask for much
– just two exhibitions, one in June and one in December – and the
rest of the time, they left me alone. But they gave me a monthly
stipend. The amount for one month was equal to my entire annual
salary back then.

Bad Ems was the reason I had to be brave and quit my teaching
job in China. This was when the school had started to push back
on my requests for time off for exhibitions. When I resigned, the
school was astonished. The principal asked me, 'What will you do?'
I said: 'I don't know – but I know I have to quit.' So I went
to Germany.

There was an amazing library there, and I went every day,
even though I didn't understand the language well. That year, I really
learned a lot. On weekends, I would travel to Berlin or Frankfurt
to see exhibitions. I really became more and more open.

YM   *And you had already started using clothing in your work
      by that time?*

YX   Yes, I used clothing in my first solo exhibition, in 1995, the same year as *Washing River*.

YM   *Where did that first solo exhibition take place?*

YX   In an art museum that's gone now. In the high school affiliated with the Academy of Fine Arts, there used to be a small space called the Contemporary Art Museum. That was where I showed *The Doors* (p. 11), *Dress Box* (p. 95) and a sweater piece, *Yarn*, where I unravelled a bunch of sweaters and re-knitted them.

In China, people of my generation needed ration coupons to buy fabric. When we were kids, we couldn't wear new clothes. Only during Lunar New Year. Every New Year's Eve, we'd wait excitedly, sitting by my mum's sewing machine, watching her sew and sew and sew the clothes she made for us. Once they were done, I'd put them on and run downstairs to play. That's how it was every New Year. But for the rest of the year? No new clothes, because we had to use fabric ration tickets – and so I had to wear my mum's old clothes, my sister's old clothes. When they were worn out, my mum would cut and patch them for me. I found it interesting to watch her.

I remember a time I waited until my parents went to work, then went into the trunk where my dad locked his treasured garments. I took out one of his shirts and started sketching on it – even though I'd never studied art, I liked to draw. Then I cut it up and altered it. But when I tried to put it on, it didn't fit. The tailoring was off. So, I rolled it back up and stuffed it at the bottom of the trunk again. No one ever found out. But to me, that process was incredibly meaningful.

My mum worked at a garment factory which produced custom-made clothing for foreign export. She did the cutting, and after each job there'd be a stack of offcuts which would be sold to the workers. Mum would bring them home, and I would draw my own designs, cut them myself, and wear them. Of course, none of them fitted, but I was so happy to wear something I made. In the '70s I used to make drawings of myself wearing the clothes I'd made.

At first I was using my own clothes in my artworks. In *Dress Box*, the first piece of clothing you see was made from those factory offcuts. At that time, I wanted pastel colours, which were trendy, but we didn't have any. So, my mum dyed the fabric and made me a Chinese-style padded jacket.

YM   *So your work started with something very personal. But later on, the clothes became those of other people, right?*

YX   Yes, exactly. *Dress Box* was extremely personal. Later, I thought I could also work with other people's experiences. So I started collecting clothes to use.

	And since then, it's transformed into many different forms, from suitcases to bookshelves to large-scale installations, like the heart in this exhibition or the airplane. Yet all of it started from clothing, from Dress Box.

YX	Like you say, it's all still within the framework of clothing, isn't it? I started adding other threads, exploring other materials such as cement, and later on ceramics and glass. But about working with clothing … Society is fundamentally made up of people, and although a lot of its elements change because of how people develop differently – different systems, different structures, between China and abroad – in the end, it's still people who shape those systems. I believe it's people who change the world.

I think the information that clothing carries about people is especially important. Collecting people's clothing and stitching them together becomes a new kind of collective. Even though, as a viewer looking at the clothes, you may just see the material, in fact, they've been worn by different people. And that makes them completely different. They carry so many invisible things, and I find that very interesting.

I also wanted people to be able to enter into works, to have a direct relationship with them. So I created the *Cavity* series – 'cavity' as in a body cavity. I describe the pink piece, *Introspective Cavity* (pp. 116–18), as a womb, but it's not modelled exactly after that form. It's more about the concept. It's about returning to the mother's body – *Introspective Cavity* is a place of reflection, a very intimate space, a space for rethinking.

If you return to the mother's body, what are your deepest thoughts? Your original thoughts, even. What happens if you go back to the beginning, to rethink things? That's the space I made. And later I made more similar pieces, including the brain, and the heart that I'm making this time – it's also one of these cavities, a place for heartfelt conversation. You return to the heart, and everyone gathers inside the heart to talk, to have conversations. I think that's really interesting.

YM	*Earlier, you mentioned that cement was an important material for you. Did that originate from the work* Ruined City *(pp. 65–69)?*

YX	Yes, although I did also use cement in *Dress Box* – which was sealed with cement. I see that work as combining two types of building materials, one for constructing the individual, and one for constructing society.

When I was making *Ruined City*, Beijing was undergoing massive demolition and construction. There were buildings I'd see still standing on my way to work, and by the time I came back, they were gone. It felt like the air was filled with the scent of cement. That's why I used cement to make that work.

24

I'm also especially interested in cement as a material. Later on, I made a whole series related to cement. Cement powder has got this very smooth, fine texture. But when it sits in the air, over time it slowly absorbs moisture from the air. Then a thin crust forms on the surface – it hardens. And once you mix it with gravel and sand in the right proportions, it becomes concrete, which is used to build houses. So I really love that material.

> YM   *I like your description that clothing is for making people and cement is for making buildings. I think some of your work has a strong connection with cities and urban environments. Do you agree?*

YX   Cities are symbols of speed. In the city, it feels like everyone has to keep moving. And there's this pressure – it presses down on you. I felt that sense of tension very strongly in Tokyo. A kind of tightness. People living in cities often have a yearning for rural life. But once you go out there, the reality is that although you can relax for a while, you can't stay for long – you still have to come back to the city, to work, to make a living.

I made a piece called *Supermarket*, for which I created a huge supermarket cart, then invited ten people from the countryside and ten people from the city to participate in making quilts. But what we actually made were their dreams in the size of a quilt, about two metres by two metres. During the making process, I made it very clear that they could create something about their own life, or the life they yearned for. And what was especially interesting was that the city people wanted to make things about rural life, and the rural participants longed for urban life. The work reflected on the relationship between the city and the countryside.

> YM   *You also have a piece called* Beijing, *if I'm not mistaken?*

YX   Yes, a work which I made in Australia – a large rooftop structure. That piece was a large, traditional Beijing-style roof frame, and on the tiles, I printed many photos I had taken of people's everyday lives in Beijing. I've documented a lot of life in Beijing. Like I mentioned earlier, *Ruined City* was about Beijing.

> YM   *There's also the piece* Beijing Opera *(pp. 70–75), which takes its name from a traditional style of performance known as 'Peking Opera', and features street scenes from Beijing.*

YX   *Beijing Opera* came about because I used to pass by the neighbourhood of Houhai every day on my way to work. Sometimes, on the way home, when I felt more relaxed, I'd stop to see what was happening, because people often gathered there. Often, there would be a group of enthusiasts taking turns singing Peking opera. They

weren't professionals, but they were so devoted. I thought it was
so interesting, and very moving, too, their state of being when they were
really relaxed and immersed in it. Young people are all off working,
talking about the same stuff, but these were retired people, people
from a segment of society that isn't really paid much attention to.

Later, when I wasn't working, I'd ride my bike there to observe
and take photographs. I felt like I was getting to know a different
kind of society – one that exists outside of our usual social structure.
They would chat with me too. Actually, eventually they thought
I was one of them – they'd say, 'Come sing something.' I had to say:
'I don't know how!'

The photographs became *Beijing Opera*, which was shown at
Hamburger Bahnhof – Nationalgalerie der Gegenwart in Berlin.
I turned the photographs into wallpaper. In the middle there were
little stools and a small speaker beside the installation. At the
Hamburger Bahnhof, I had a whole room for the work – I really
wanted to make it life-size, so that viewers would feel they were
part of the scene, immersed in that Houhai environment – but when
M+ acquired the work later, they just placed it in a corner.

YM   *You then turned to ceramics, but that came a bit later, right?*

YX   Yes – ceramics started for me in 2005. It happened
gradually, after I'd been experimenting with various materials.
I started noticing new things in daily life, discovering different
materials. Of course, ceramics is something everyone comes into
contact with – like the bowls we eat from every day – but you
don't really think about it.

I didn't just want to make a craft piece like a bowl, a gourd
or some kind of decorative shape. I wondered: if I intervene in
the process, could something new emerge? So I decided to go and
explore. In 2015 I was invited to exhibit at the Aurora Museum
in Shanghai. They invited me to create a large piece for their main
hall. I made a stomach – also a cavity, like a digestive cavity, but
filled it with stones that feel like gallstones. That's when I decided
to work with ceramics.

YM   *So the gallstones are ceramic?*

YX   Yes. The work was called *Digestive Cavity*. I laid out a kind
of highway on the ground for people to step on as they entered
the work. The fabric I sewed to make the highway was donated by the
Italian sponsor, Alcantara – it was the kind used inside luxury cars,
so that relates to the highway too.

There's a floor that people step on to enter the 'stomach',
a contradictory space that is both still and fast-moving at the same
time. Inside are the ceramic stones which people sit on, which
are like chunks of rubble, demolition debris. I added some fabric fuzz.

Those are the undigested feelings. That was my first ceramic piece
that really took form. From then on, it developed uncontrollably,
constantly changing and evolving.

SD   Before that, Yin had made some small ceramic pieces, just
for fun. With ceramics, if you fire them and it's not done well, it
cracks. But she liked those cracks and textures and wanted to preserve
them, rather than have a perfect, intact piece.

YX   Actually, at that time, I didn't have a specific idea of what
I wanted to make or what effect I wanted to create. I knew I wanted
to make *something*; and quite often I knew the result wasn't quite
right. So even when the exhibition plan was already set, but during
the process something else appeared, it turned into something else.
I think the constant emergence of new ideas happens while working
– sometimes accidents occur during the firing process that make
you rethink things. So I keep going, because there are always new
things to try.

YM   *And of course, later, your ceramic work became more fixed
in form. You also started to work with glass more recently.
Was that due to the exhibition at the Shanghai Museum of Glass?*

YX   Actually, before that, we went to Murano in Italy to see their
glass craftsmanship. Song and I each made one piece. I especially
liked the Roman glass vessels which I studied in the Murano Glass
Museum. They say Roman glass technology wasn't very good,
because it had lots of impurities, and also because it was buried
underground for a long time, with acid and alkali, which gives it this
distinct patina that I loved. For my work there, I made a bookshelf
and filled it with Roman glass vessels, which were all rod-shaped,
and which I crushed in such a way that one side was kept intact and
the other side was all straight – so that when you view the bookshelf
from one side it looks like it's filled with books, and from the other
side it shows the shape of the objects.

YM   *When you add other things inside ceramics or glass, it's often
something soft, to contrast with the hardness. Ceramics are hard,
cloth is very soft, for instance.*

YX   I like contrast and opposition. Also, one more important
element – I especially like things that have life. Clothes have life,
and combining them with ceramics creates a feeling of being alive.
When I first made clothes, I felt like the collar and the cuffs were
like breathing holes. Then when I was working with ceramics,
I decided to add in those cloth scraps.
    Apart from cloth scraps, I also threw in other daily objects,
like a ruler, a knife or a clock in my ceramic pieces (see pp. 79–87)

– I like how they change during the firing process. It's not like this
piece of ceramic is perfectly flawless, but the ruler I put inside
originally had clear measurements which disappeared with firing.
New cracks appeared, which resembled new measurements,
and the ceramic got cracks too. I think imperfection is perfection.

And for my glass pieces (see pp. 88–93), I added fruit – it has
life. Also, during the process, each layer of glass contains different
fruits, and the weight of the many layers presses it down. So even
before firing, juices flow out from the crushed fruits, which I find
very touching. It moved me. And after firing, the black areas inside
are the same fluid (juices), carbonised now, but also still showing
a trace of life. During firing, gas escapes and creates bubbles,
altering the glass surfaces. Actually, for me, it's like the materials are
communicating with us.

YM   *How about the series* One Sentence *(pp. 98–103)? You once again
went back to working with clothes.*

YX   The starting point for *One Sentence* was simply thinking
about life. Why do you live? I'm alive because my parents gave birth
to me, so I have no choice but to live. Then in life, you definitely
continue living – not just eating and drinking to sustain life. You
have to do something. What will you do? Every life is so different, but
in the end, I think it's about what you understand of the world and
what you leave behind. One day, you'll be gone, but before that, what
important things do you want to say to this world in one sentence?
So, that became the name of the work.

The series is made up of 108 circular metal boxes, like film
canisters. Each contains the clothing of one person. I arranged each
set of clothing from inside to outside – from underwear to outerwear
– and then shredded it, and wrapped it into a colourful ring.
Each one is different – some people gave me more clothes, some gave
me less, and of course I didn't choose the colours – but each one
looks something like a film reel. When each was finished, I measured
its diameter and then made the box. On each one there is a serial
number and a description of the clothes inside the box. And so, there
are 108 sentences – 108 life statements. When I was collecting the
clothes, some people said, 'Should I write a statement for you?'
'No,' I said, 'I think your clothes themselves carry your statement.'

YM   *I want to ask about the influence between you and Song Dong
in your creations. You are life partners as well as artistic partners,
and when we talk, it's often with both of you together.*

SD   When two people live under one roof, they definitely
influence each other.

YX   Sometimes before he says something, I already know what
he wants to say, and he knows what I want to say. At some point,
we both realised life is short, and as long as the two of us are together,
no matter where, that's home. So if I go out, as long as he has time,
he accompanies me. Wherever he goes, if I'm free, I go with him.
That's how it is.

SD   At the same time, we are two independent artists.
We don't want to become the same person. From the start, the two
of us were very clear we had to be independent – we couldn't be
each other's appendages. Later, in 2001, we created a working method
called 'The Way of Chopsticks'. Sometimes I want to do it one
way, Yin wants to do it another way, the ideas are different. For one
piece, she wants to do it this way, I want to do it that way, but if it
can't be done together …

YX   … then we just split it in half, cut it evenly. He takes half
to do his work, I take half to do mine. There are clear rules: we don't
have to tell each other or negotiate, we keep it secret and don't
influence each other. Then, at the exhibition, we put the two parts
together. We thought it was really interesting and it continued
on like that.

SD   We always say that we are each other's workers, and
we can't control or interfere with each other's work. I might think
something should be done differently, but sometimes she says:
'That's my work, you're saying too much.' I express my views
by talking, but she prefers to show it through her work. I am also
greatly influenced by her. She sees many things that I usually
overlook as a man. For example, when she is sorting through photos,
she can spend a whole night looking at just one picture. She
notices all these details I never would. I guess when she looks at
a photo, a movie appears in her mind.
    Another thing I really admire is that Yin always wants to break
the rules. When we were making ceramics, she once found a worker
waving a big magnet back and forth inside the kiln. She asked
why, and the worker said that the biggest taboo in ceramics is having
iron inside, because if there's iron there will be defects, black
spots burned in. The next day, Yin directly put an iron ruler into the
ceramics and fired it, and it left a mark. I thought that was amazing
because I hadn't thought from that angle. It led to later works
like rulers, containers, and mirrors fired inside the ceramics.

YM   *The more you're not supposed to fire it, the more you want
to fire it.*

YX   But it's not just about breaking the rules for the sake of it.
I think because of the ruler I started to reexamine my understanding
of a process. Who defines how things are measured? And the mirror
is actually an introspective thing. I like an inward, introspective space.
A mirror is flat but it's also a container, and so I bought a mirror
with a metal frame. And actually, the mirror's reflective surface is also
a kind of glaze. So after firing it together with clay, it developed these
blackened edges, these fine cracks, and the mirror surface's colour
is slightly different from the edges. I find that particularly interesting.

YM   *You mentioned that your first glass piece was actually made
into a bookshelf. Can we talk about your interest in books – and
the bookshelf pieces?*

SD   The biggest impact on us back in the '80s was being able
to read different books. Before, it was all the same – mainly ideologi-
cal books like Marxism-Leninism and Mao Zedong Thought. Then
suddenly you could buy all sorts of philosophical books. Universities
back then were intellectually active, so for electives, we'd choose
philosophy – Pre-Qin philosophy or different Western schools of
philosophy. Besides art classes, I think these courses had the biggest
impact on us because we got to encounter different people's ways
of thinking. Before, I thought there was only one way of thinking
about life, so it really opened up my horizons. I loved reading those
books. There was a saying in China: 'Study for the rise of China.'
This was a phrase [former premier of China] Zhou Enlai coined
during his own schooldays. And in the 1980s, when I was at university, when I rode my bike to school every day, wearing my school
badge, I felt everything was progressing steadily. I felt very hopeful.

YX   Back then at school, we would put books on a flat cart.
Going to the cafeteria, passing by others, riding a tricycle, the books
were always on the flat board at the back. That left a deep impression.
Later, I also felt that people's clothes, like books, are like files: they
can be read, so I placed them on a bookshelf. I think a person is like
a book, too.

YM   *I remember you have one bookshelf you don't sell, which is the
one you made for your daughter. Why did you make a bookshelf
for her?*

YX   That work – *Bookshelf for Song ErRui: Study Hard*
(pp. 104–05) – is very special. It has the phrase 'Study hard' written
on it. I don't think others have that. It's hard to come across. In our
schooldays, the classroom always had 'Study hard and make progress
every day' written above the blackboard – a quotation from Mao
Zedong. At the start of the school day we'd sing songs such as 'The
sea voyages depend on the left hand', and we also carried a Little

Red Book of quotations from Mao. On one side of our desk we'd have our textbooks, and the book of quotations on the other side. That was the era I grew up in. So when I see 'Study hard', it's really a hope I'm giving to my daughter.

> YM   *Song Dong mentioned the idea of recording an era. For example, at his Song Art Museum exhibition, each space is a kind of record of different times. Yin, do you think your work is like that too, or is it more about your view on life rather than a specific era?*

> YX   Although I didn't deliberately set out to create that kind of thing, I feel those elements are there in my work. I still use clothes as material, for example, and clothes from ten years ago are different from today's clothes, and carry different meanings. So, although they're all made of fabric, their styles differ, and more importantly, they carry the spirit of their times.

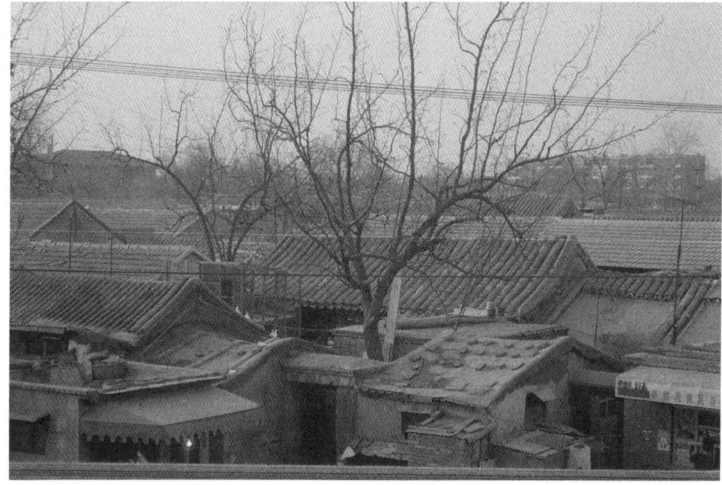

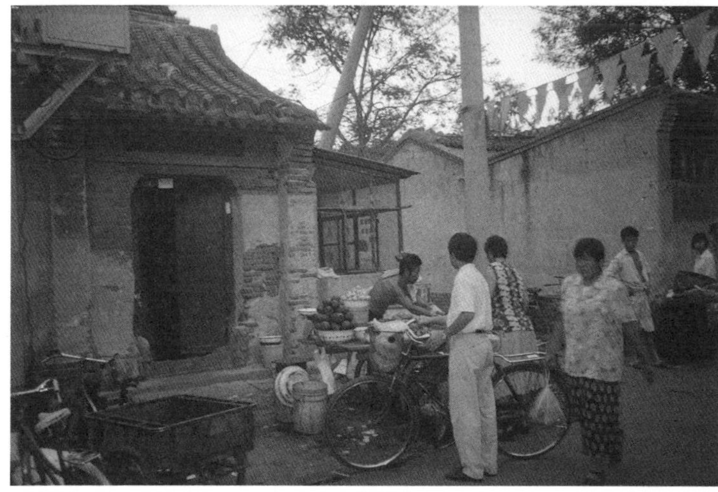

31

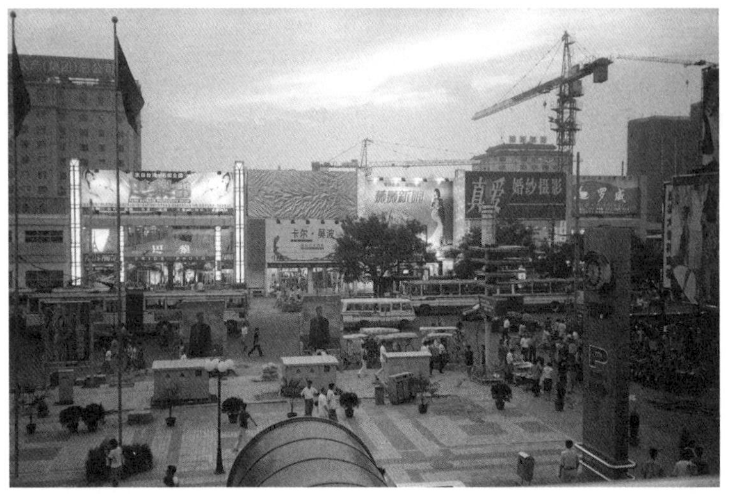

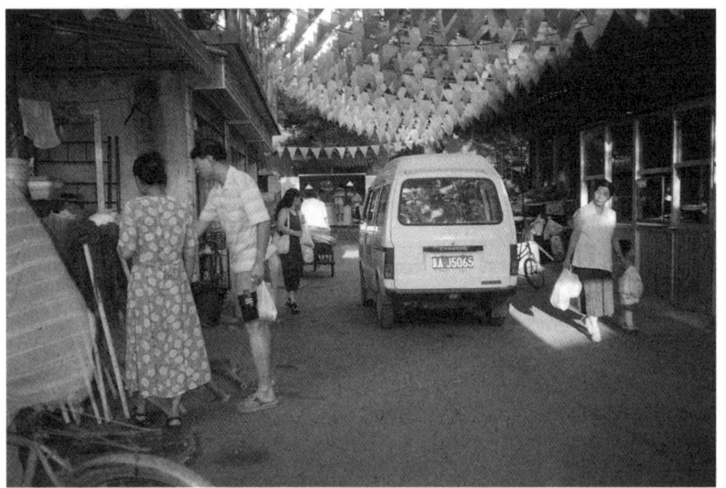

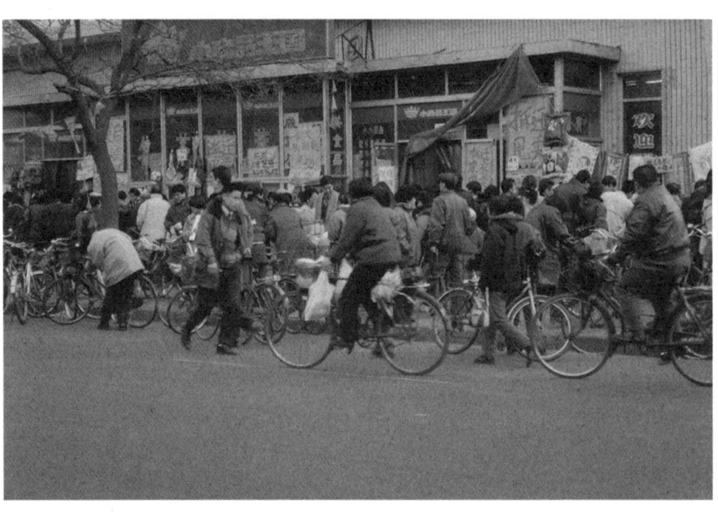

Photographs of Beijing
in the 1990s by Yin Xiuzhen

'A suitcase is like someone's home – a temporary minimised home with all their necessities inside.'

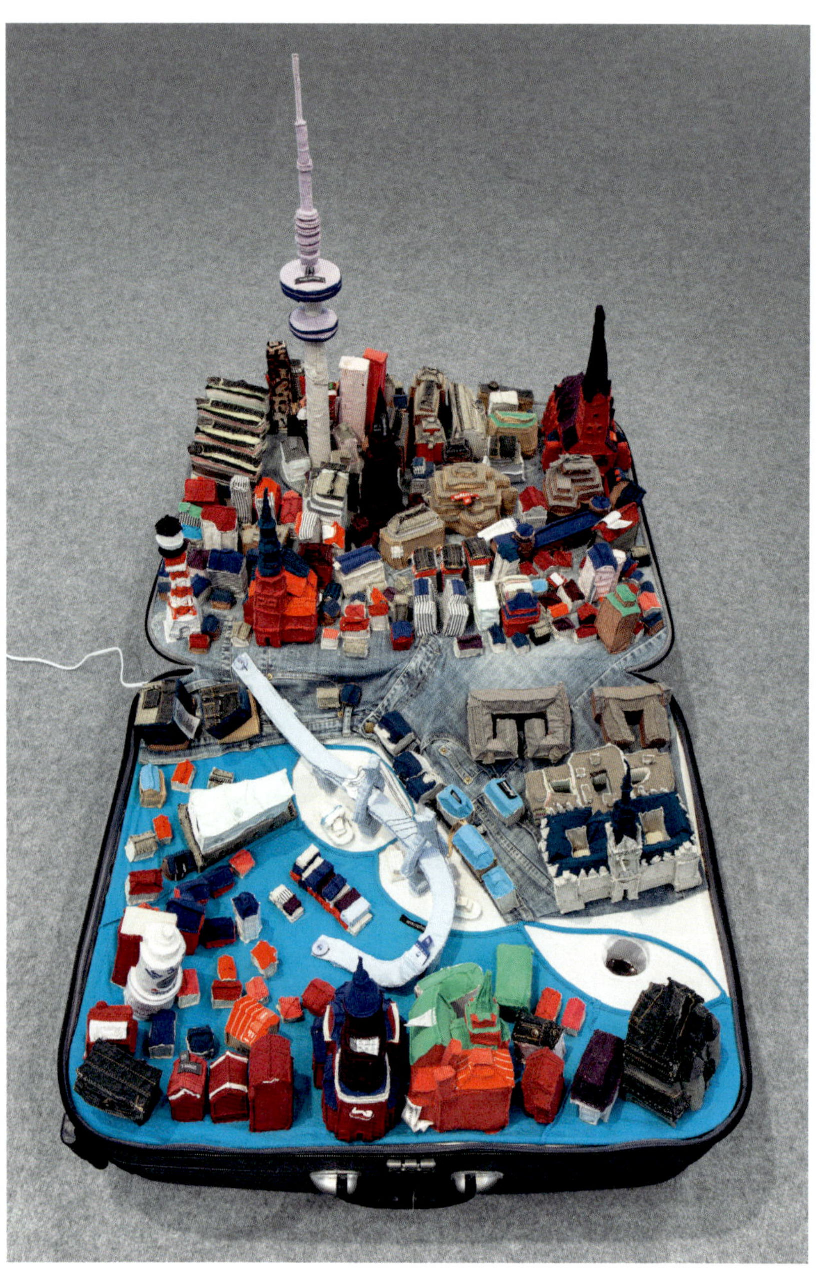

Portable City: Hamburg,
2014

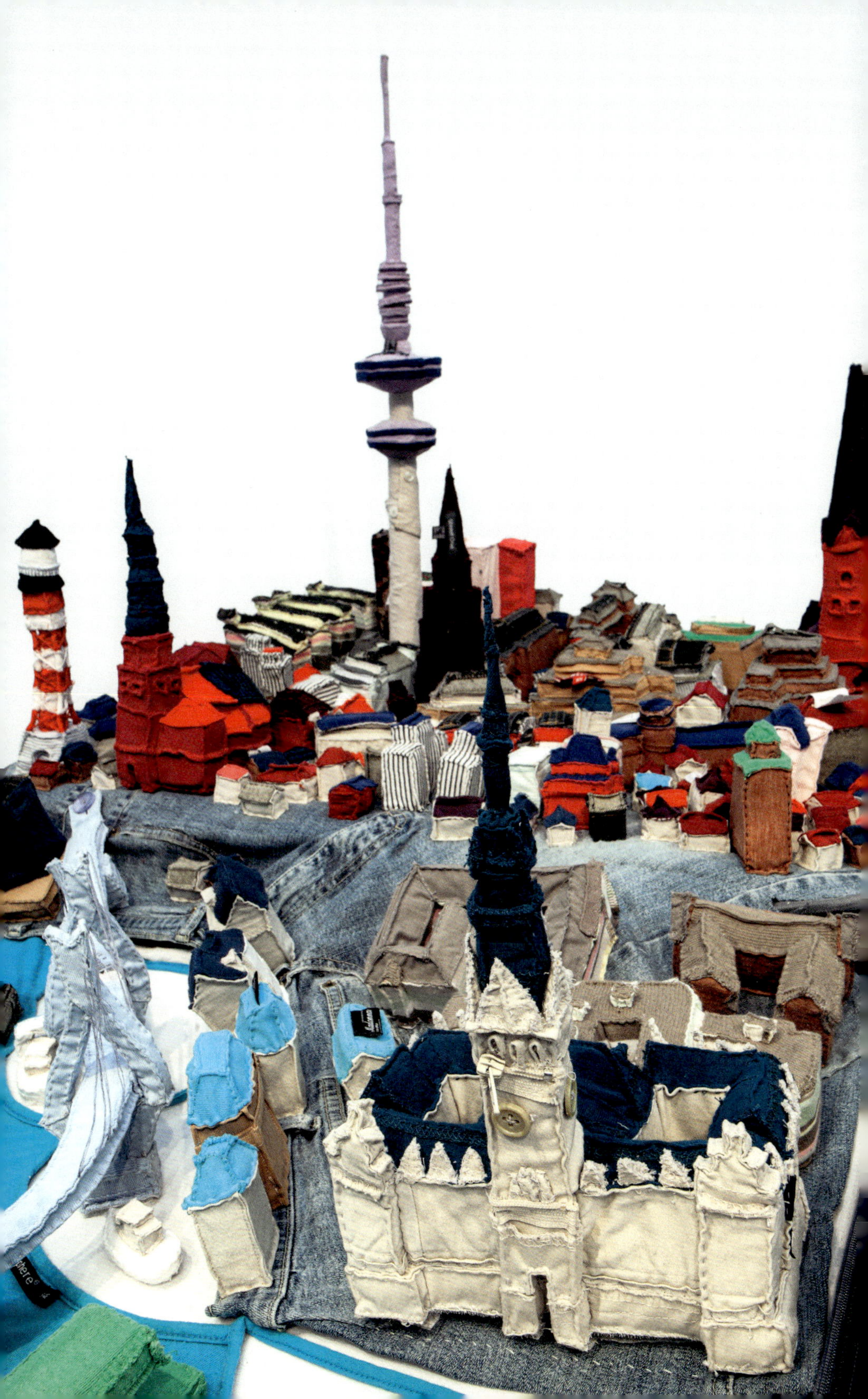

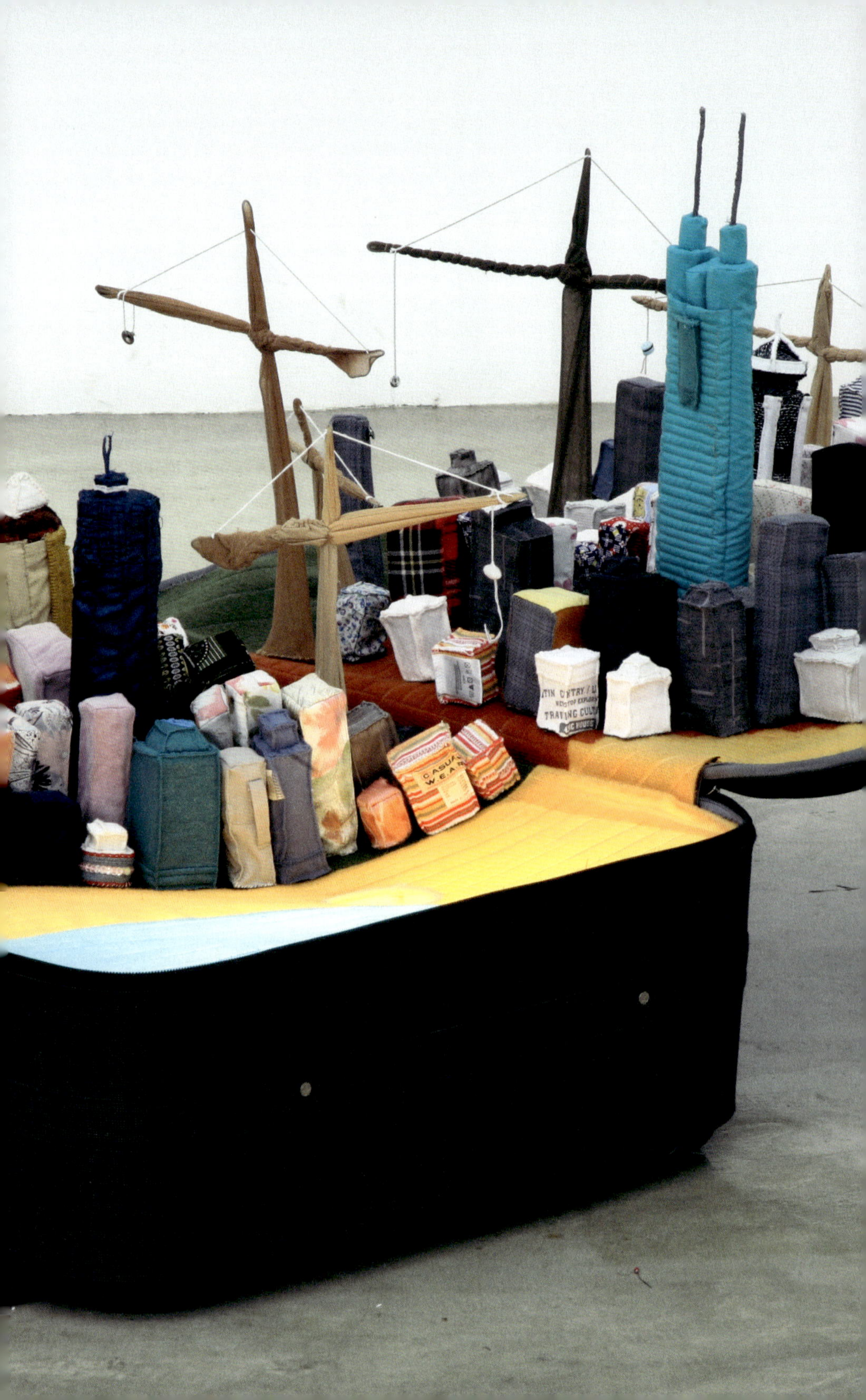

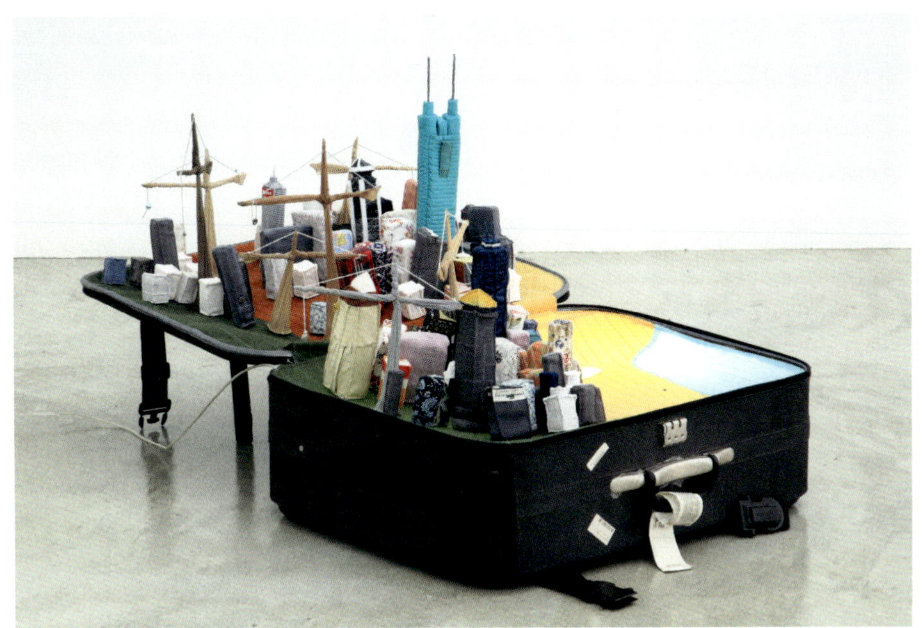

37

Portable City: Shenzhen,
2003

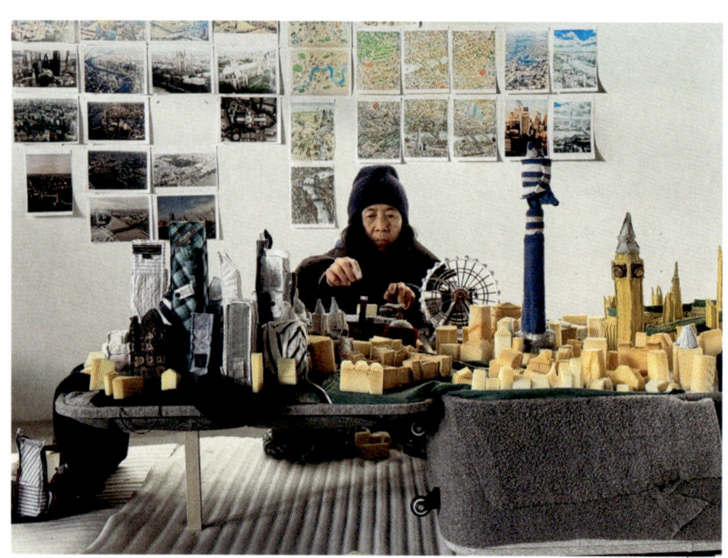

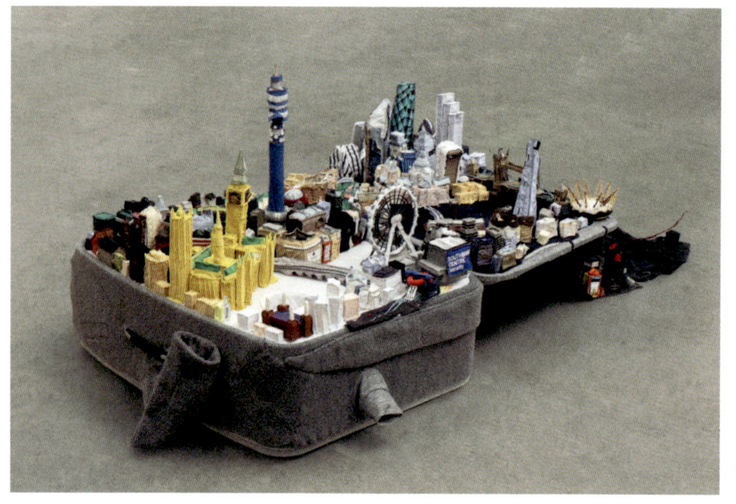

Portable City: London,
2025 (work in progress)

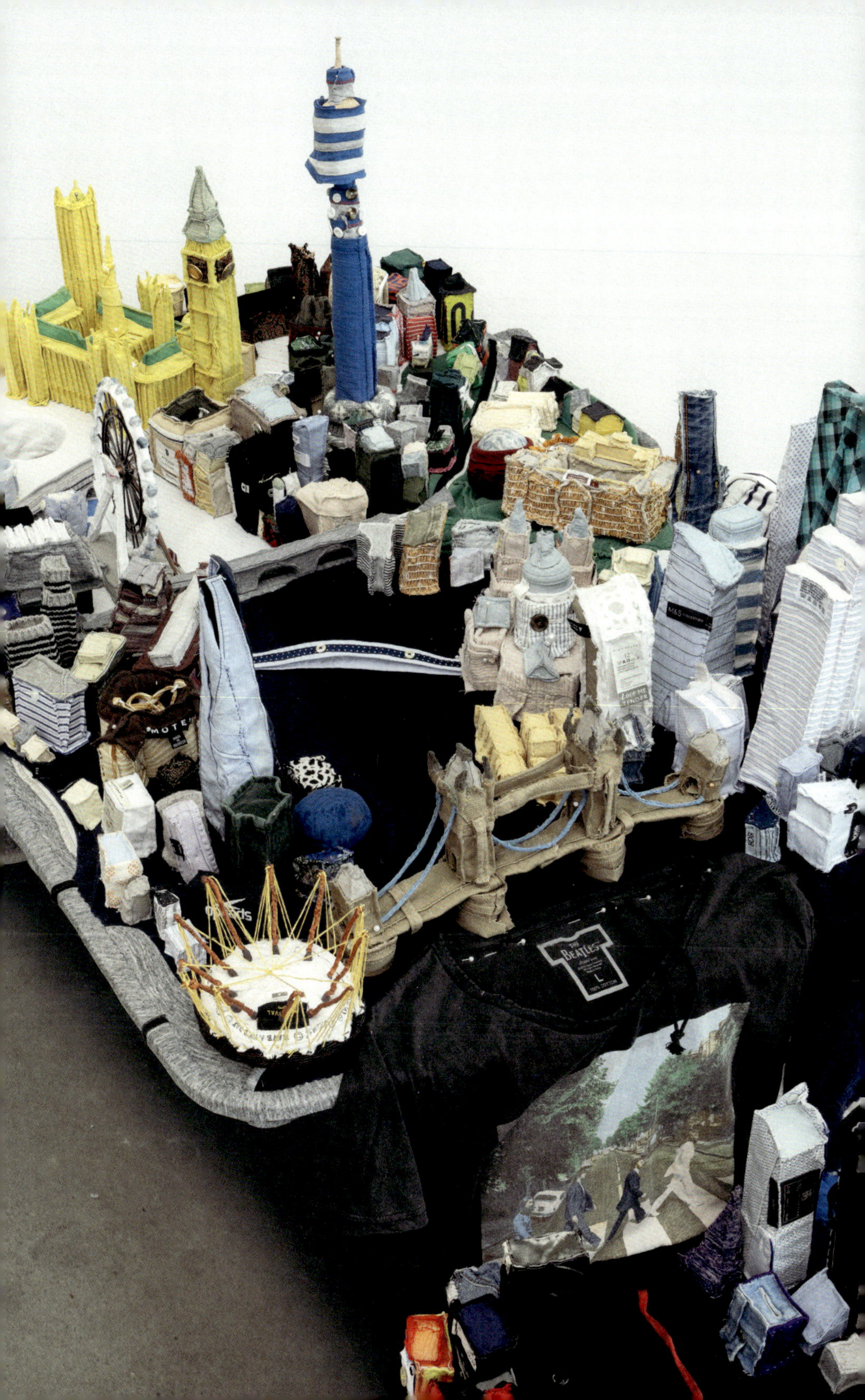

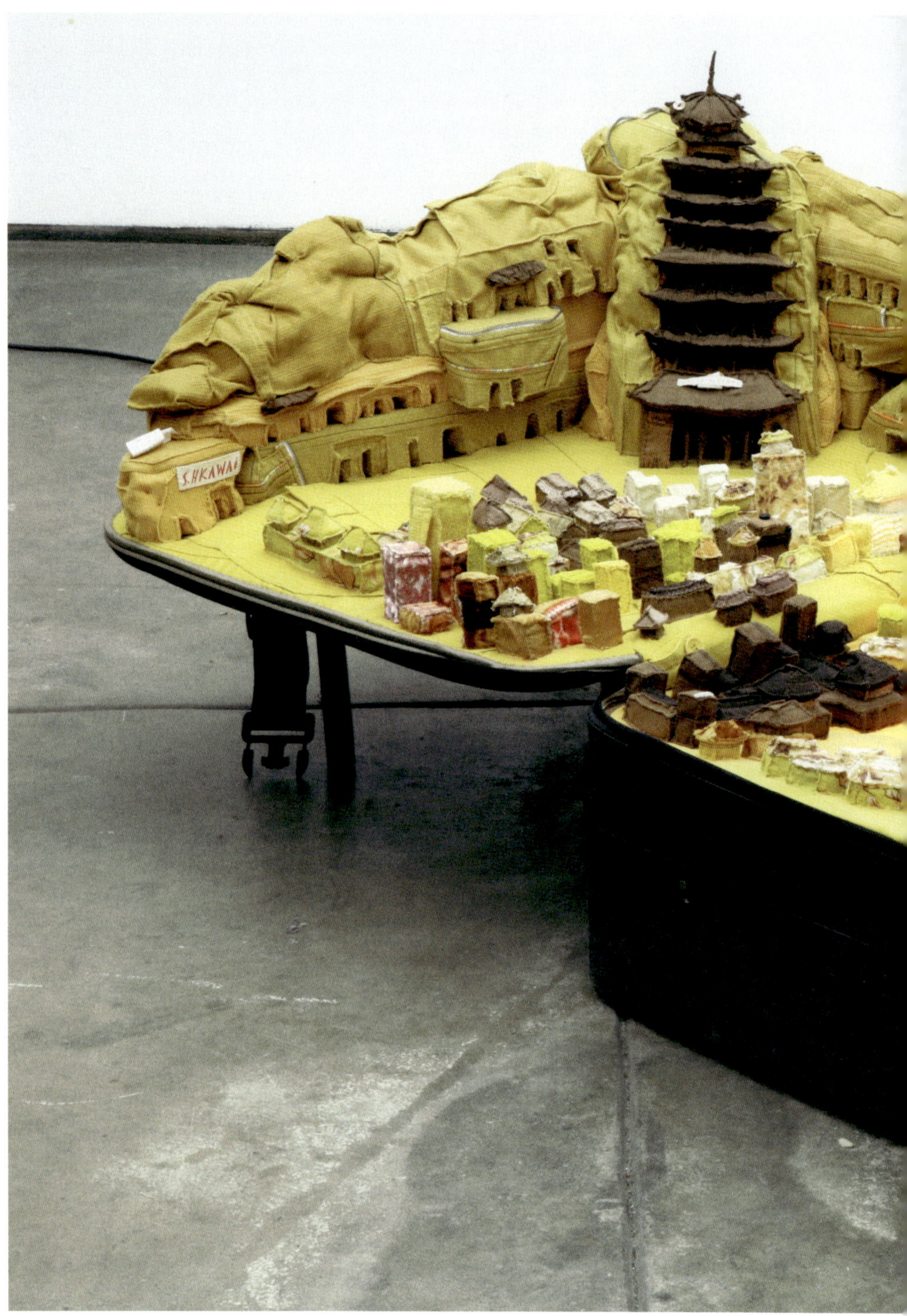

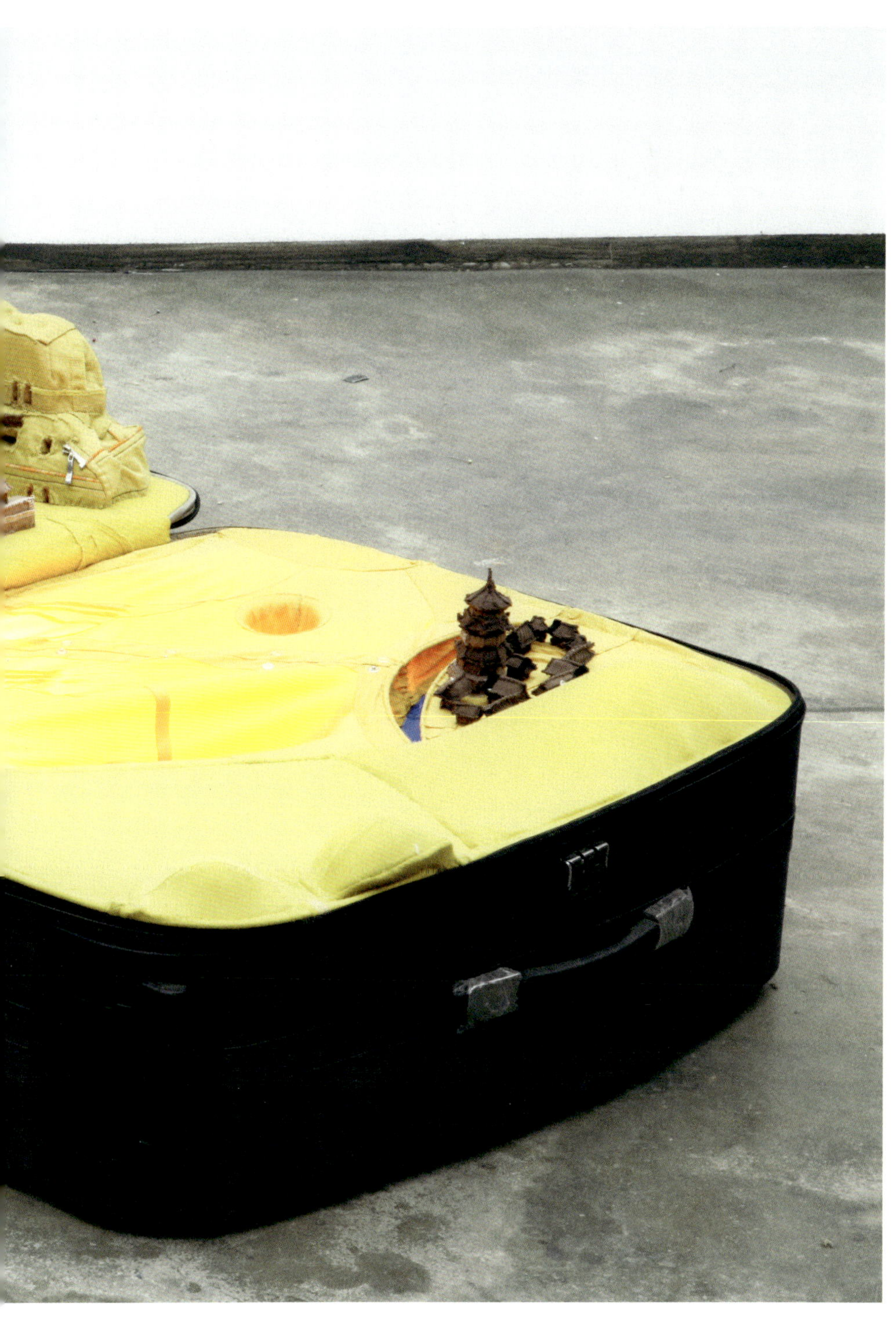

Portable City: Dunhuang,
2010

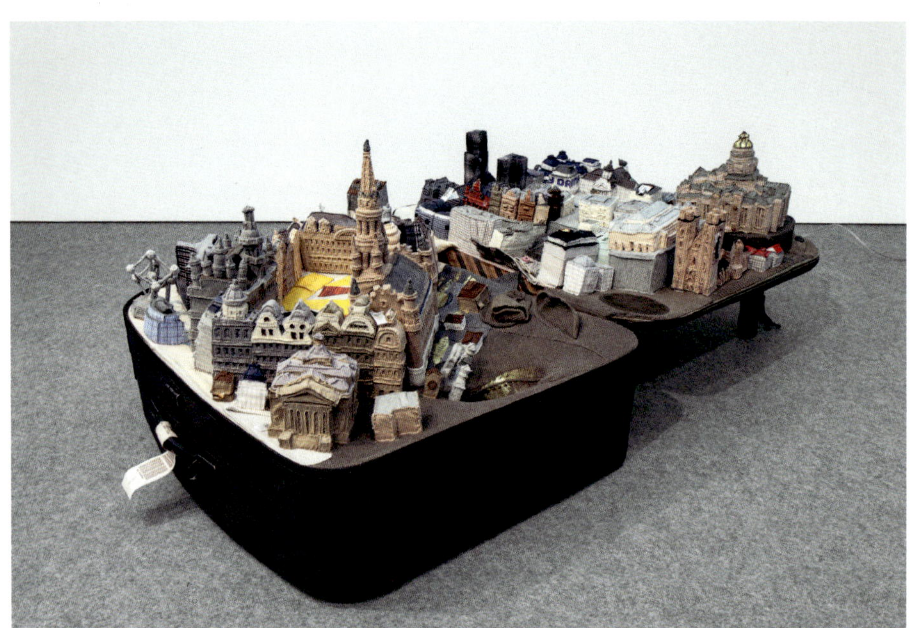

Portable City: Brussels,
2015

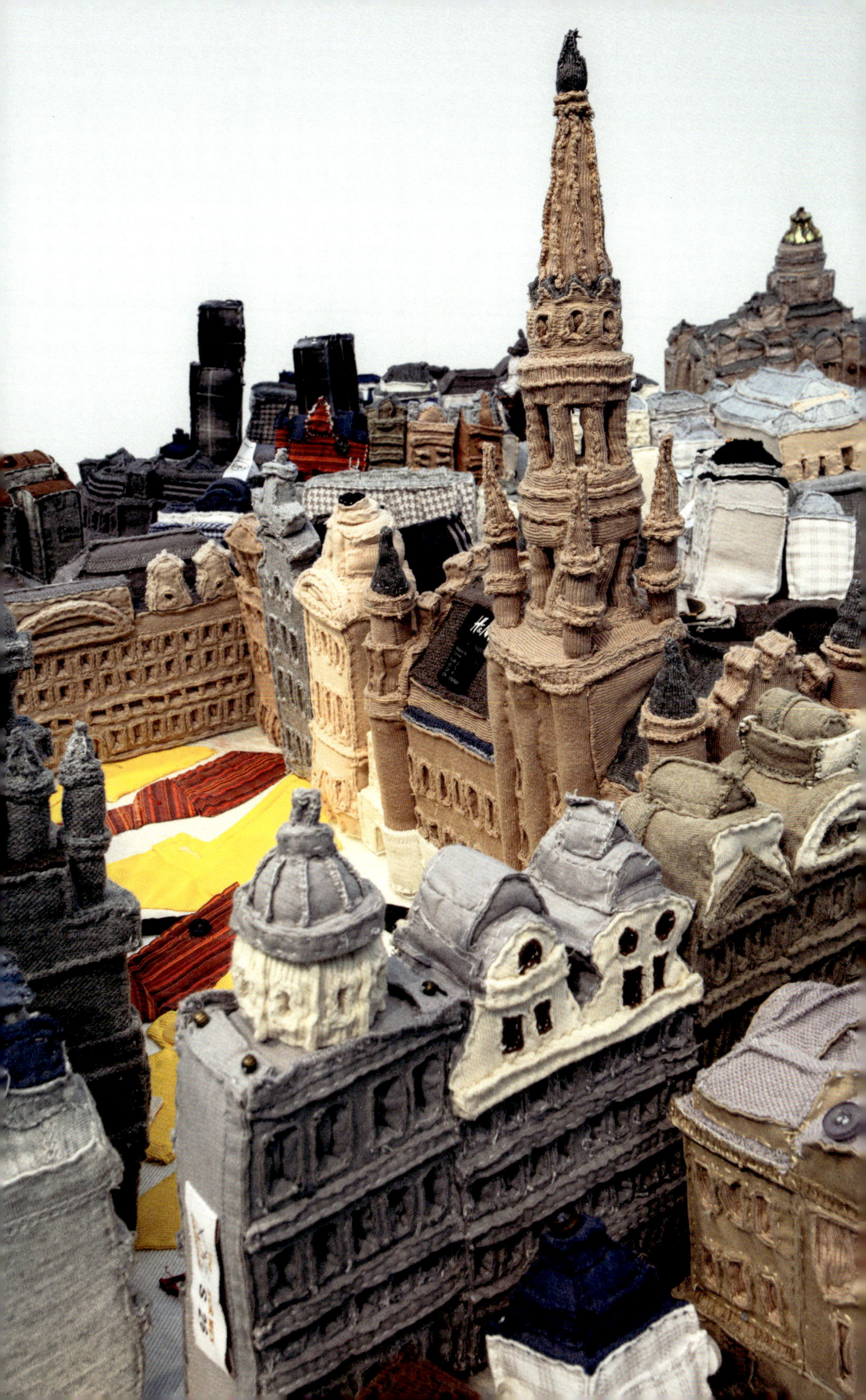

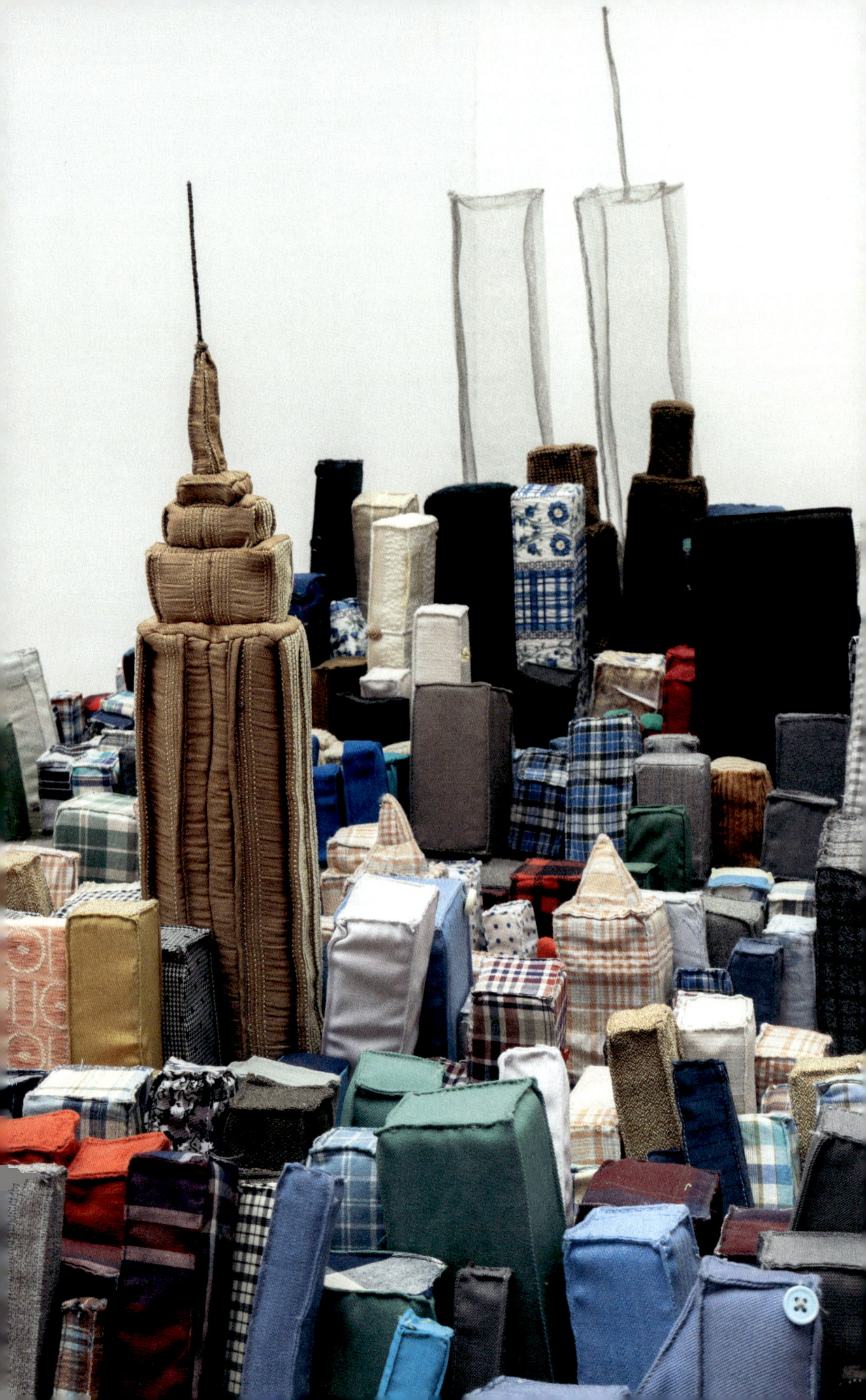

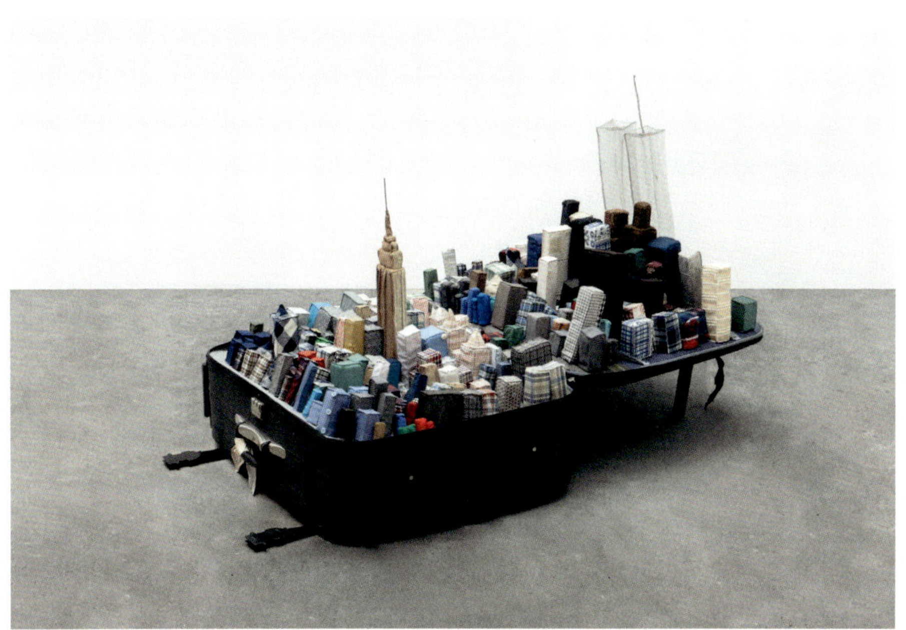

45

Portable City: New York,
2003

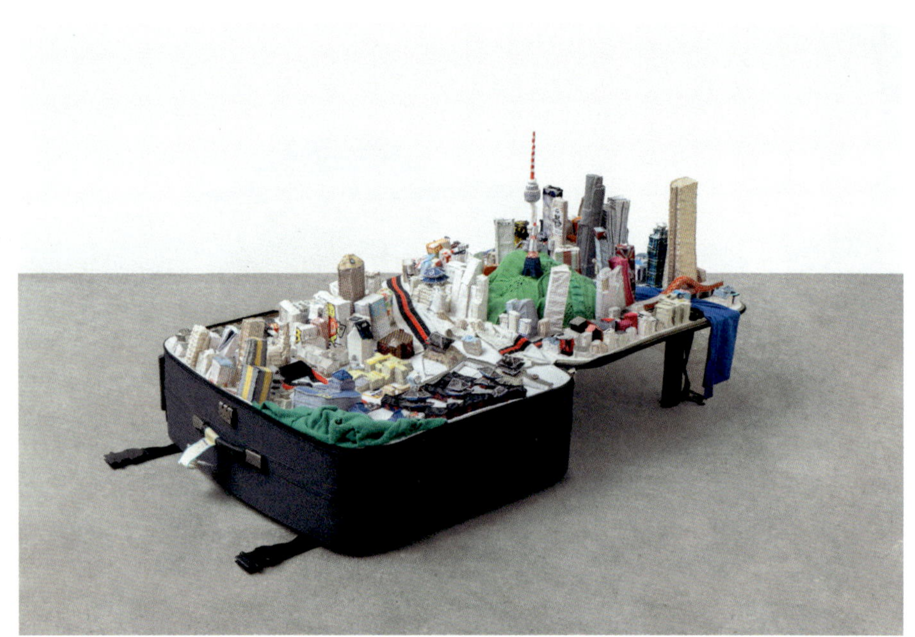

Portable City: Seoul,
2013

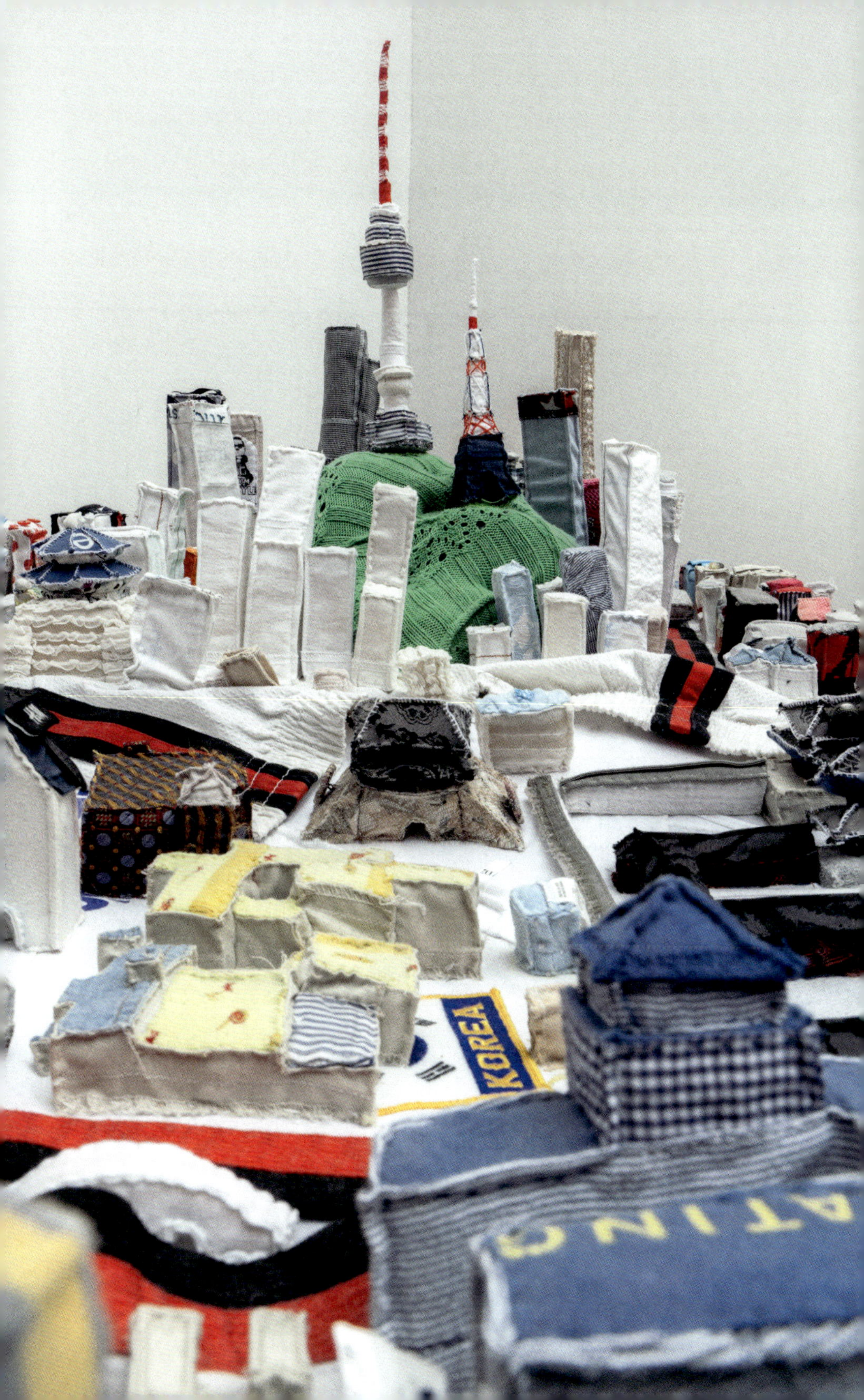

KOREA
ATING

International Flight,
2002

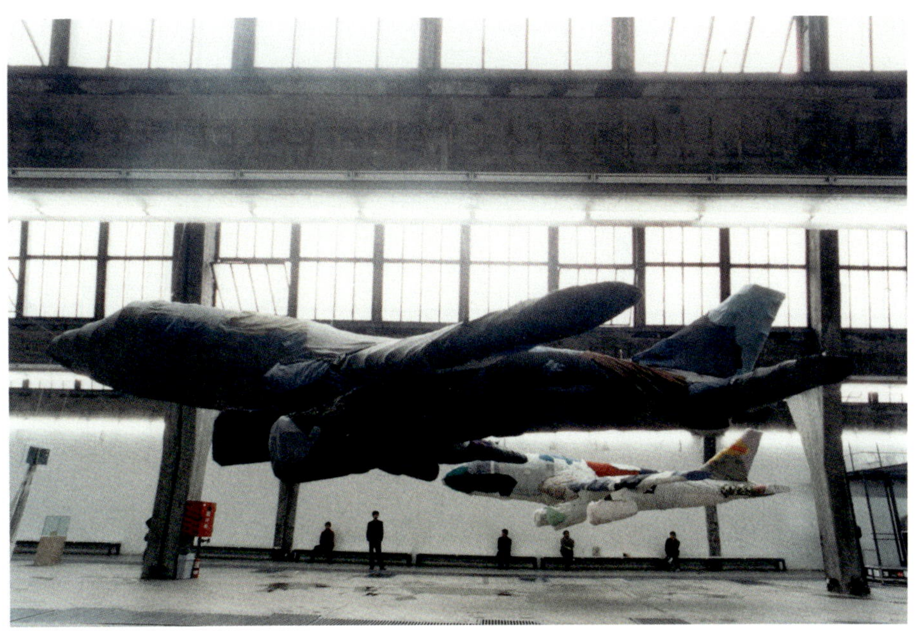

49

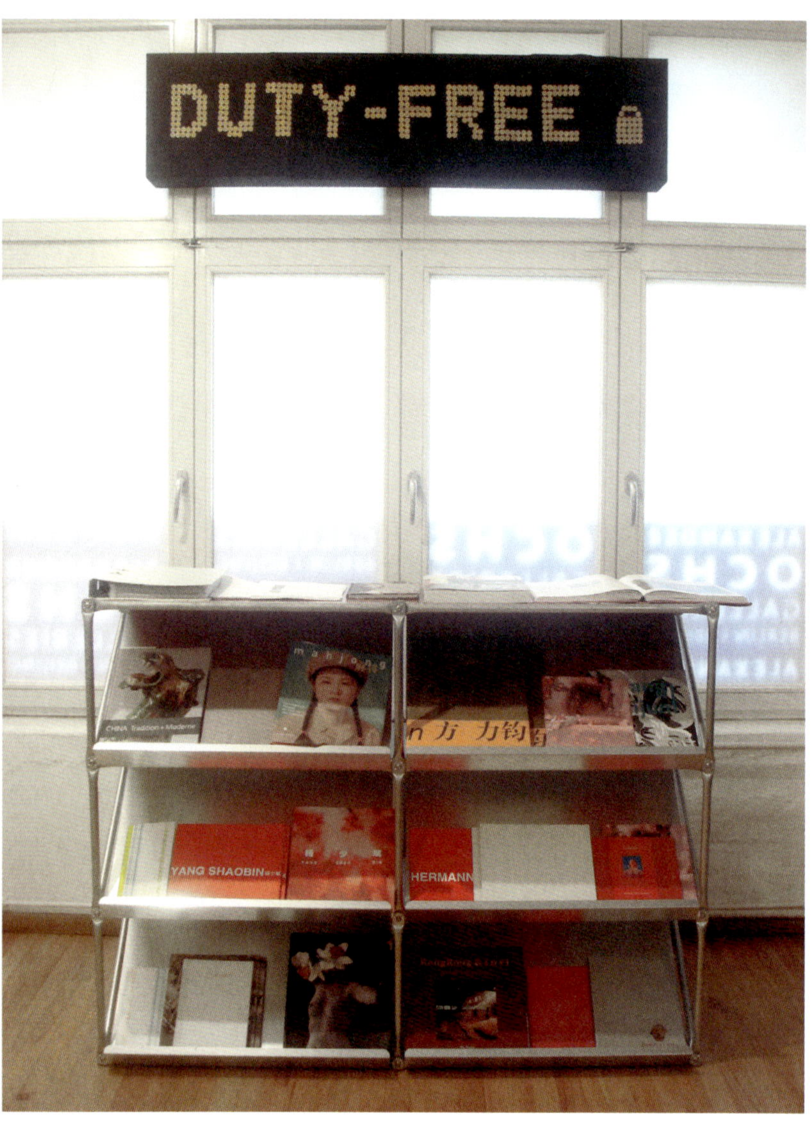

International Airport: Terminal 1,
2006

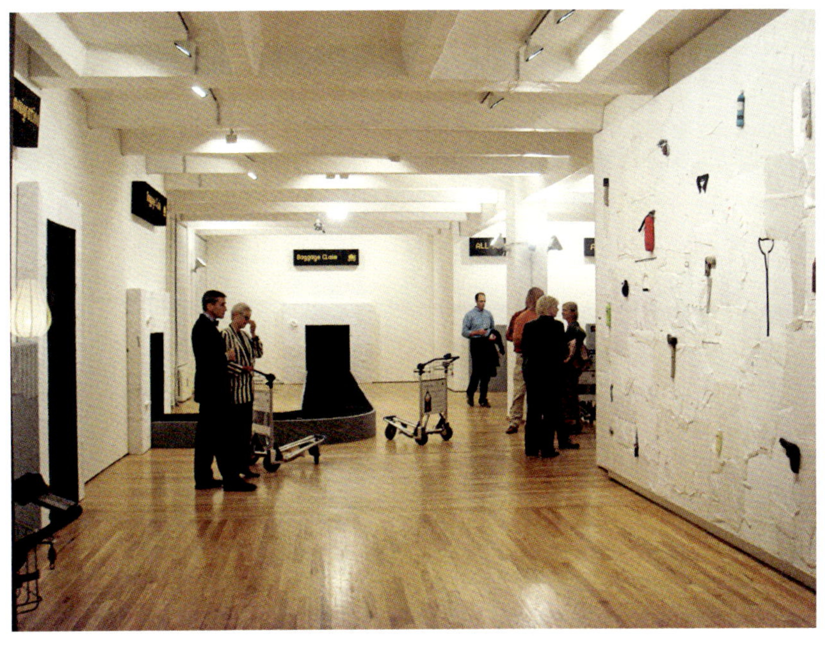

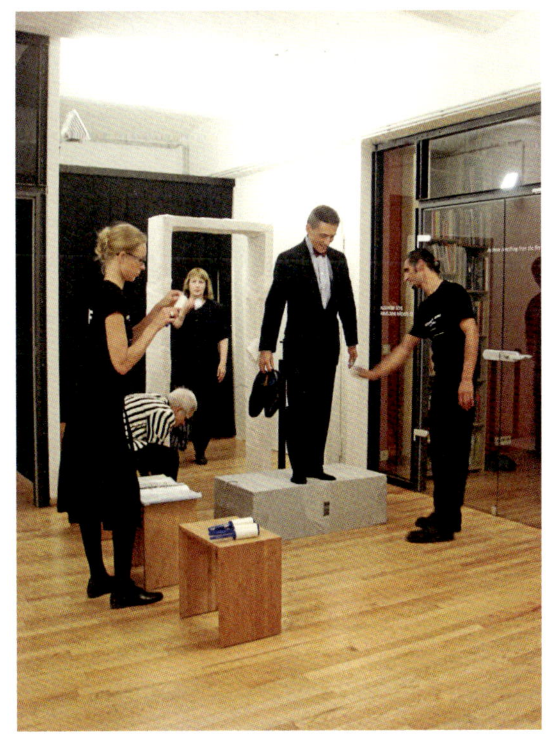

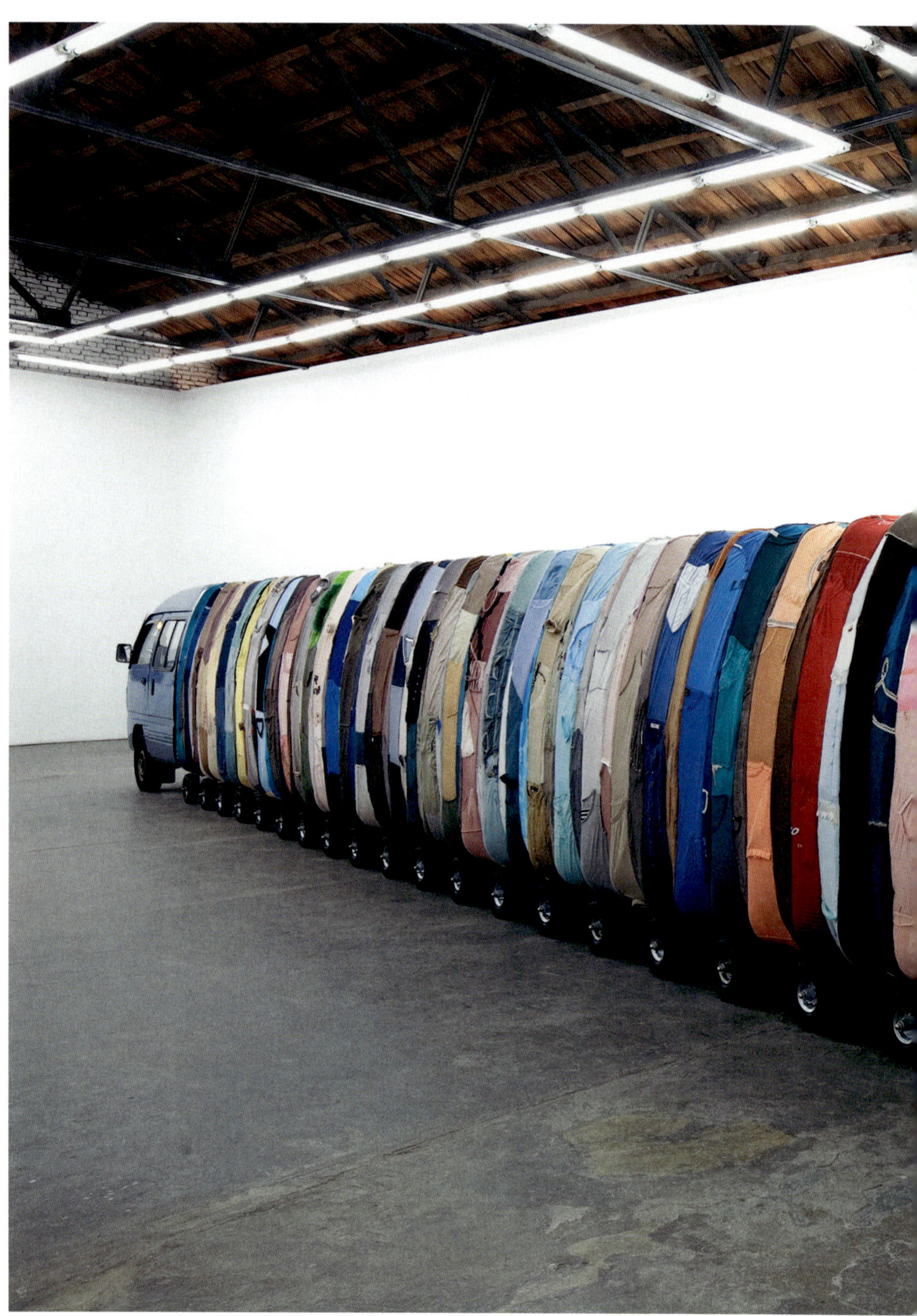

Collective Subconscious (Blue),
2007

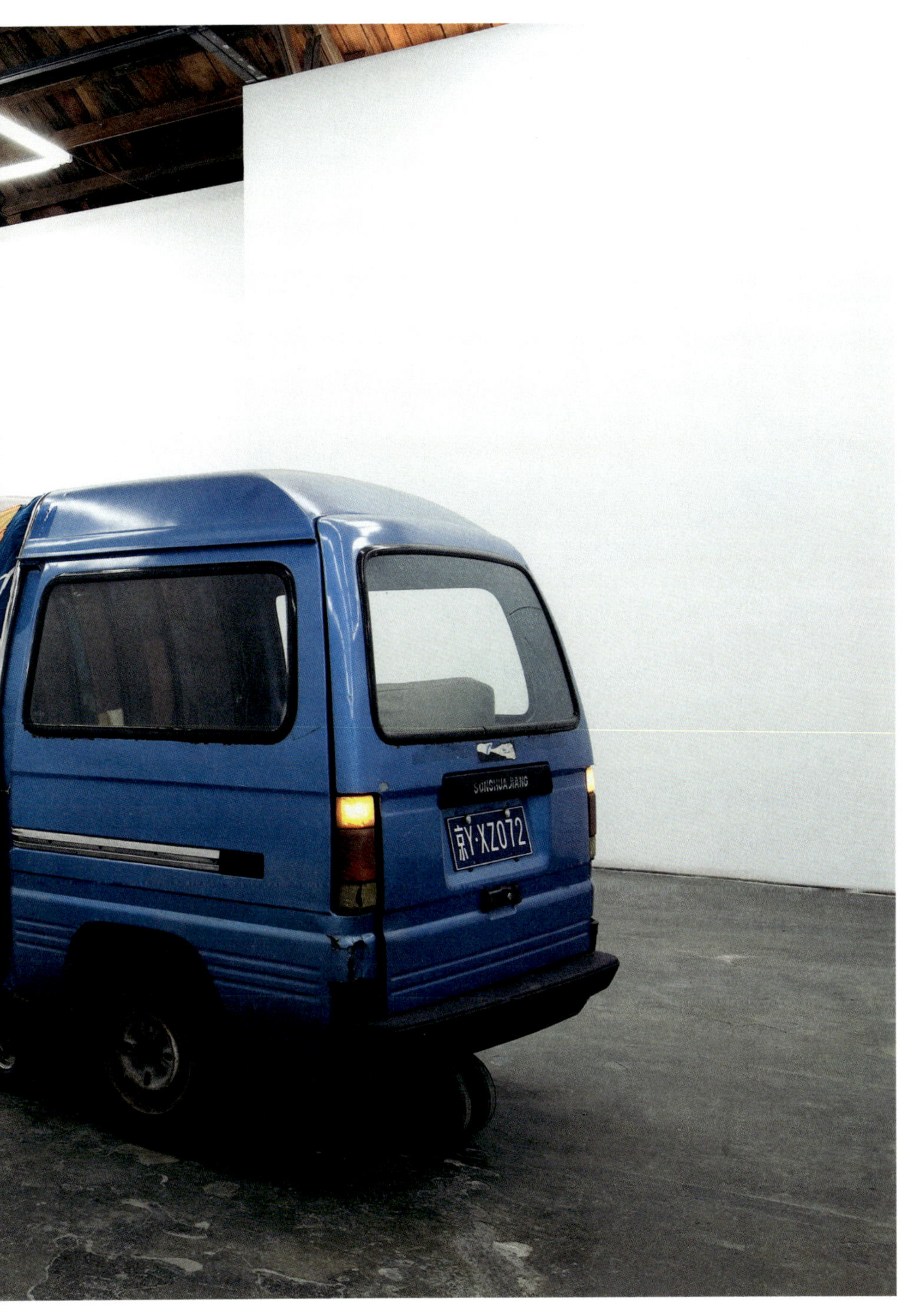

SONGHUA JIANG
京·XZ072

54

Collective Subconscious (Blue),
2007 (details)

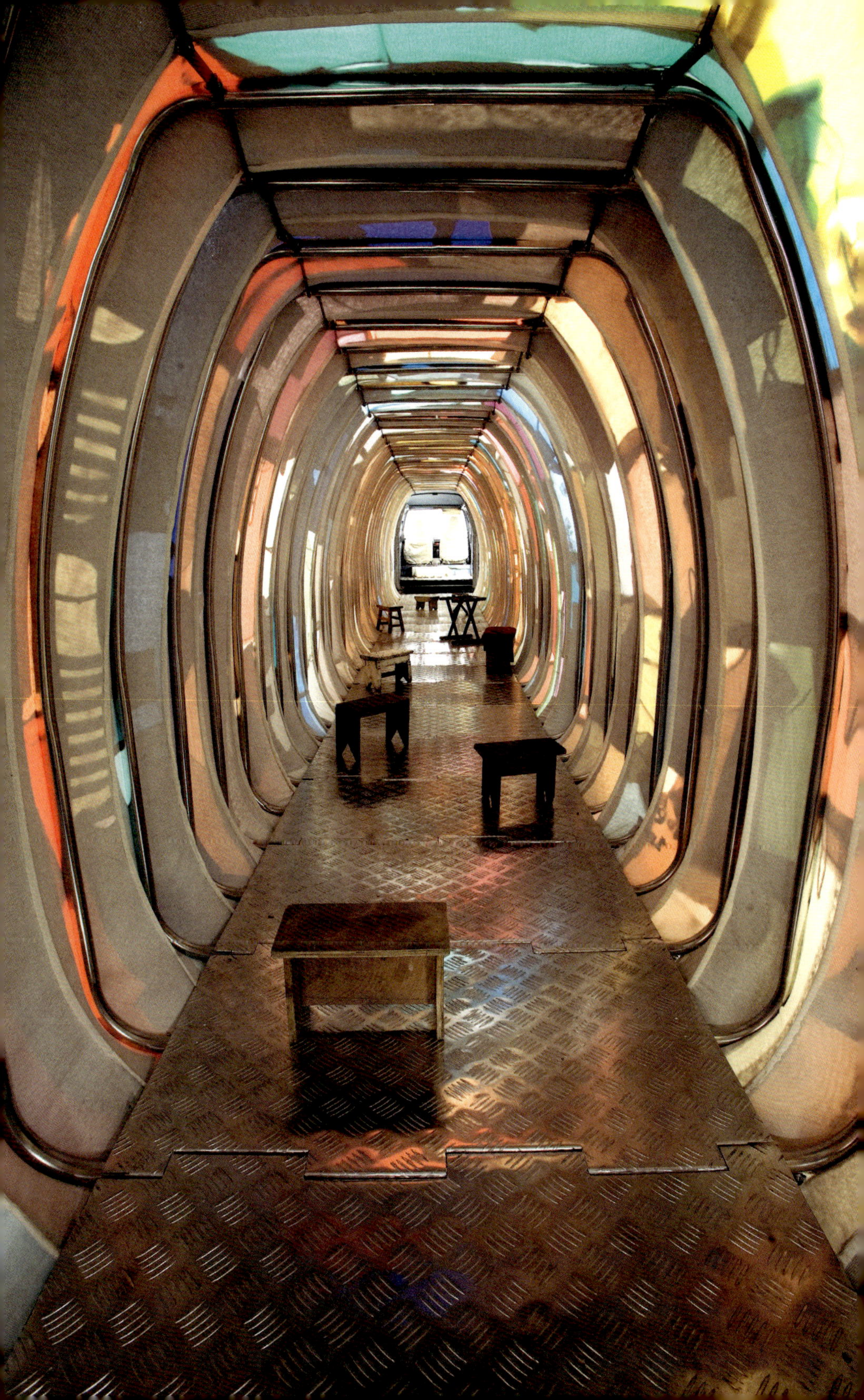

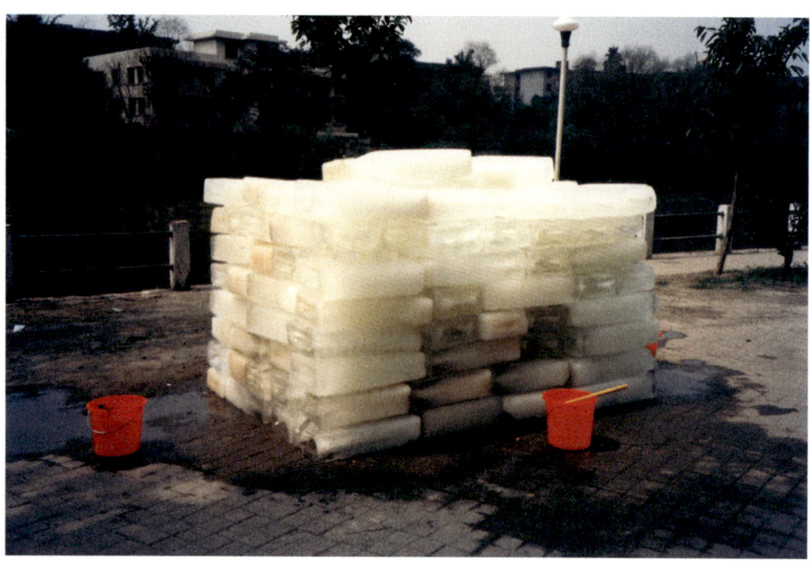

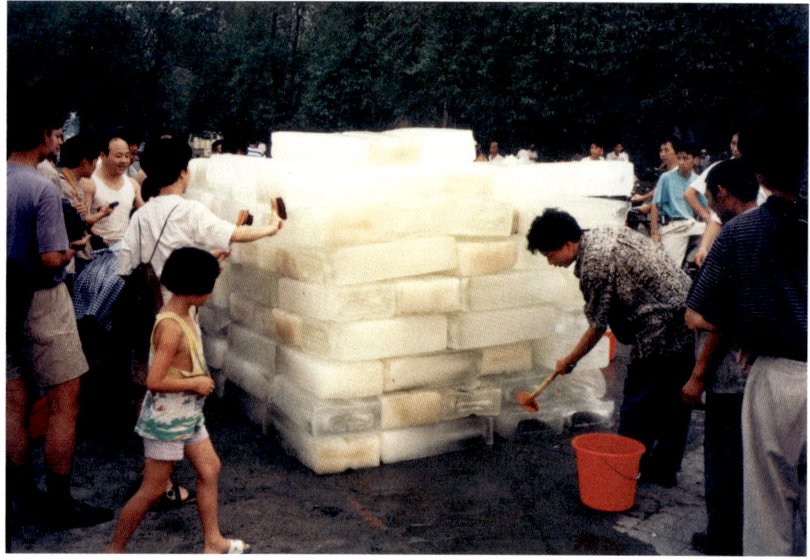

Washing River,
1995

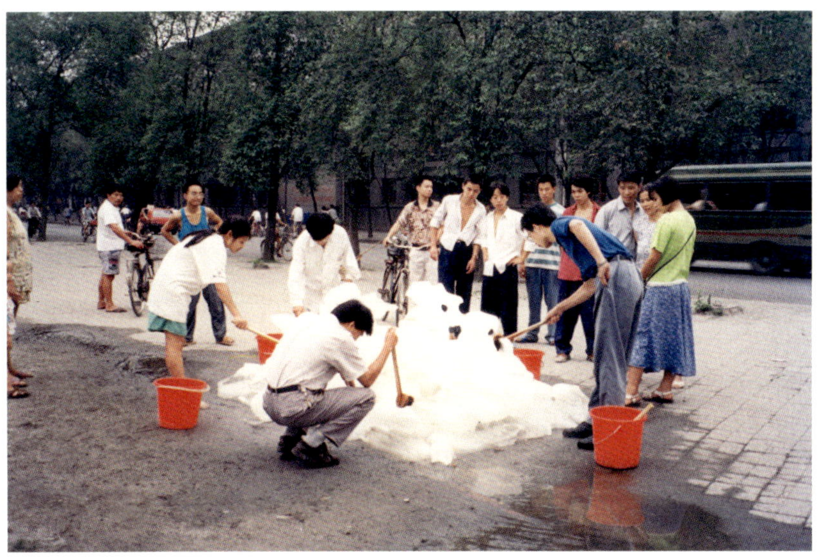

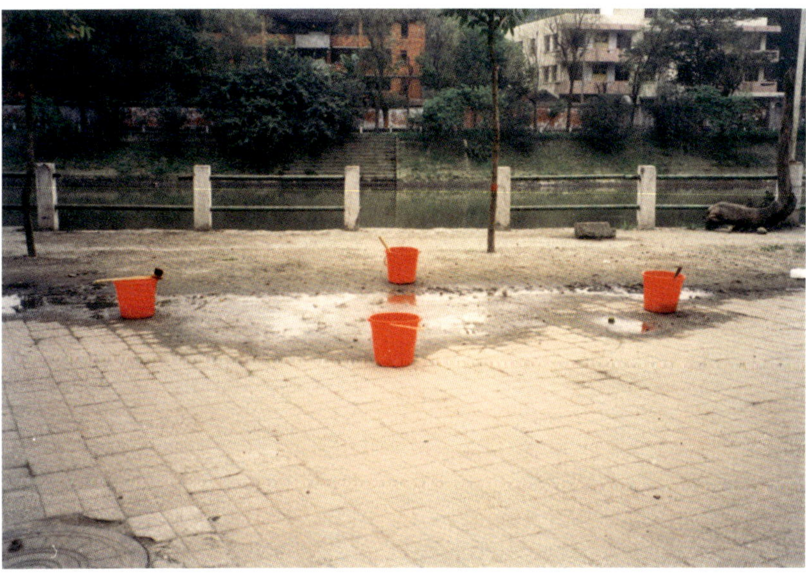

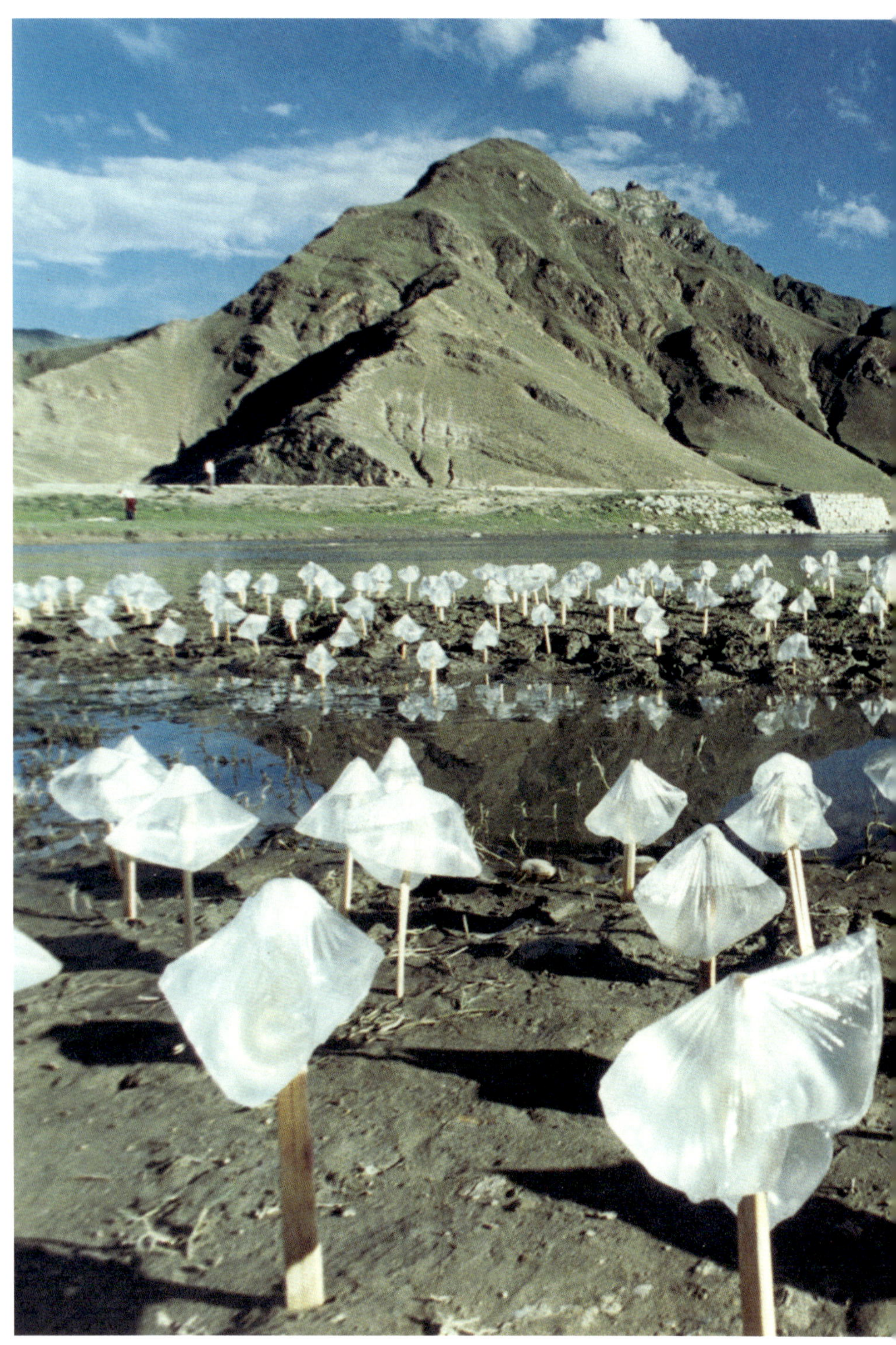

Living Water,
1996

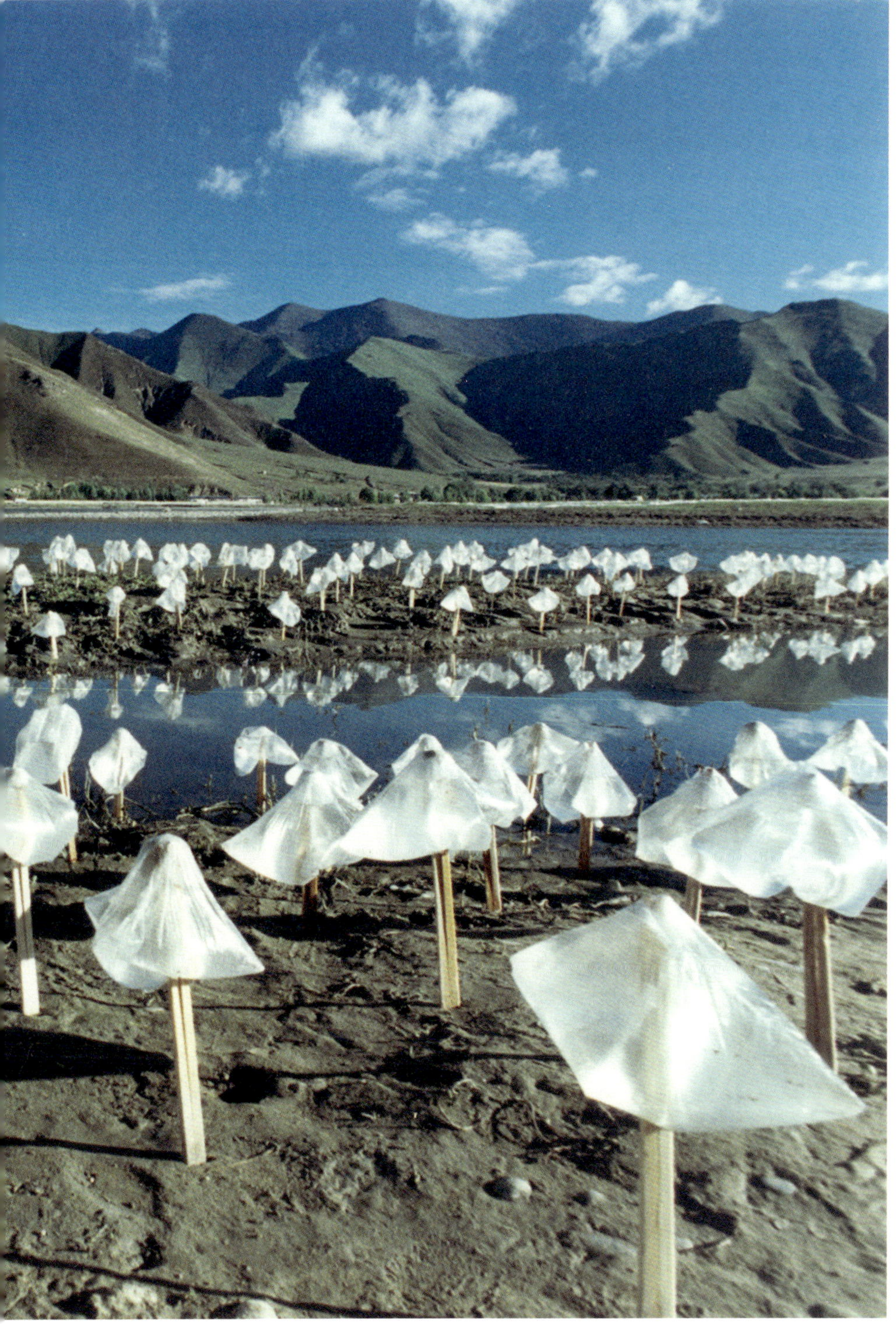

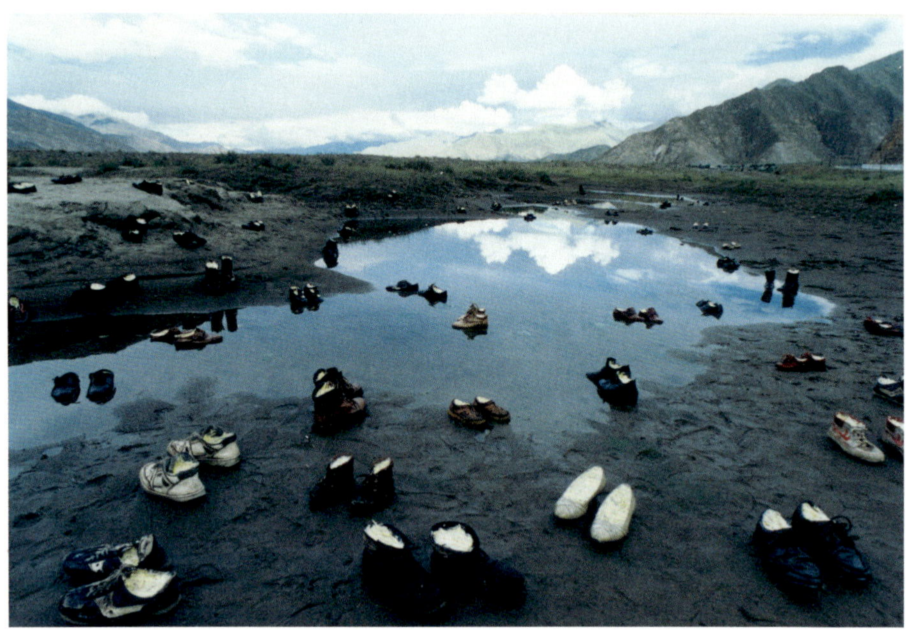

Shoes with Butter,
1996

'Why do people want to develop so quickly? ... As the environment deteriorates it will no longer be able to provide mankind with the conditions for survival.'

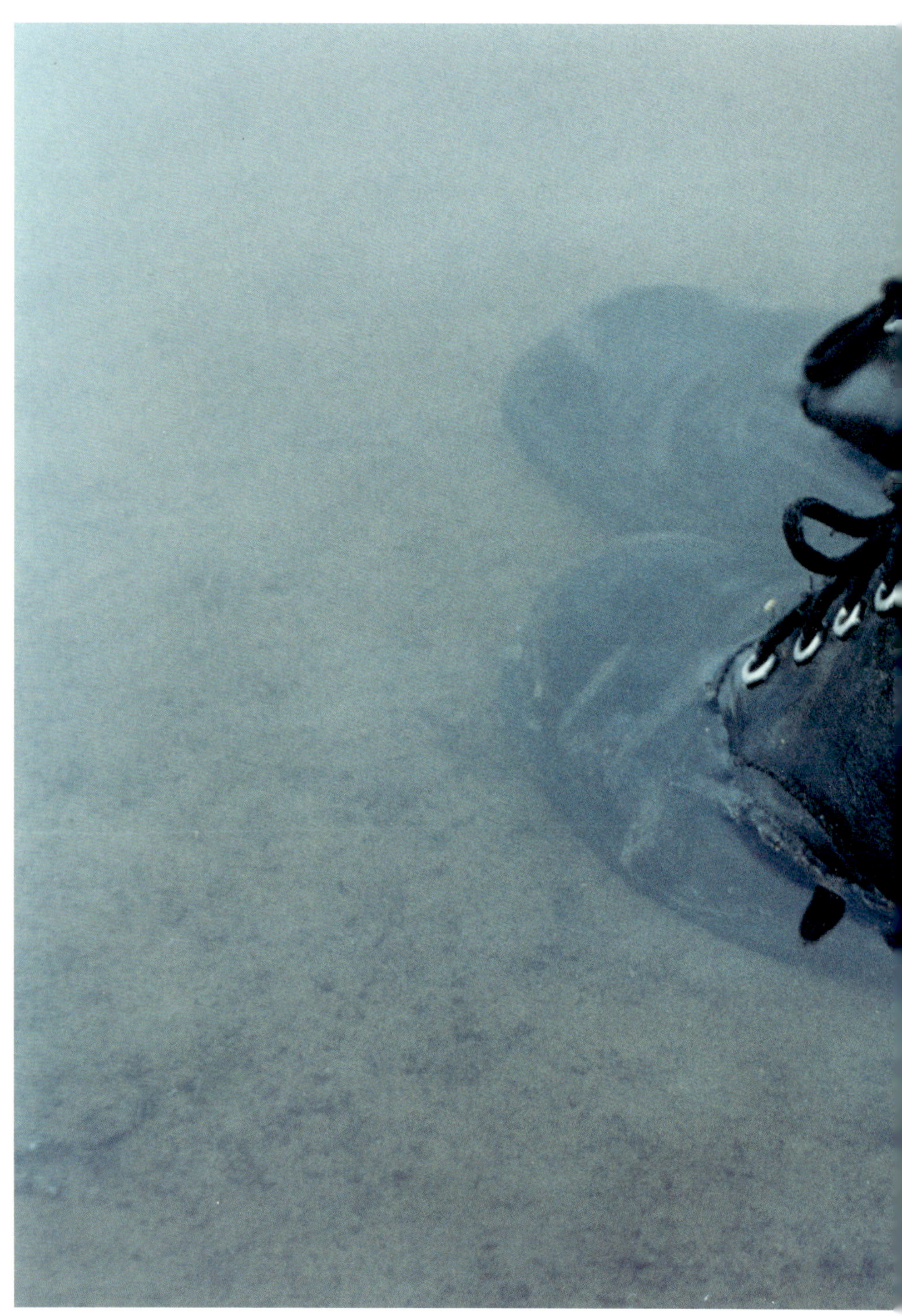

Shoes with Butter,
1996

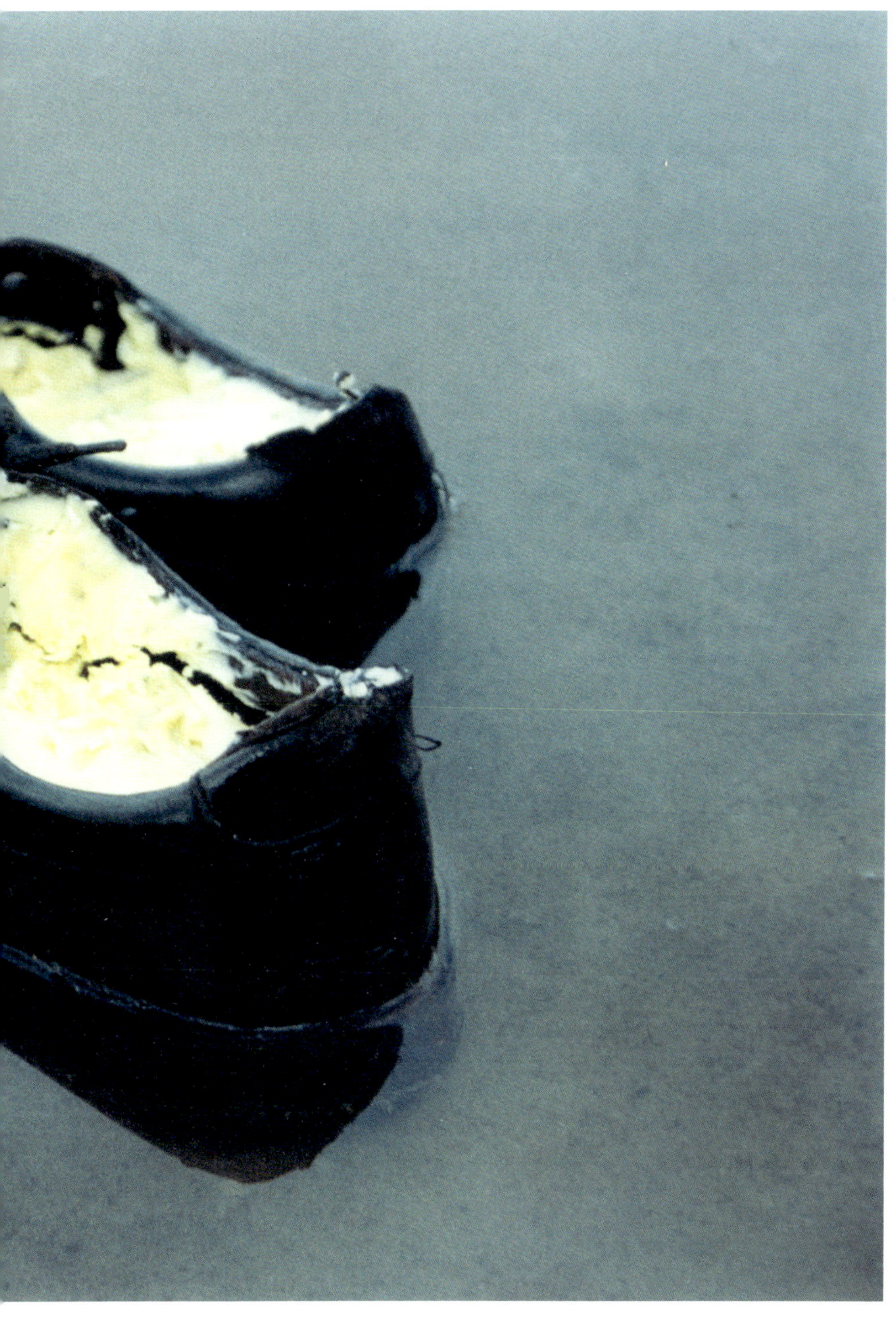

‘Demolition and construction are markers of deeper human values … we could only use artistic methods to shout out this sadness.’

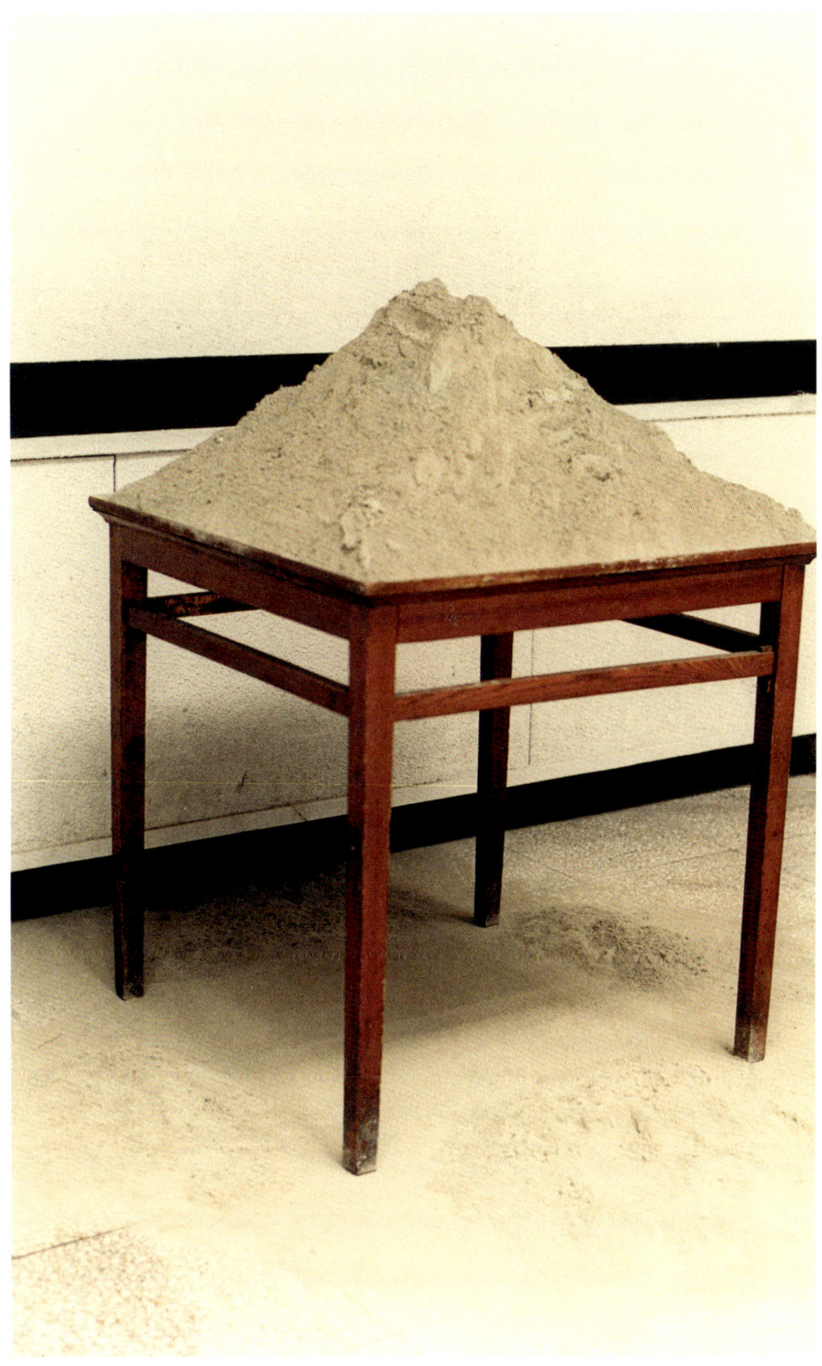

65

Ruined City,
1996 (and following pages)

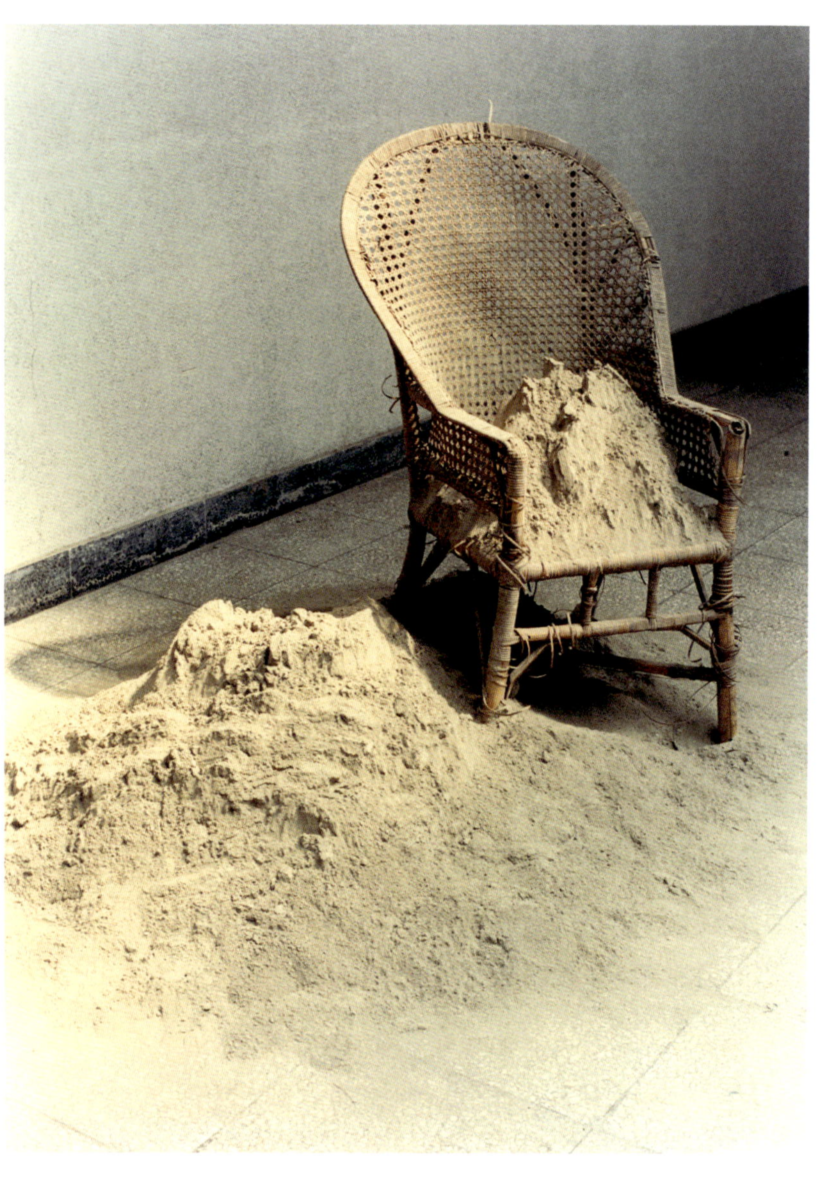

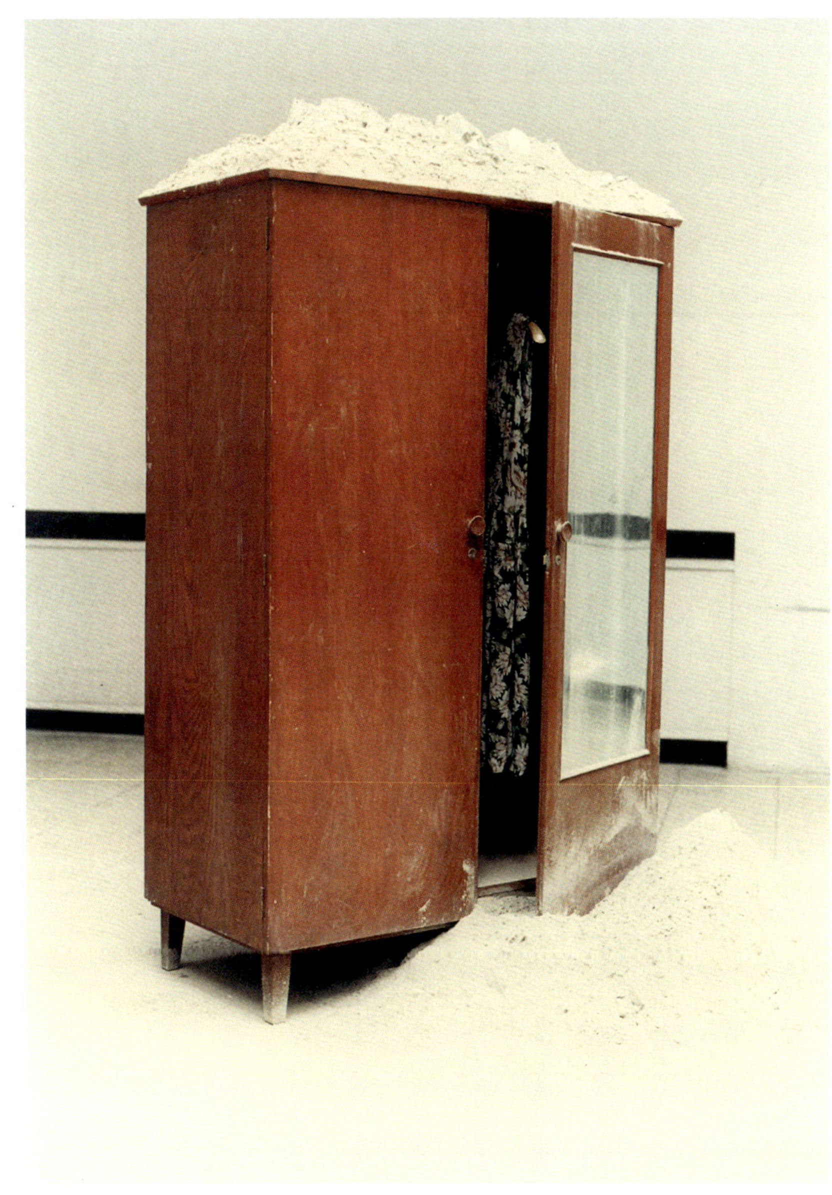

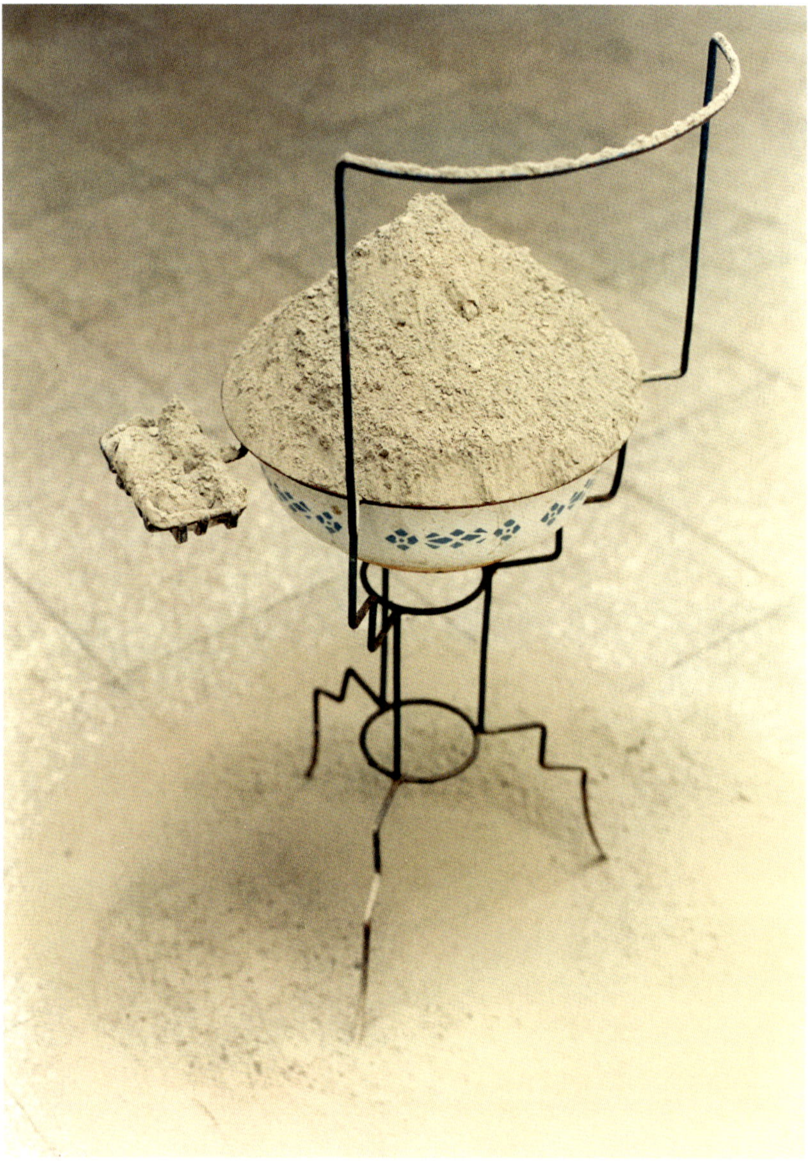

68

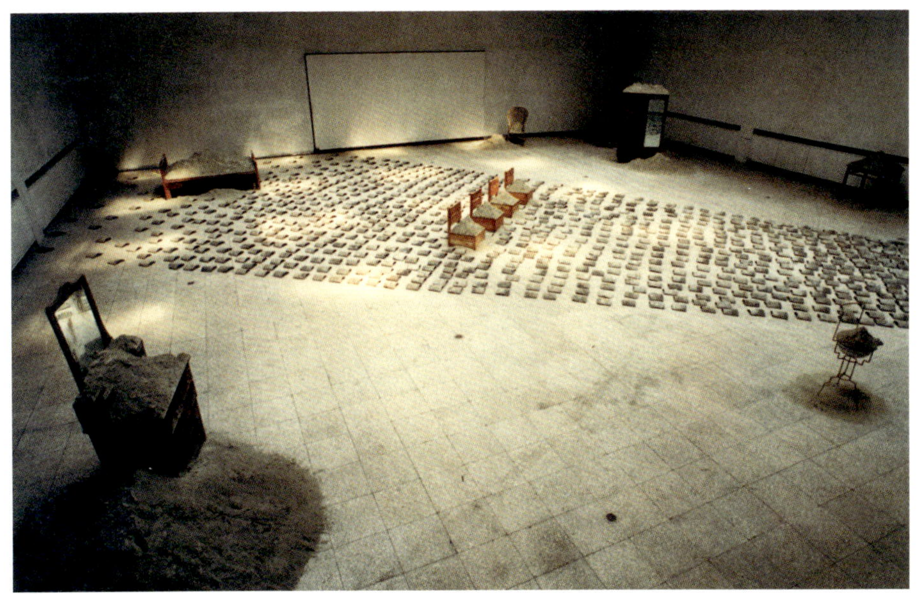

69

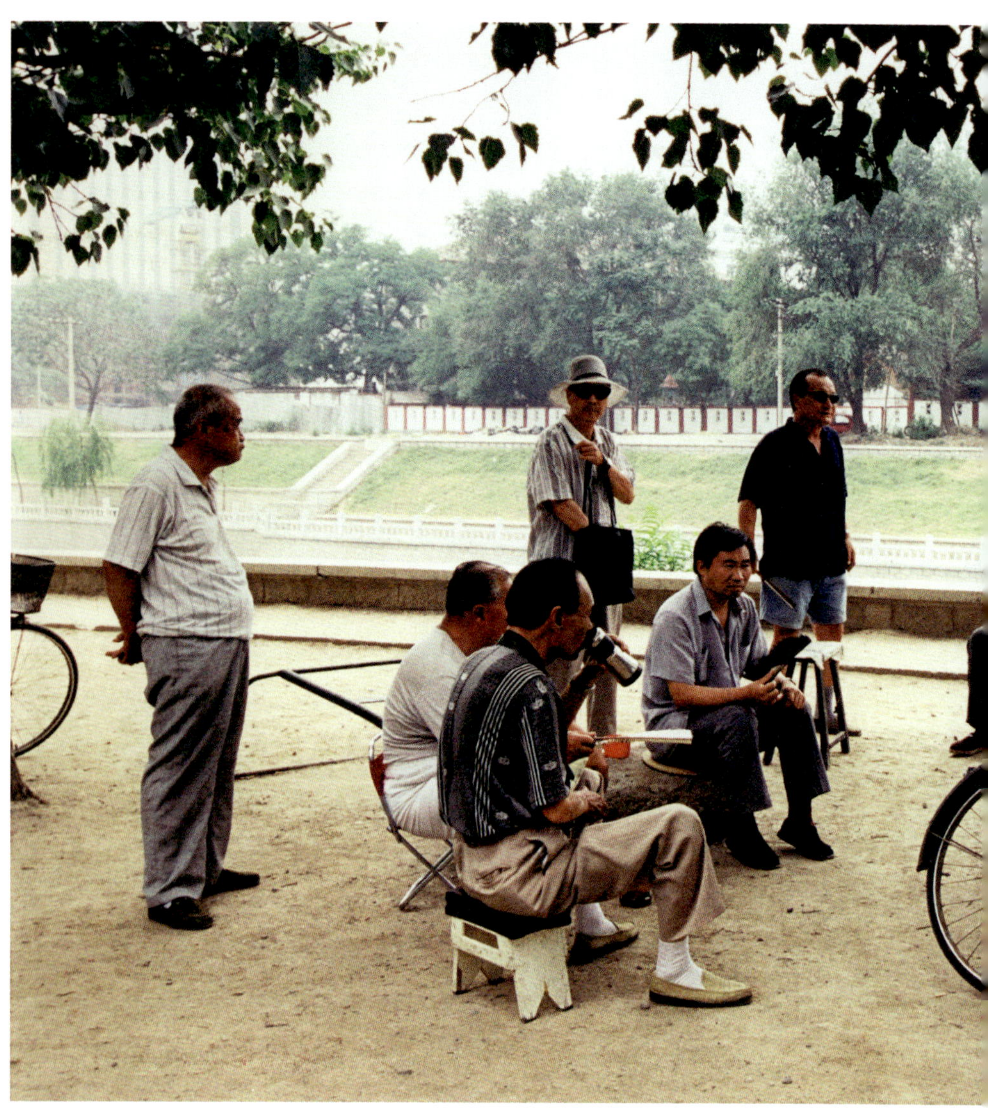

Beijing Opera,
2001 (and following pages)

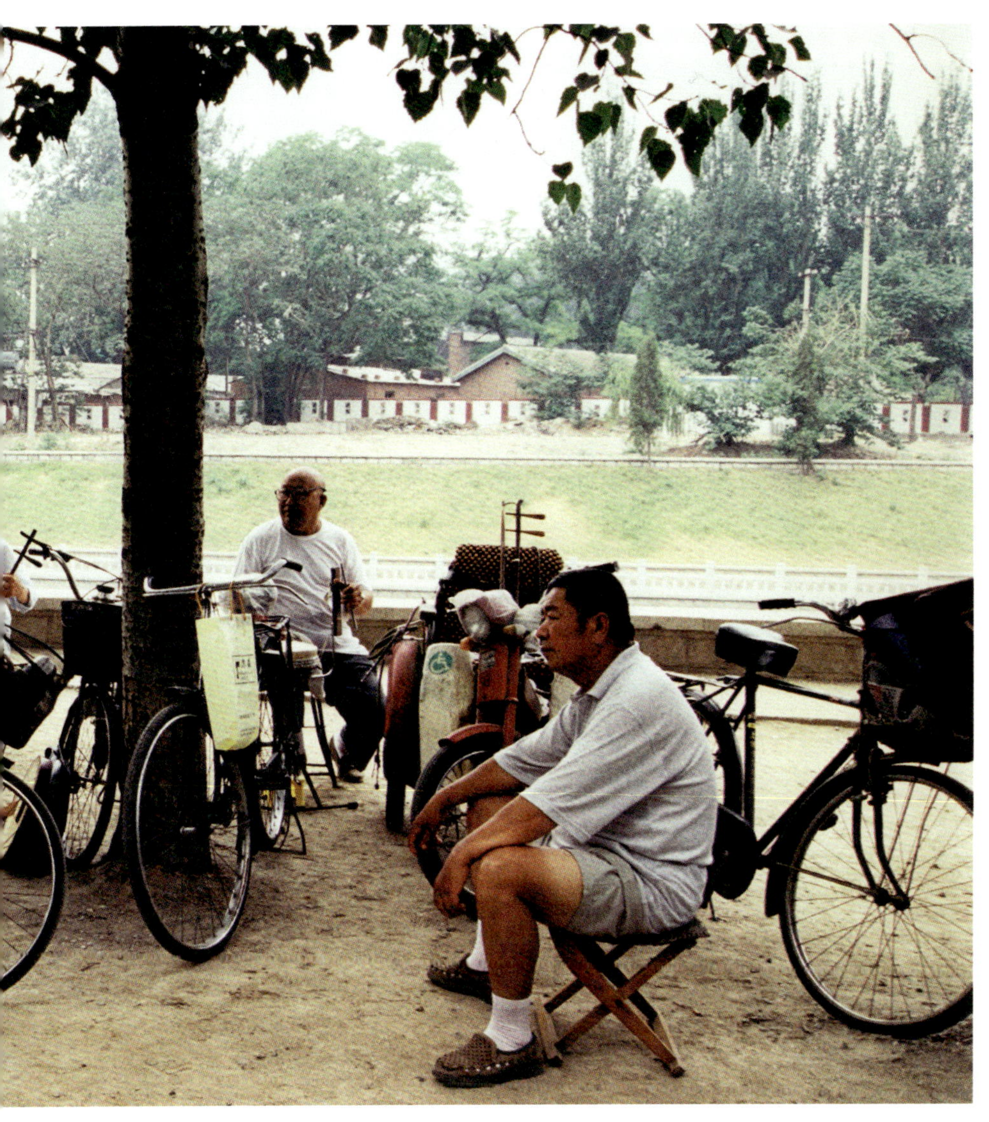

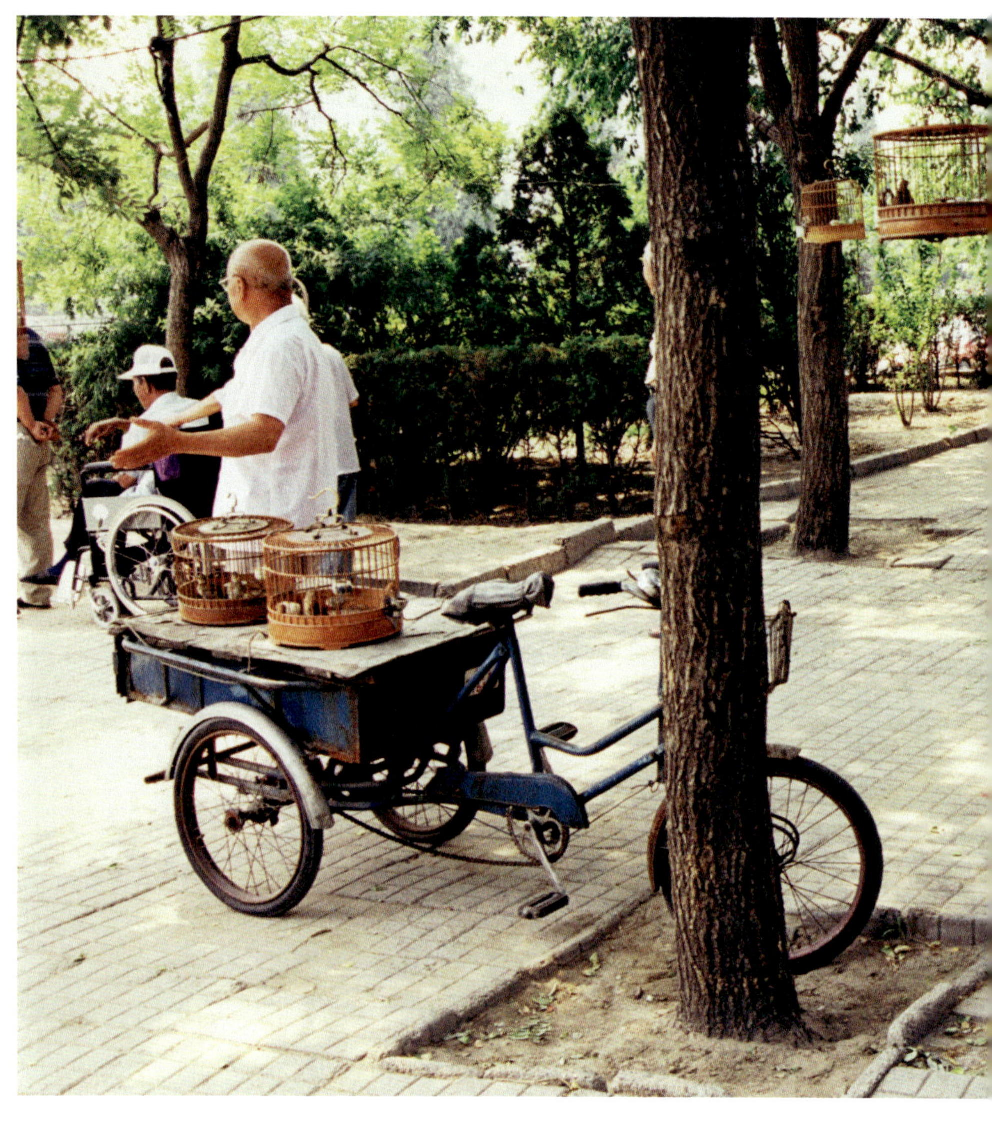

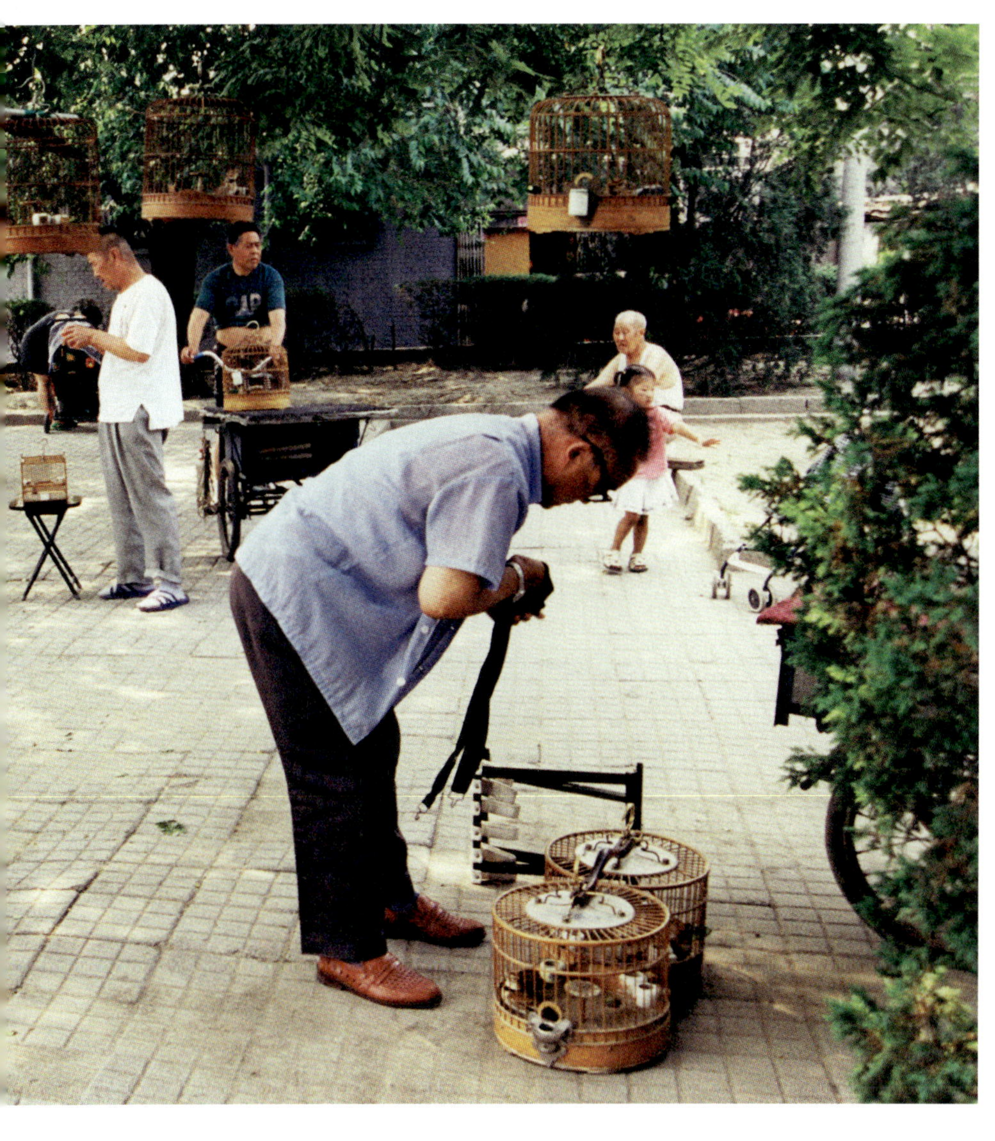

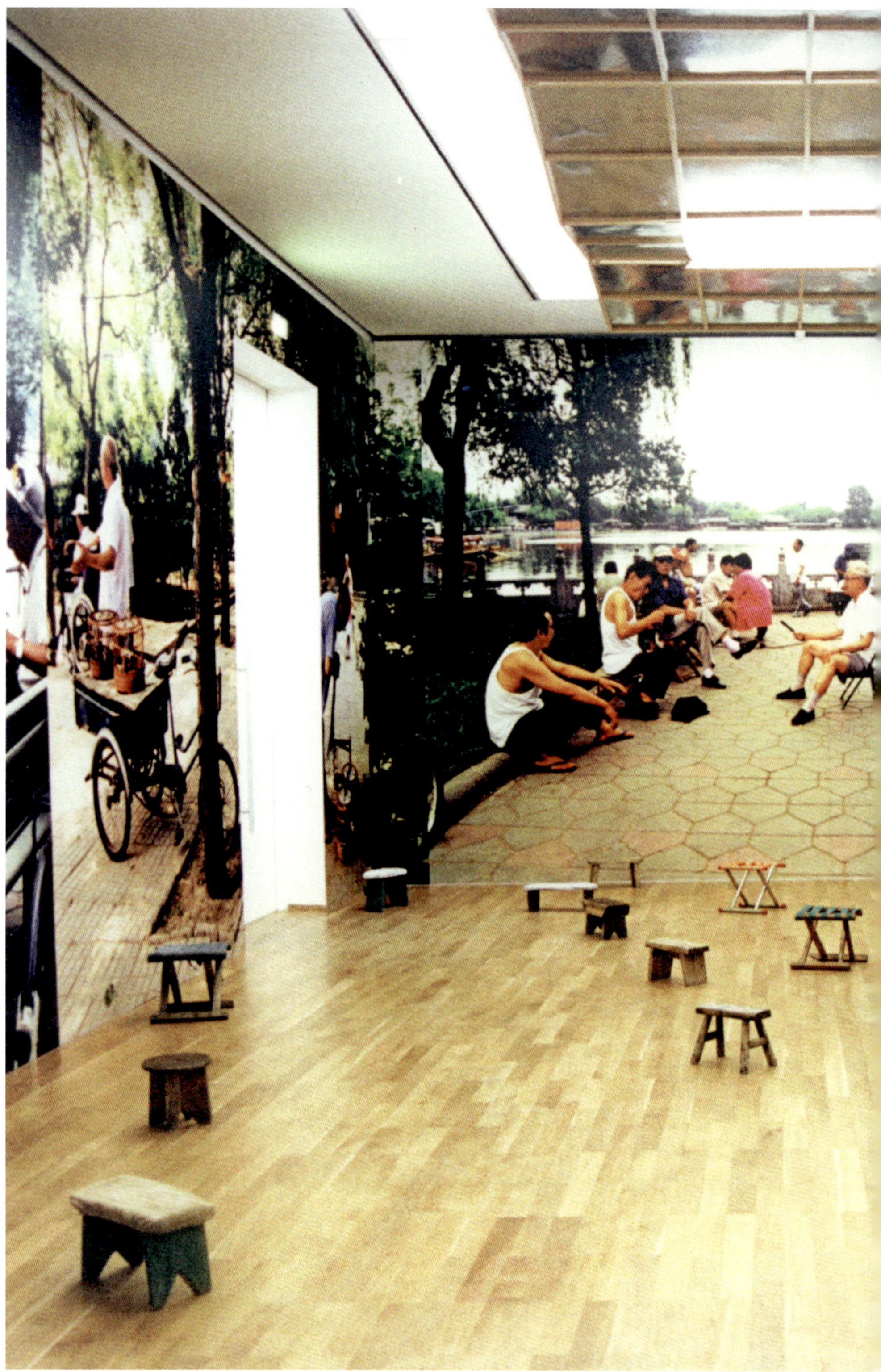

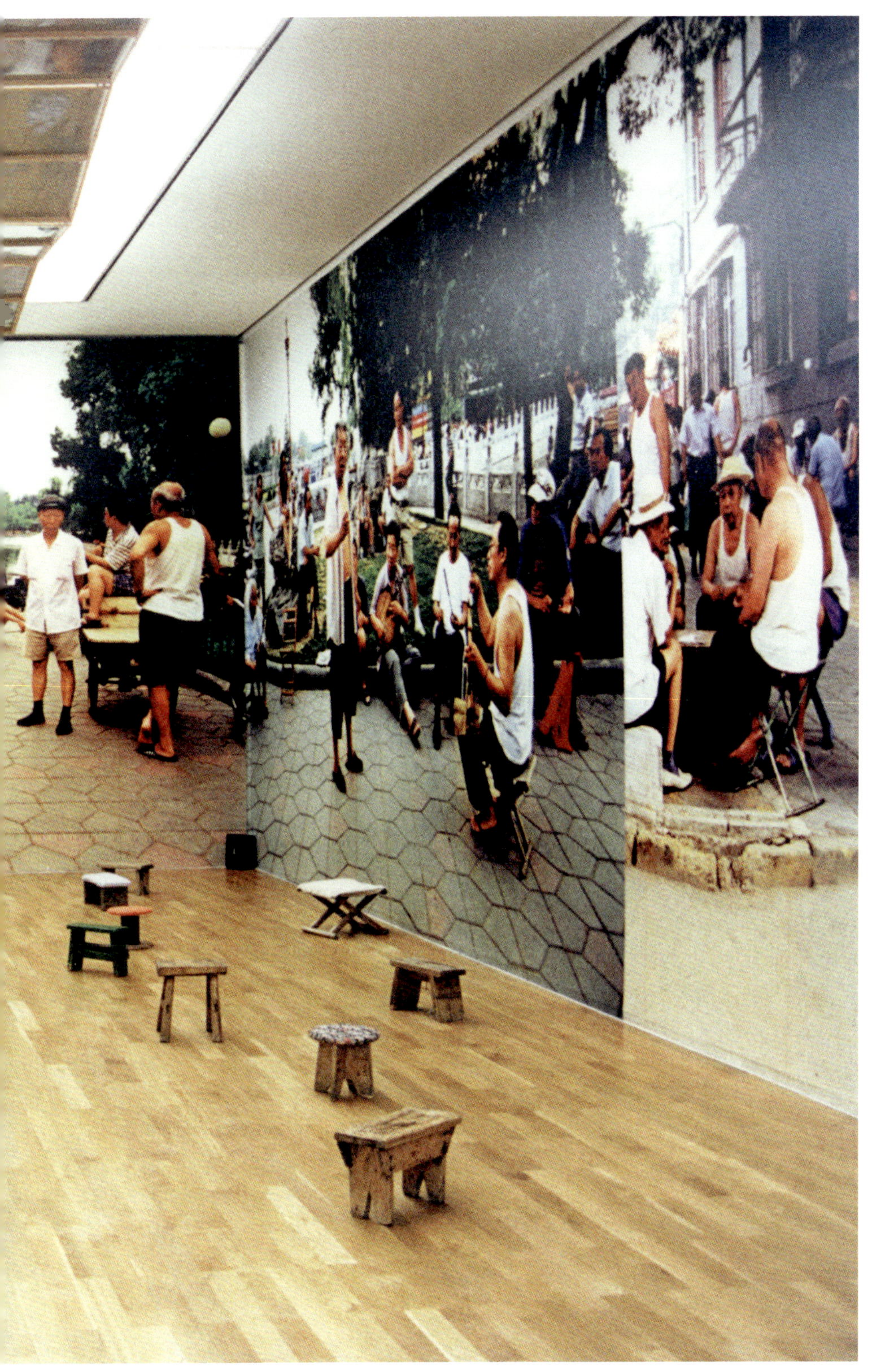

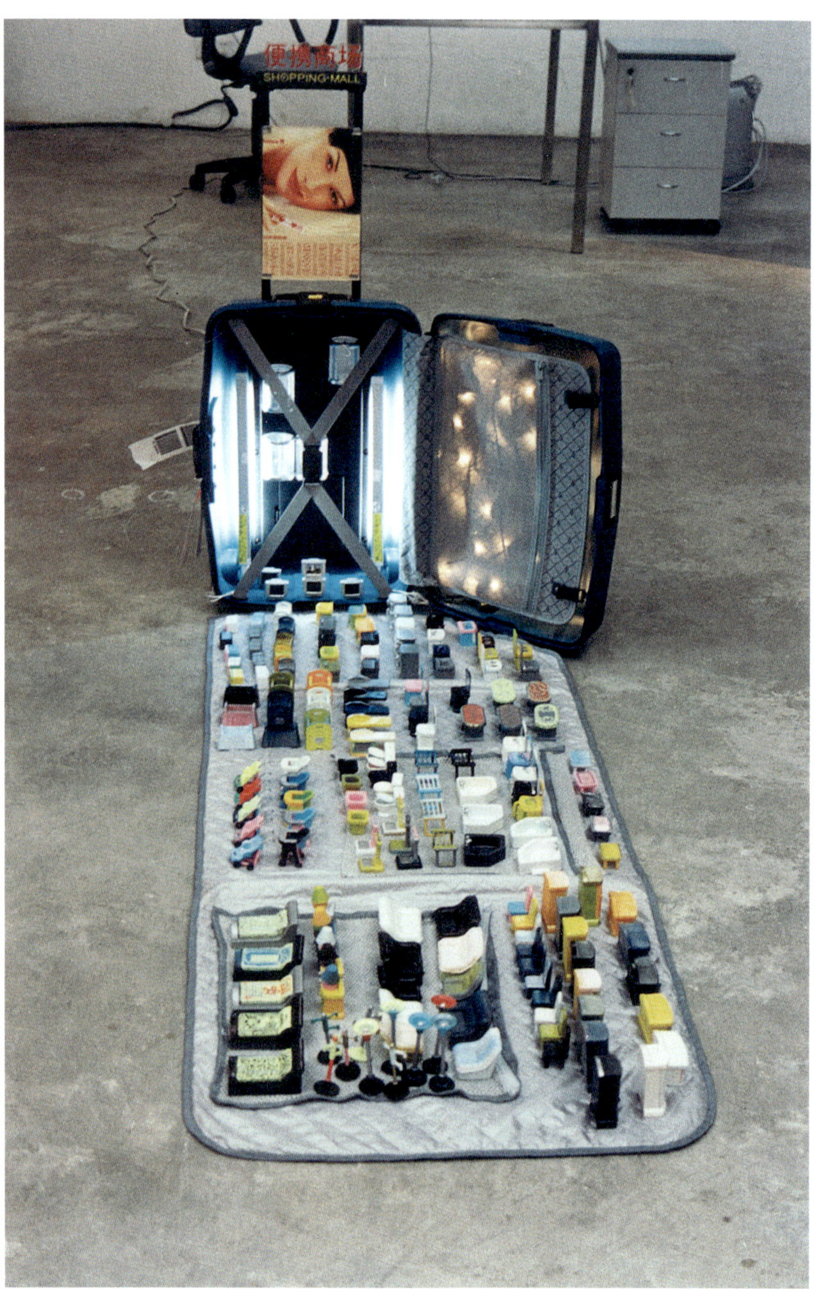

Portable Shopping Mall,
2002

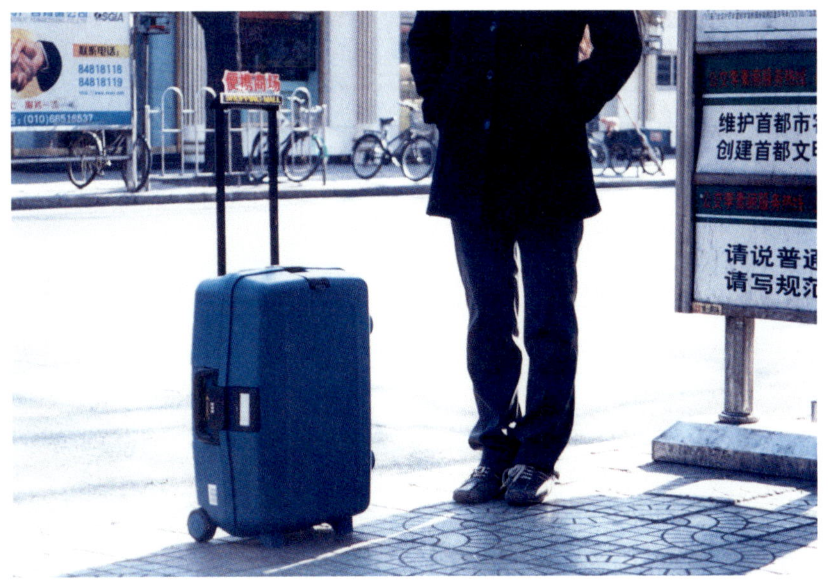
84818118
84818119
(010)68518837
便携商场
SHOPPING MALL
维护首都市
创建首都文明
请说普通
请写规范

'Two materials wrestling with each other … This contest exists in nature, between people, among animals … a struggle to achieve balance.'

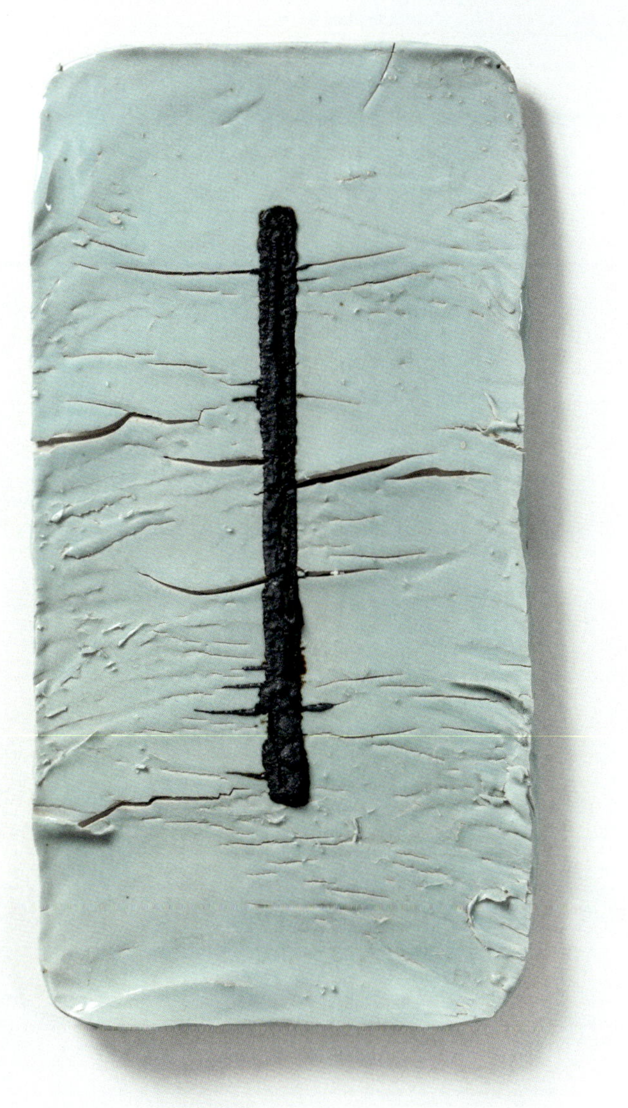

79

Blending Instrument - Ruler No. 3,
2017

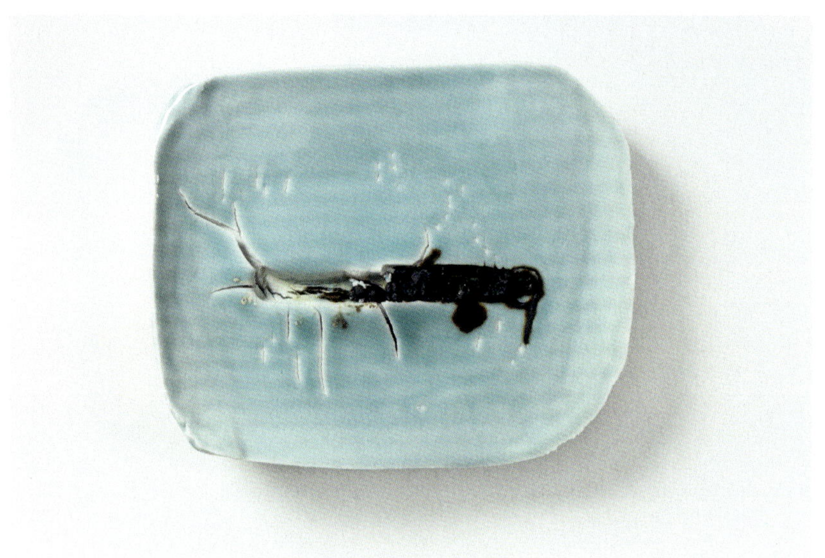

Blending Instrument – Knife No. 3,
2016

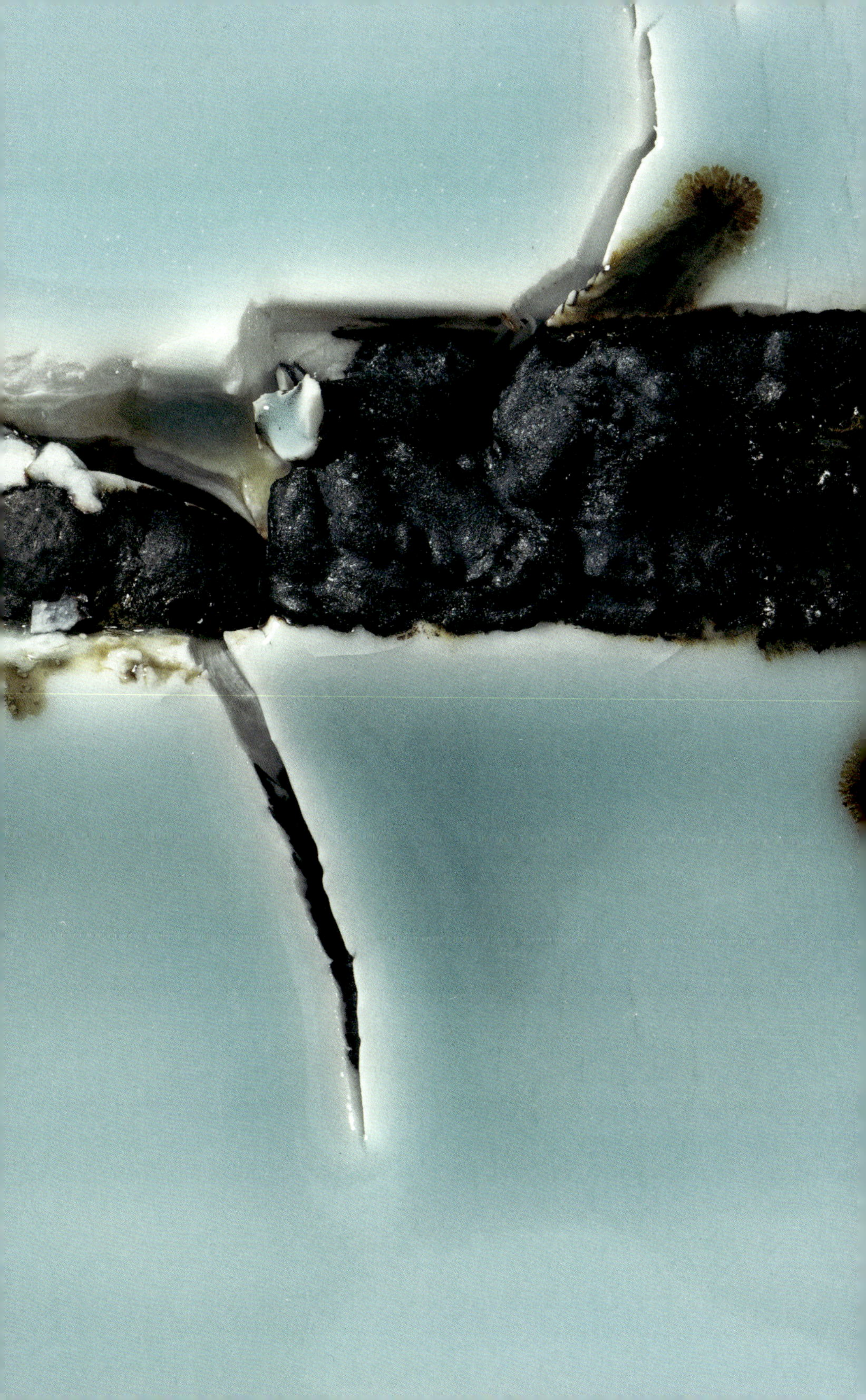

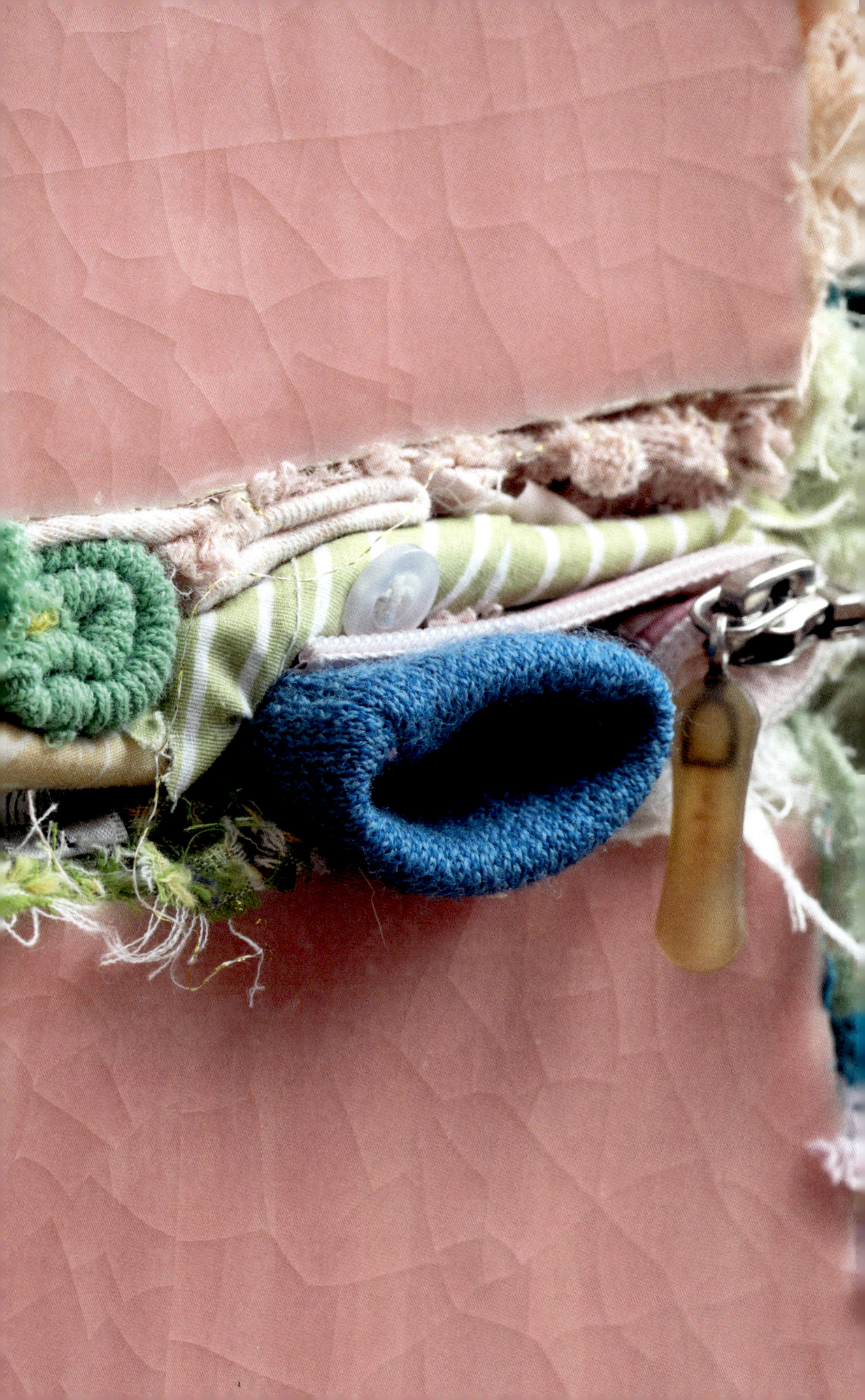

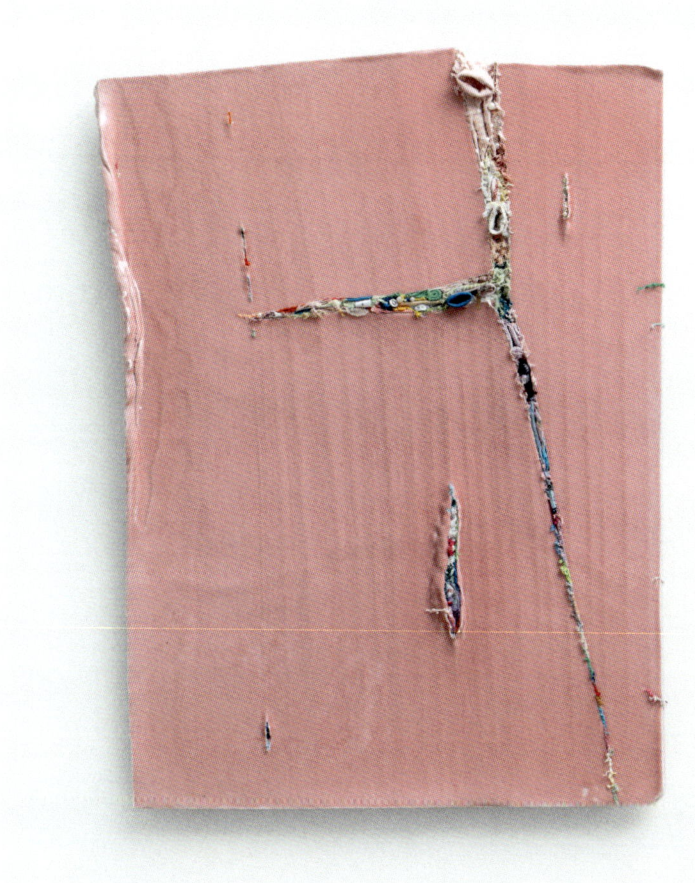

Skin of Oblivion,
2024-25

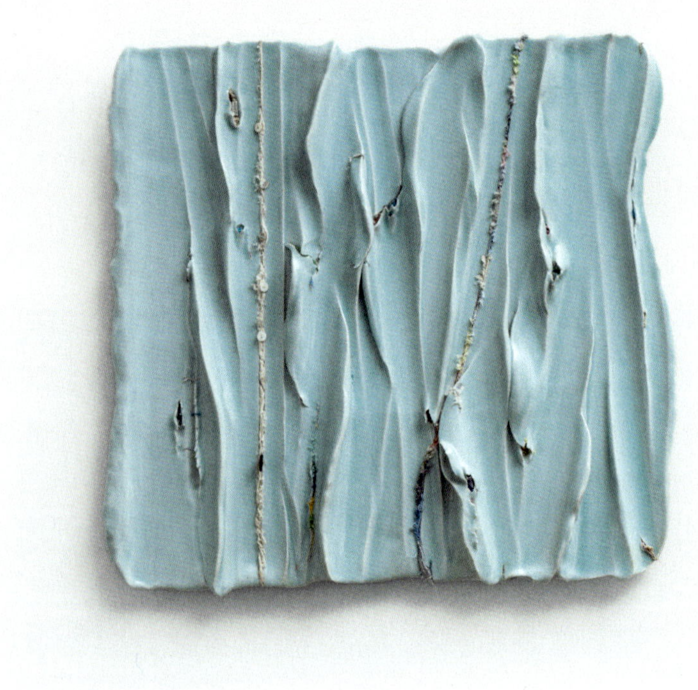

Wall Instrument –
The Surging Waves Chronicles Vol. 7,
2021–22

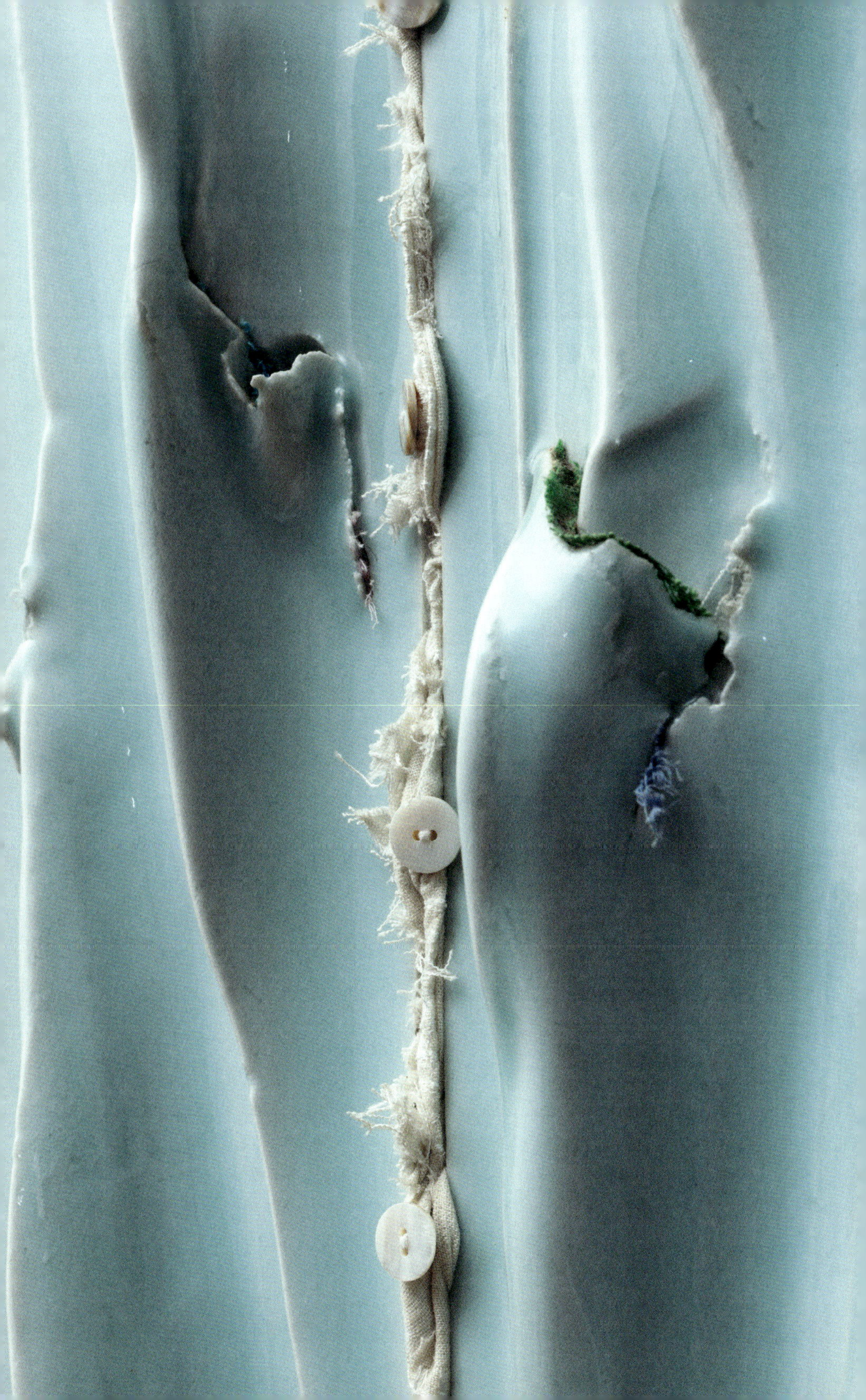

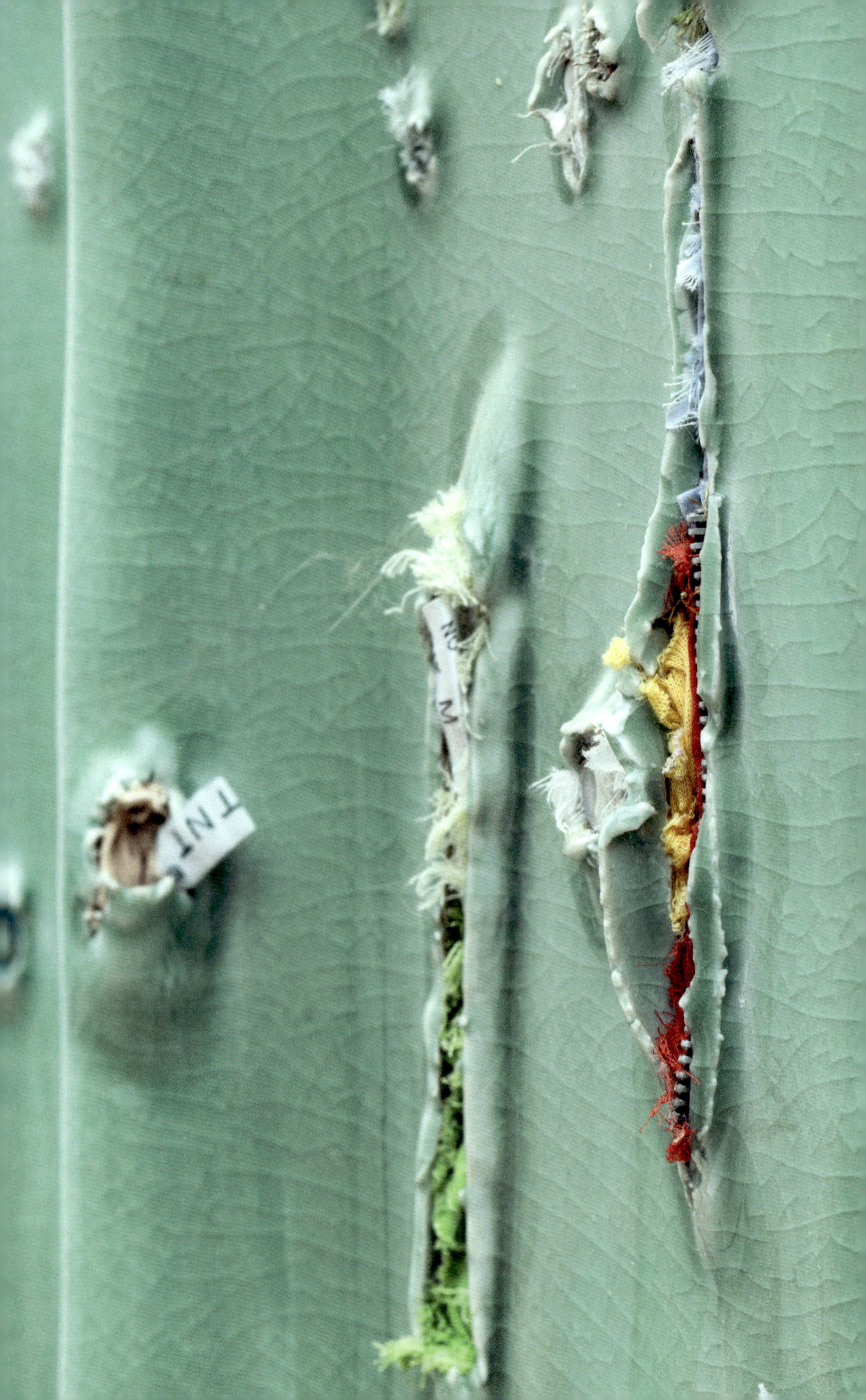

TNT

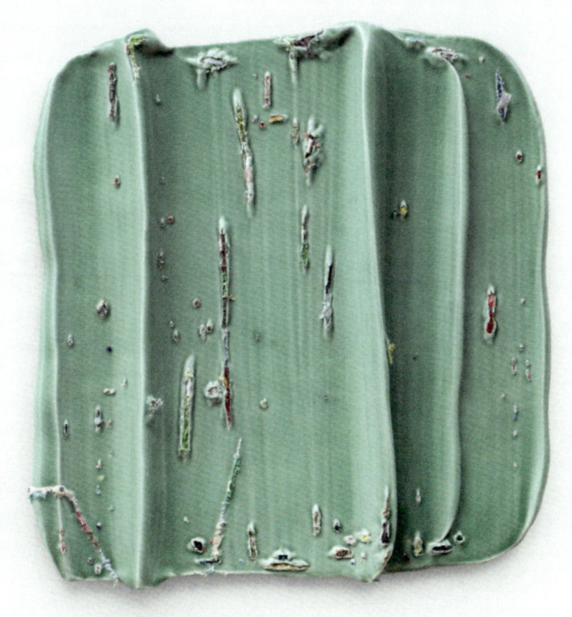

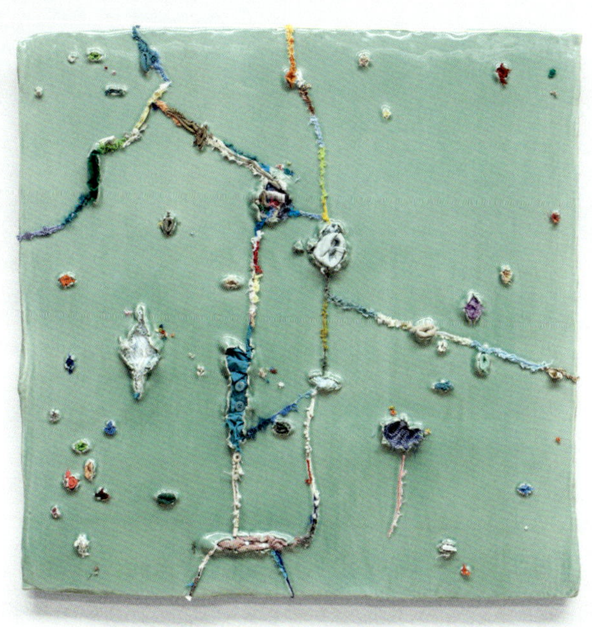

Wall Instrument No. 19,
2018–19 (detail and top right)

Wall Instrument No. 17,
2018–19

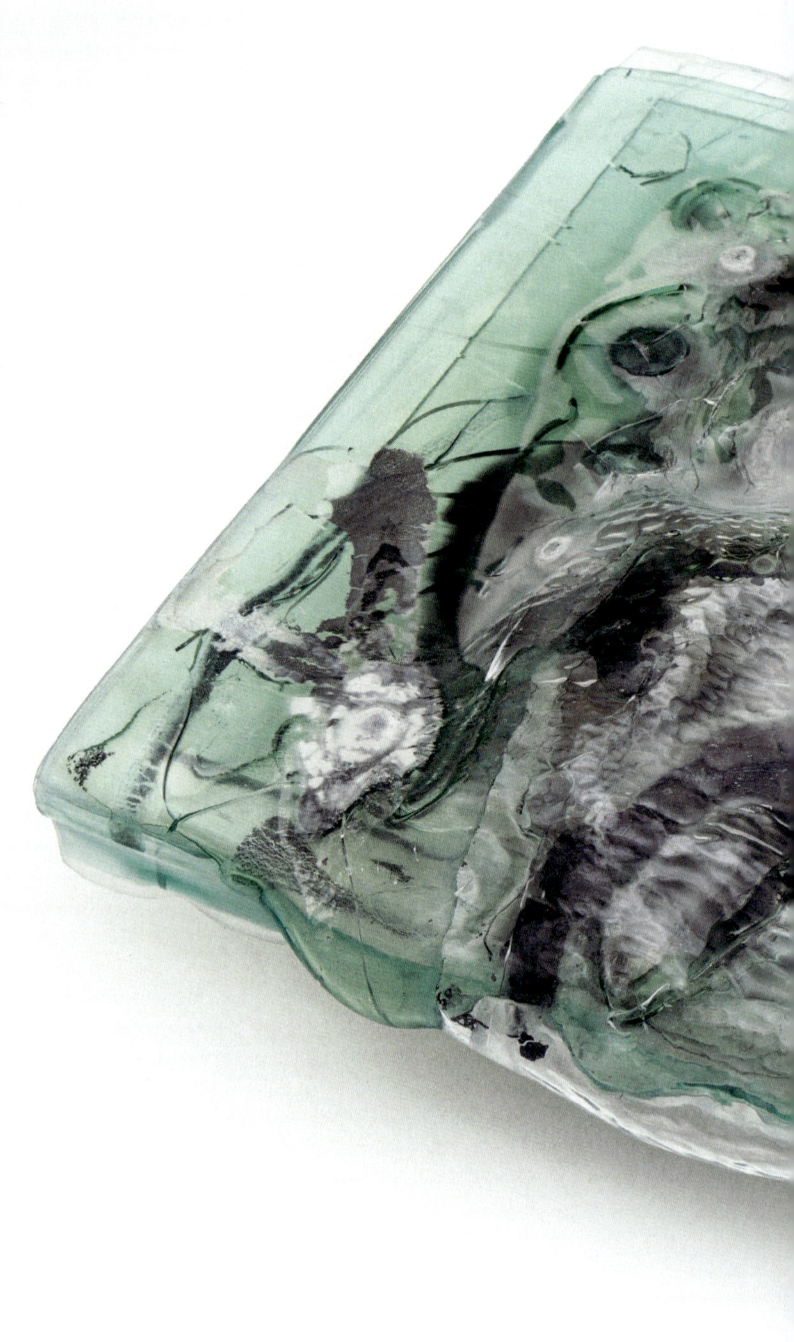

Ripple Stress Series I – No. 10,
2021–23

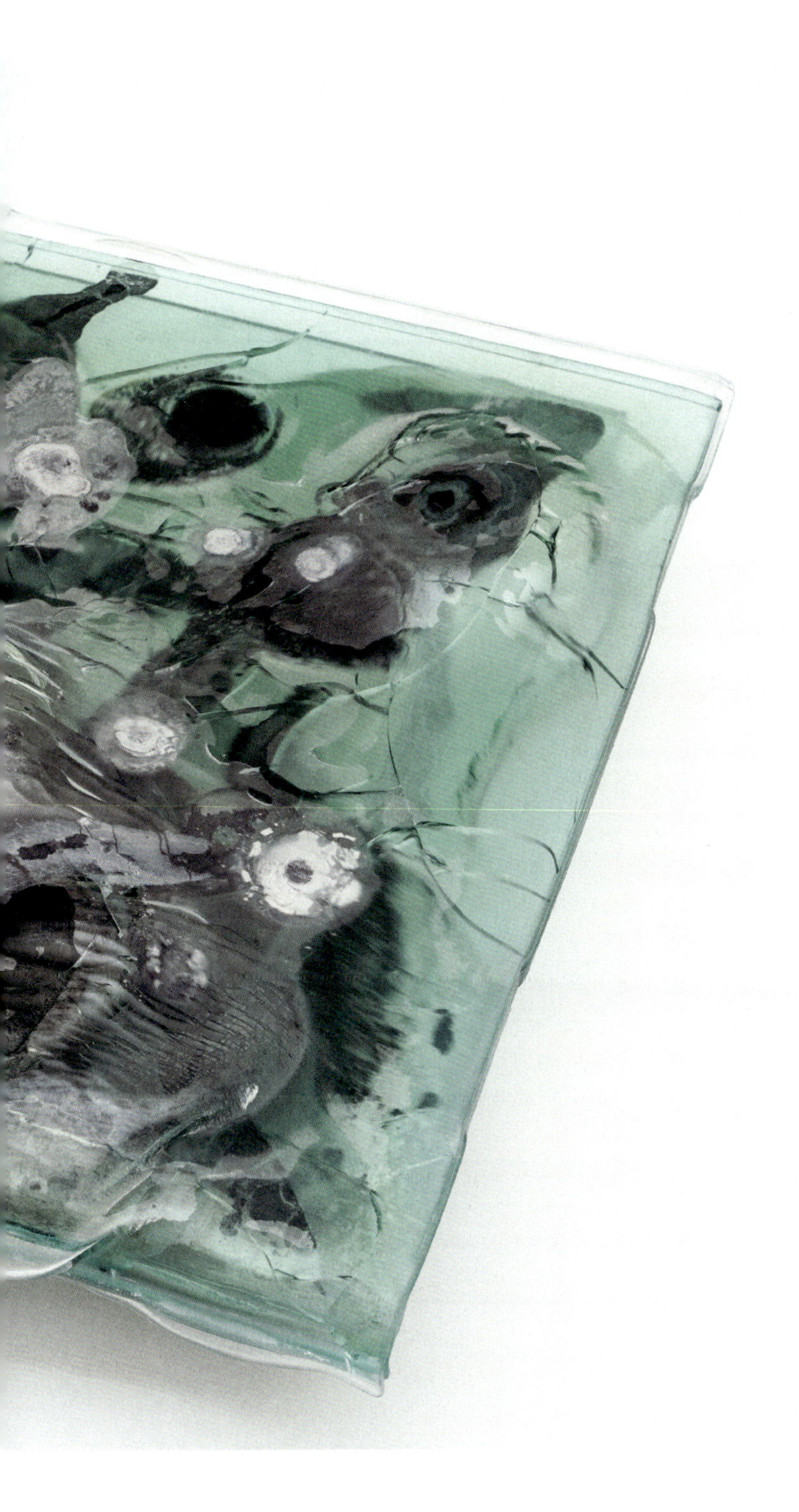

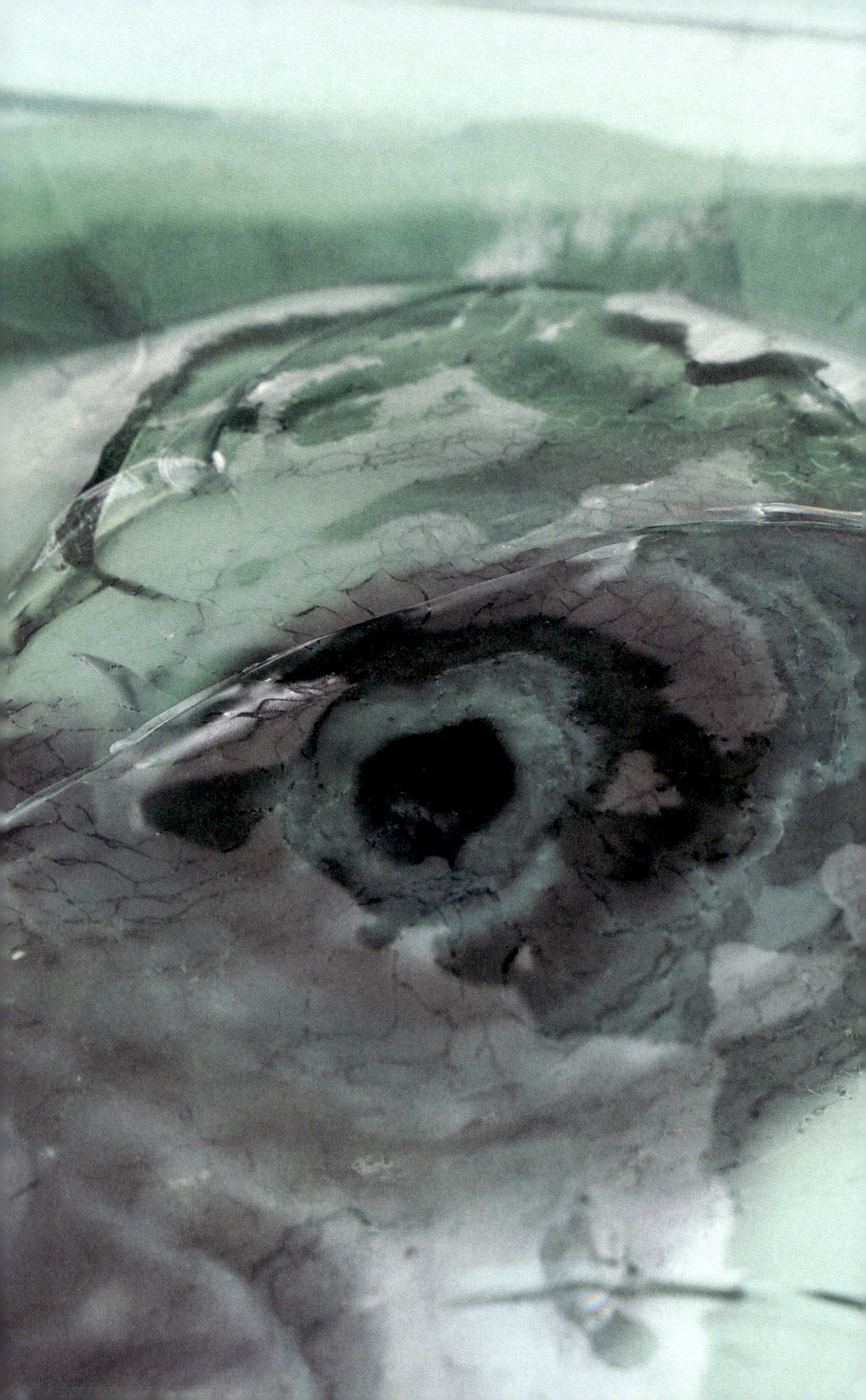

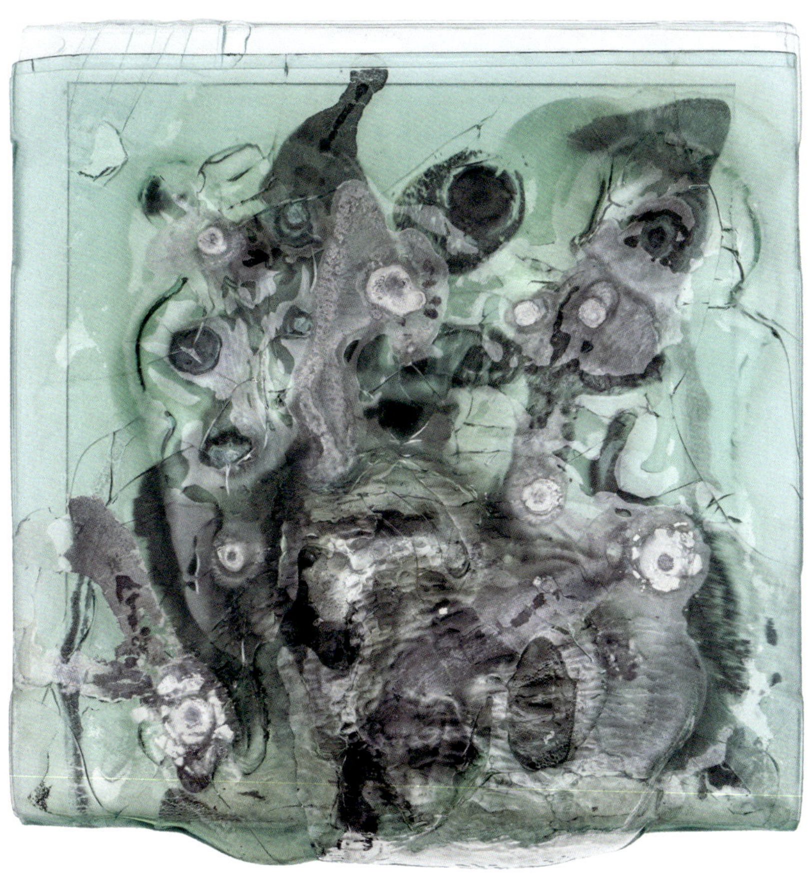

Ripple Stress Series I – No. 10,
2021–23

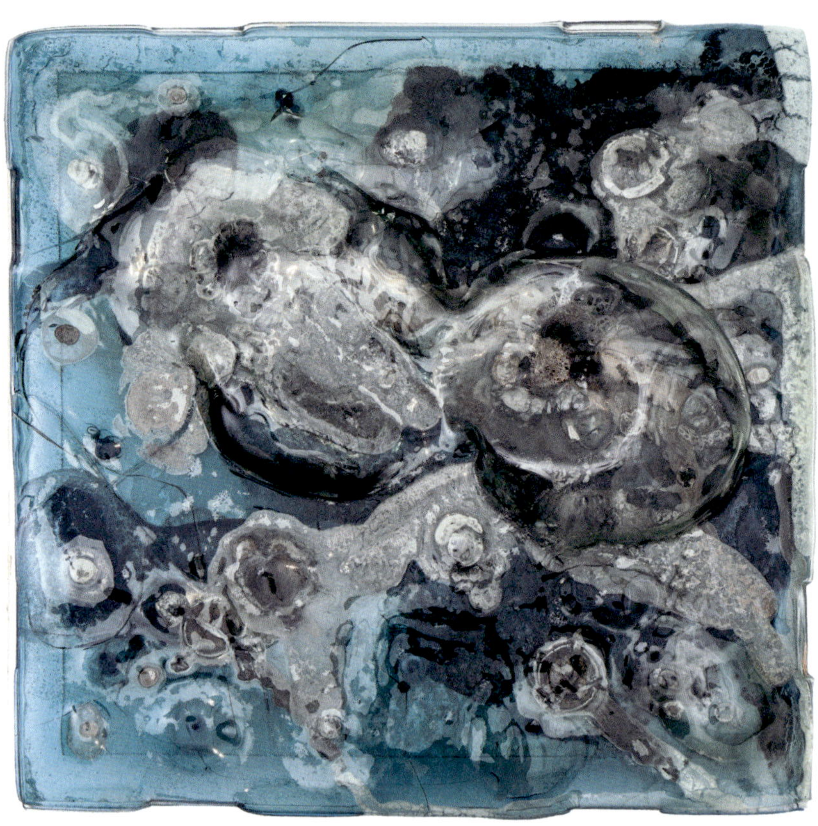

Ripple Stress Series I – No. 11,
2021–23

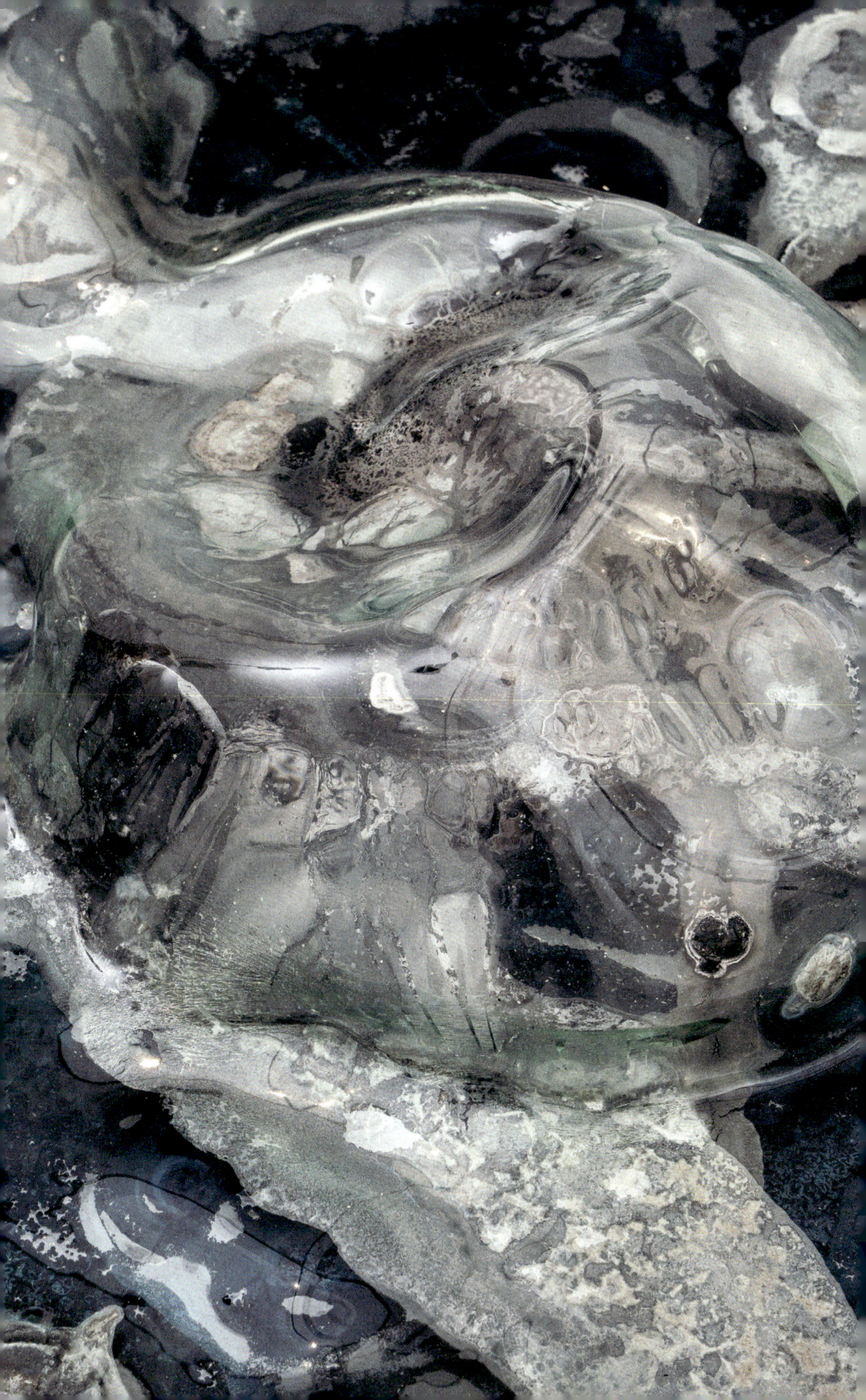

'These clothes are like shadows of memory … I sealed the worn clothing in concrete … it's like I sealed up a stretch of memories.'

95

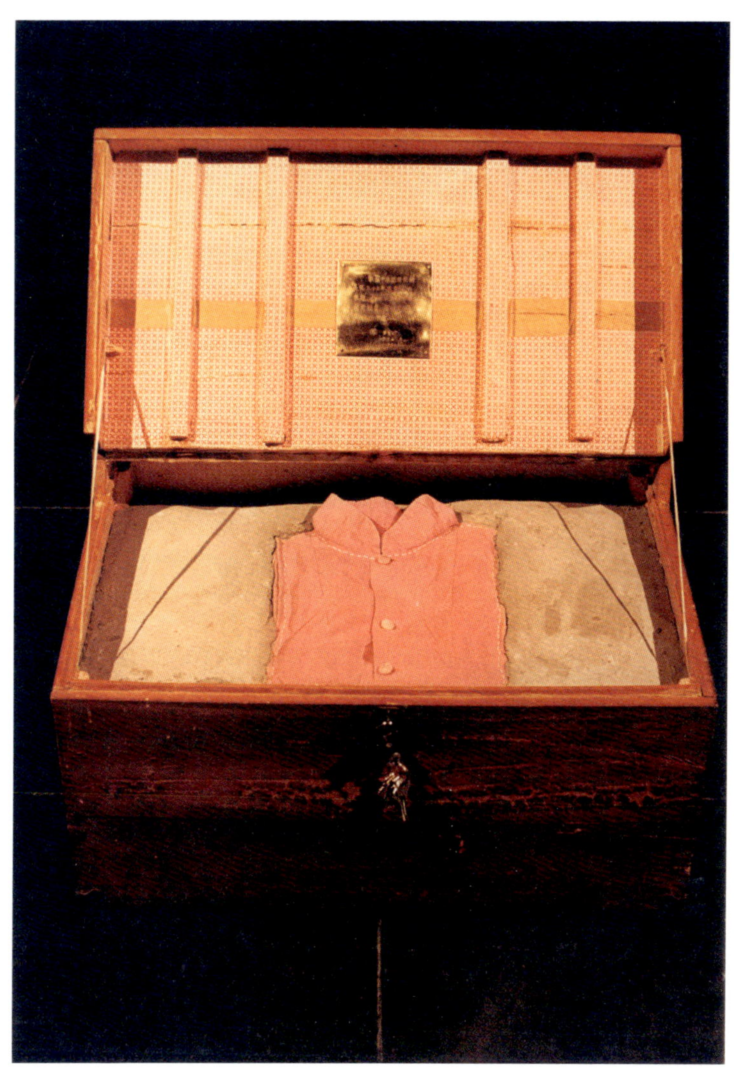

Dress Box,
1995

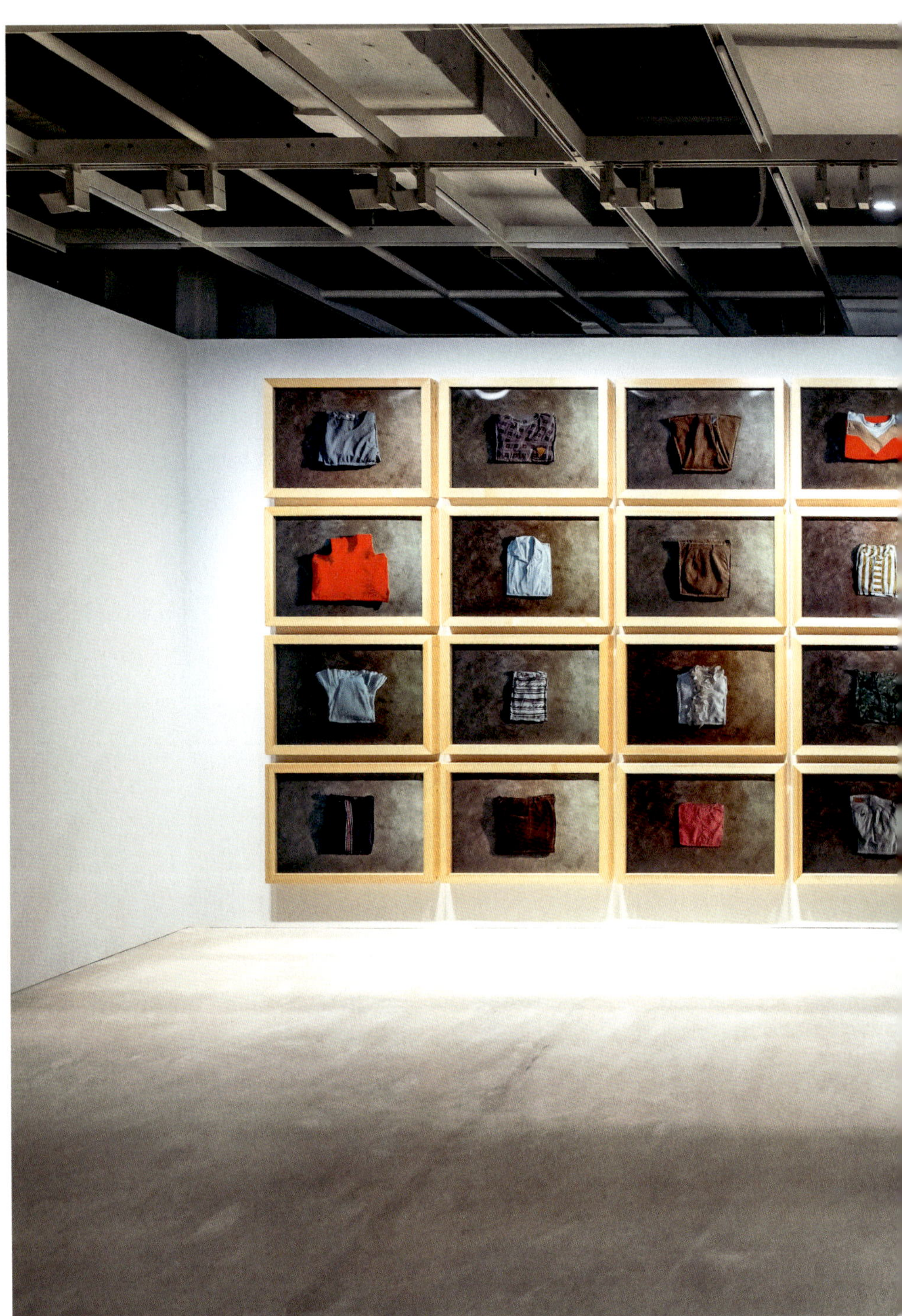

My Clothes,
1995/2021

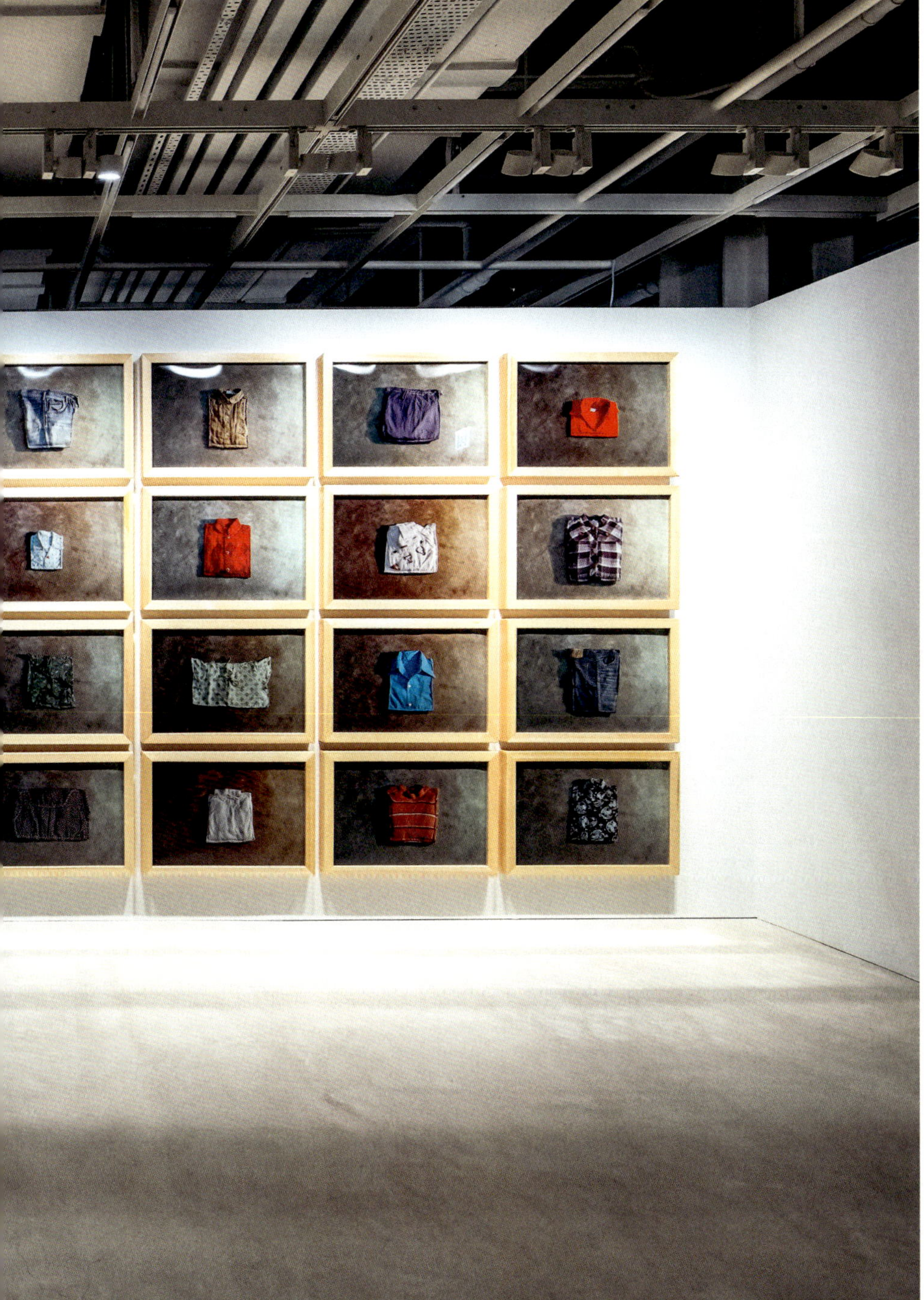

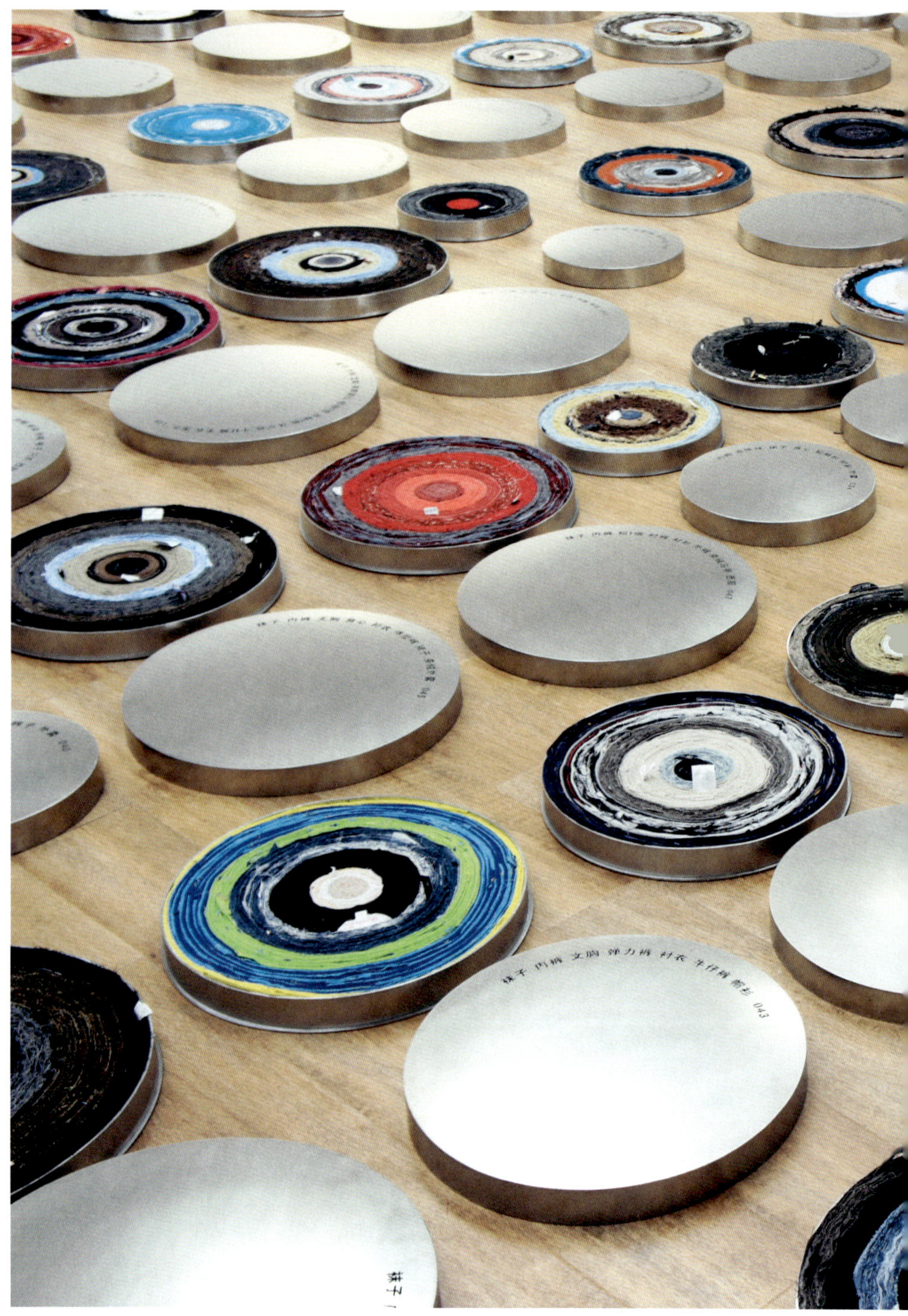

One Sentence,
2011

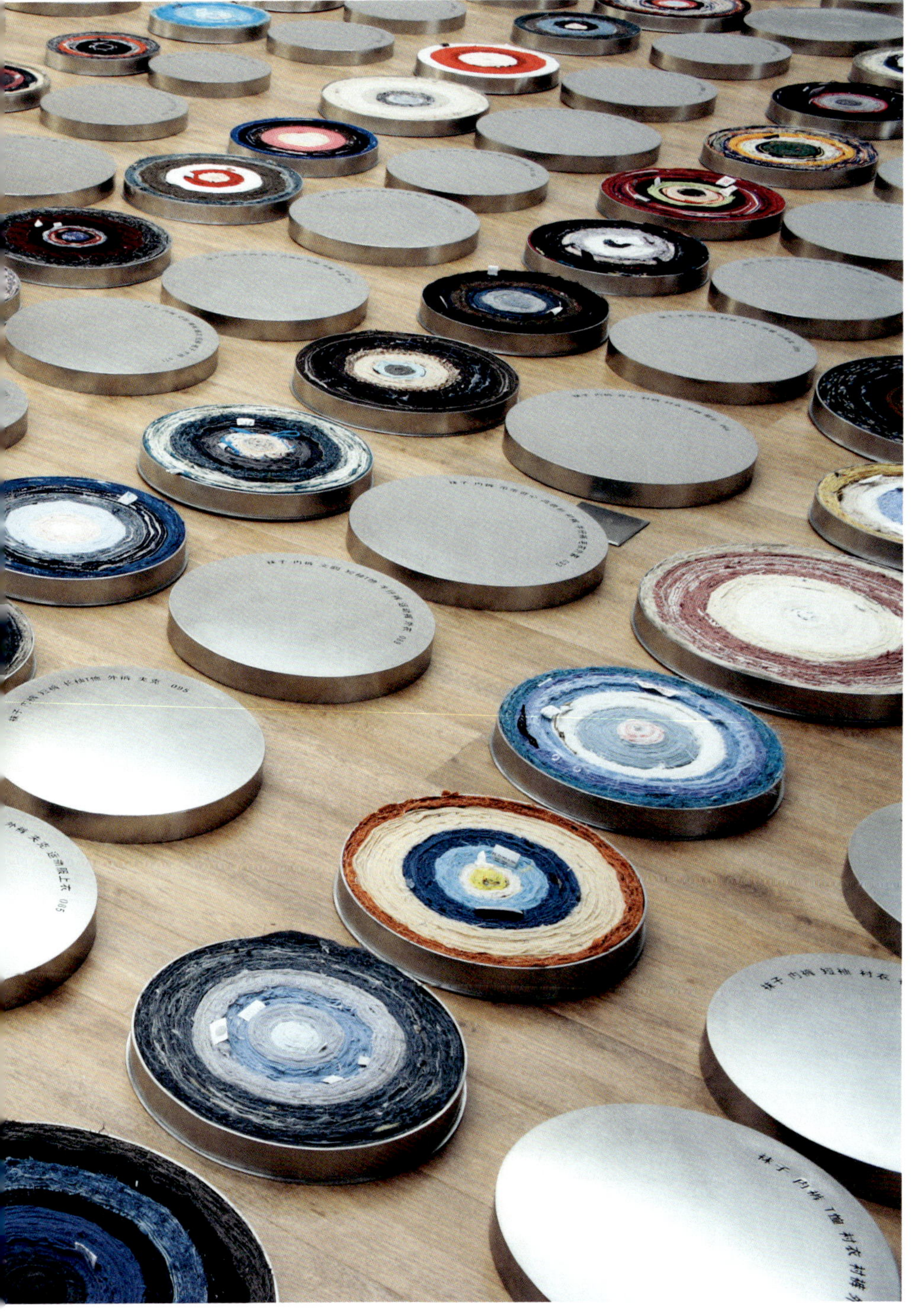

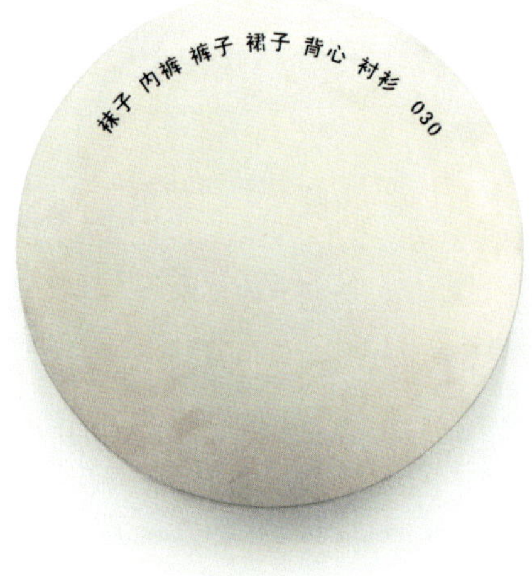

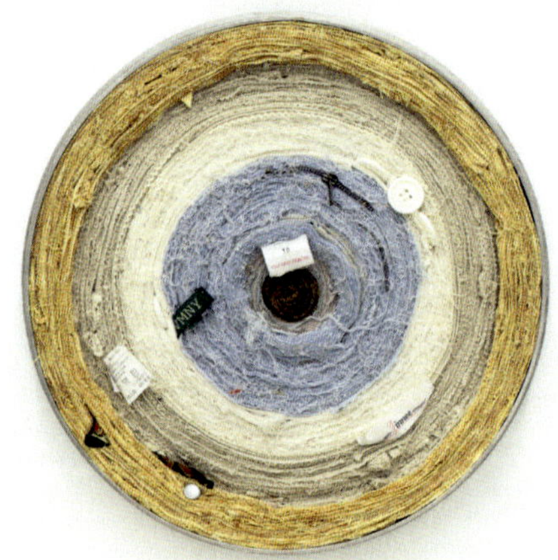

One Sentence No. 30,
2011

101

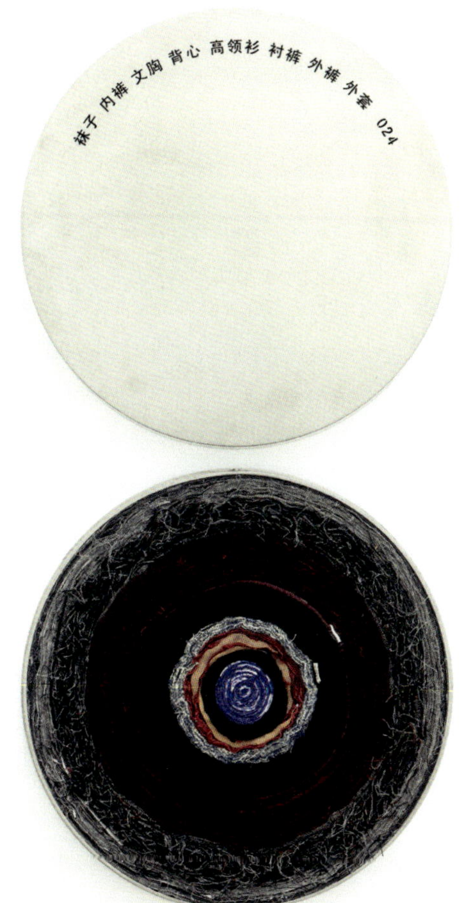

One Sentence No. 24,
2011

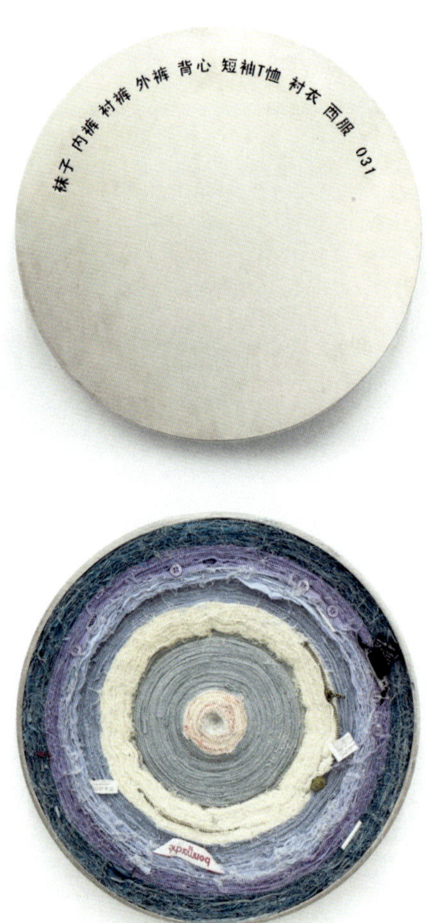

One Sentence No. 31,
2011

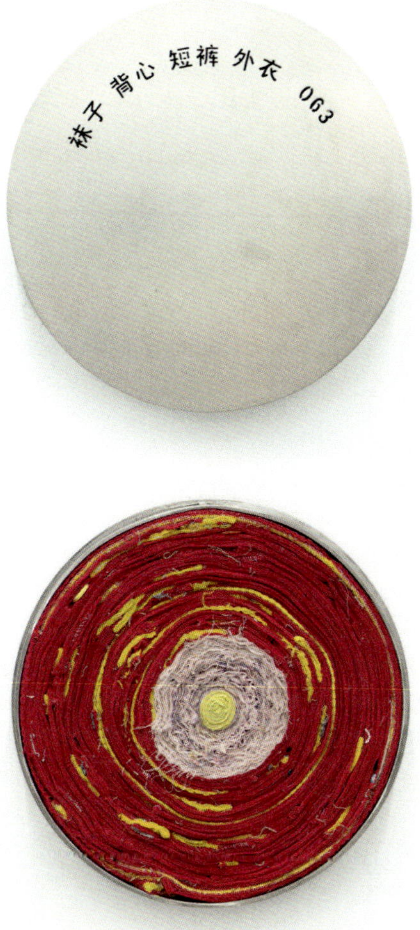

One Sentence No. 63,
2011

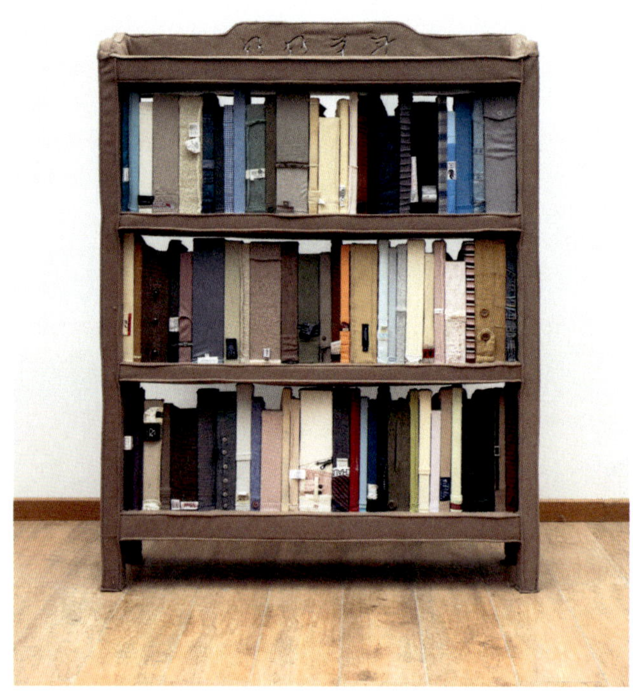

Bookshelf for Song ErRui: Study Hard,
2013

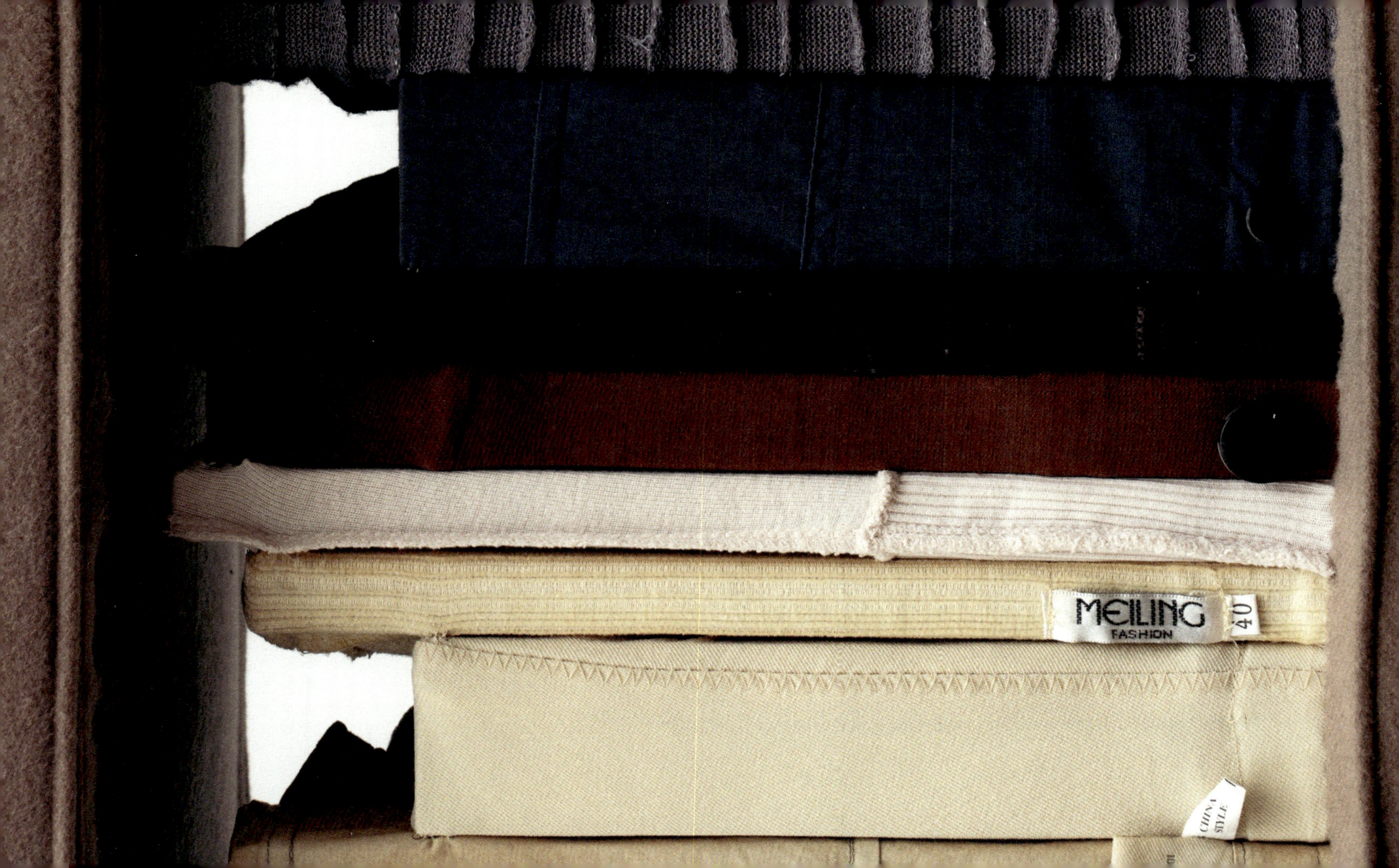
MEILING
FASHION
40
CHINA
STYLE

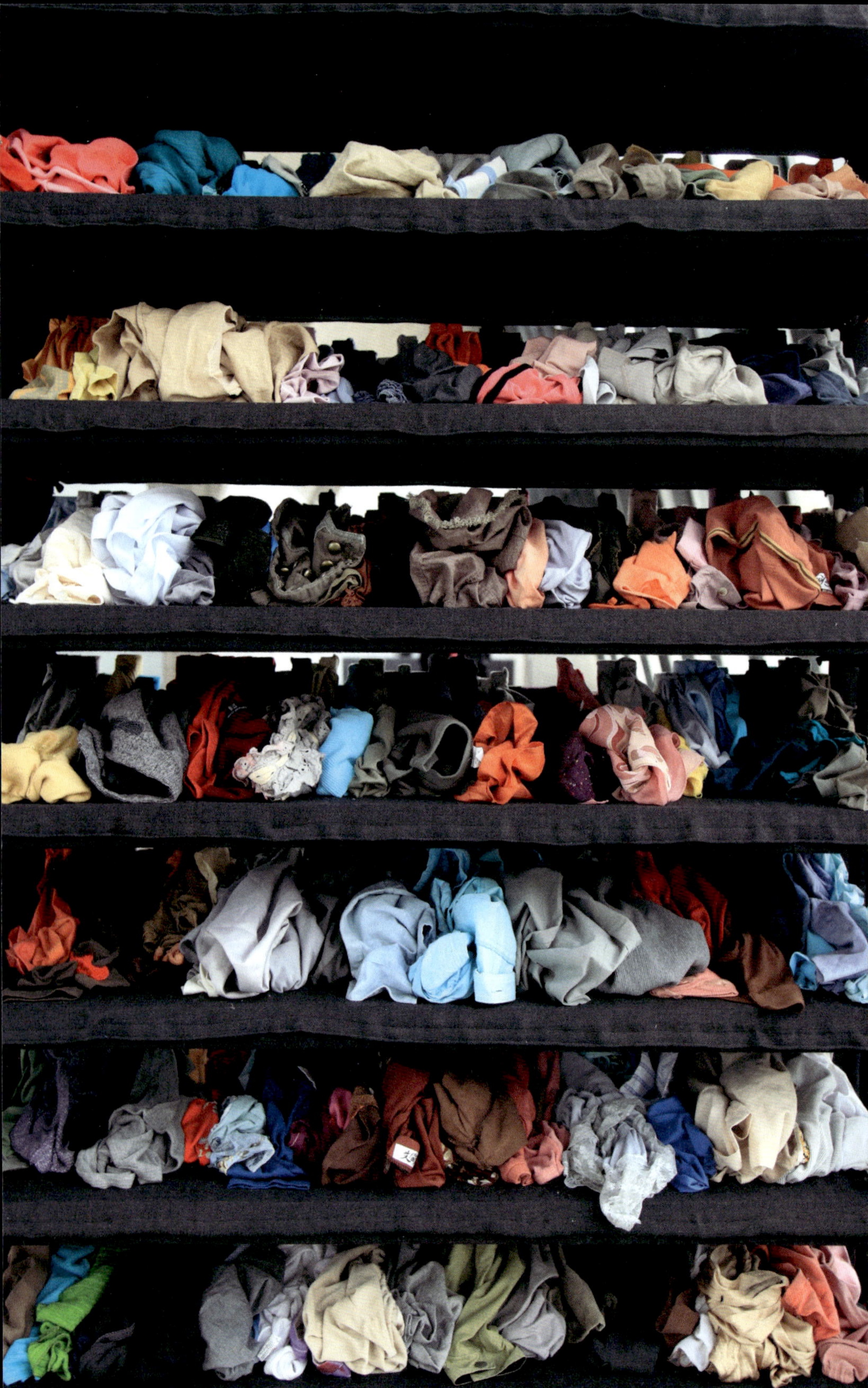

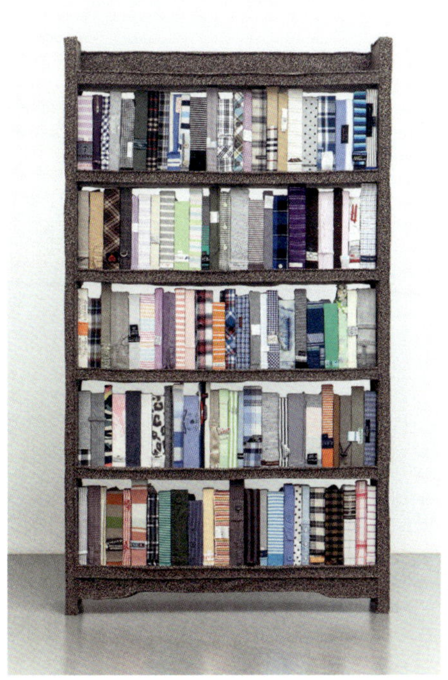

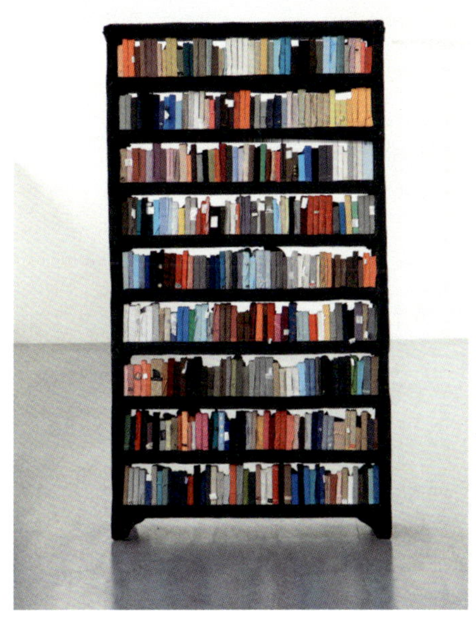

Bookshelf No. 1,
2009 (detail)

Bookshelf No. 5,
2009–13 (top)

Bookshelf No. 1,
2009

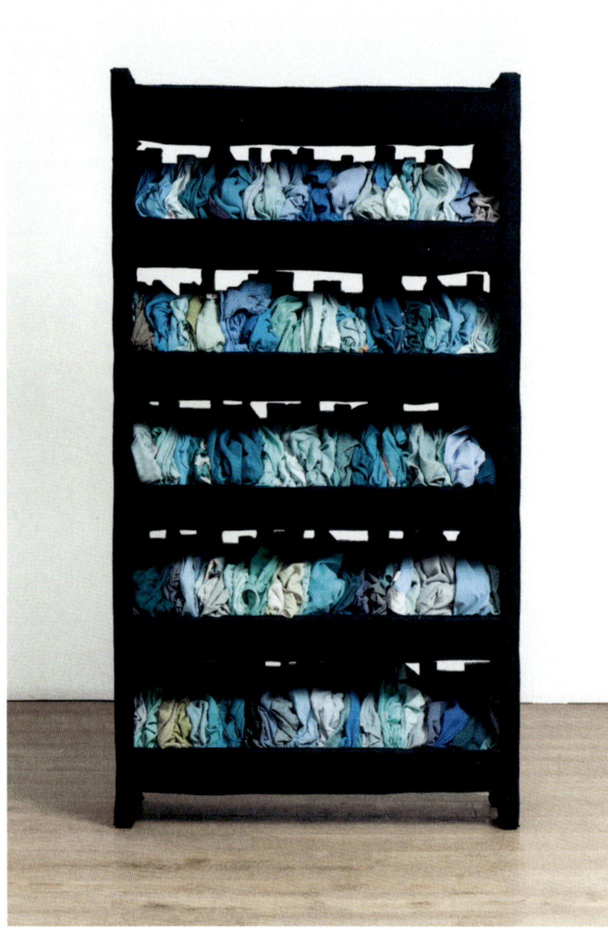

108

Bookshelf No. 10,
2012–13

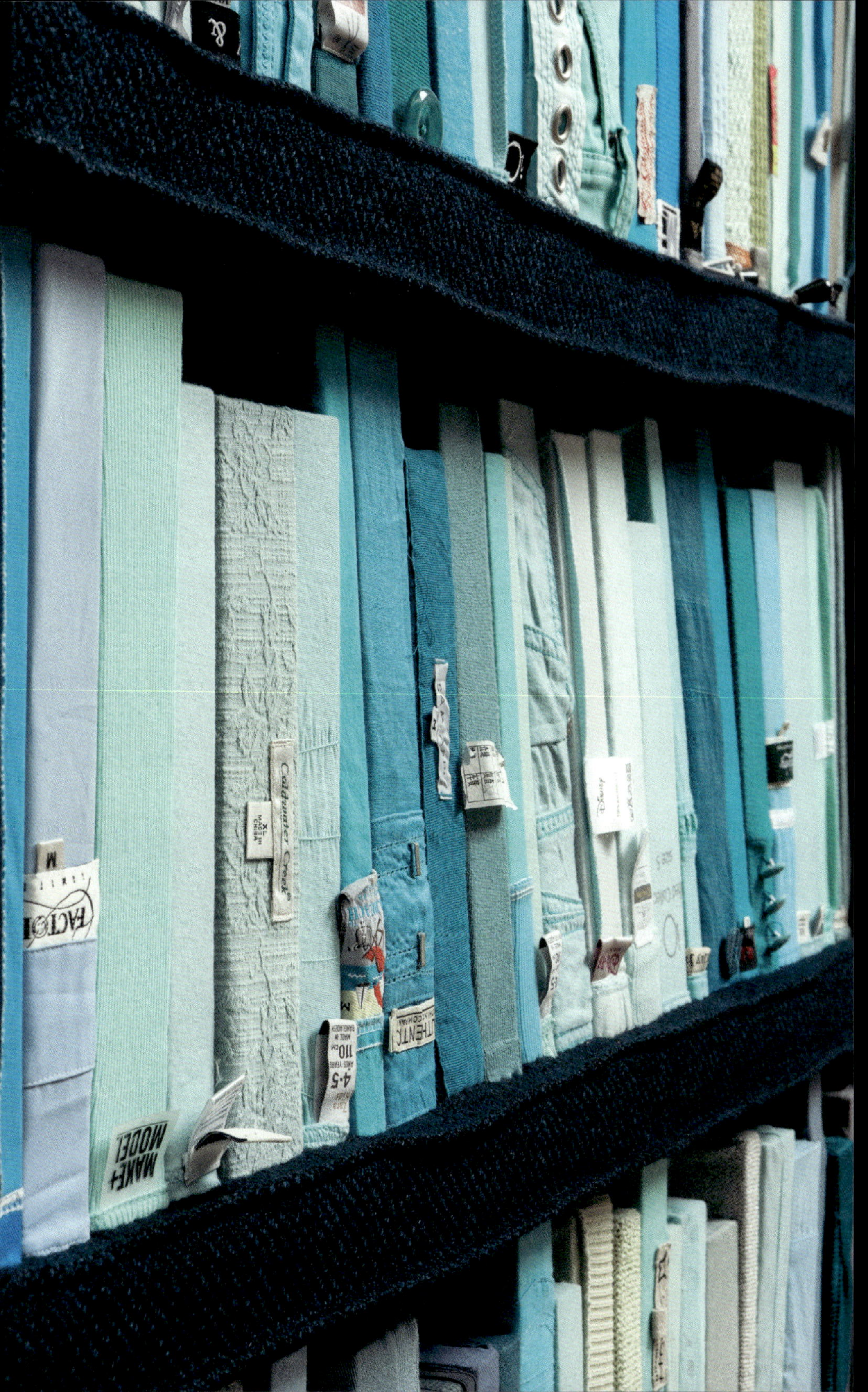

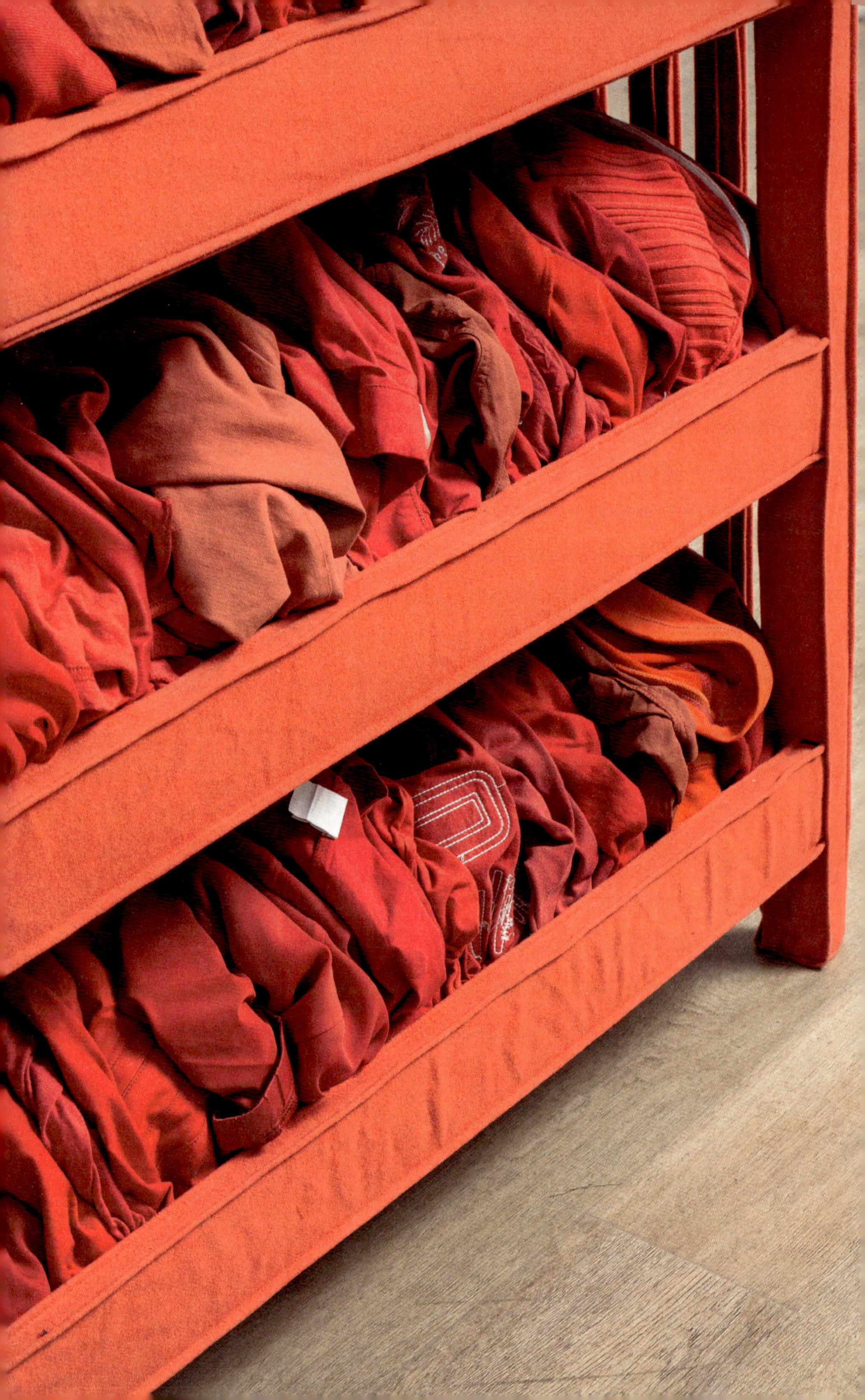

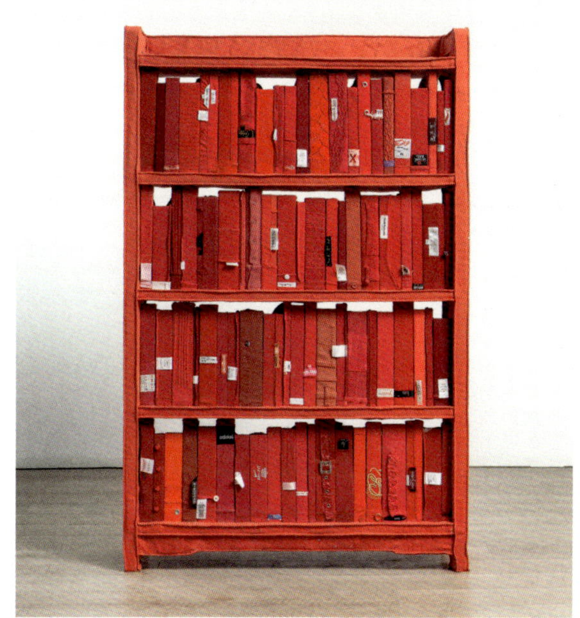

III

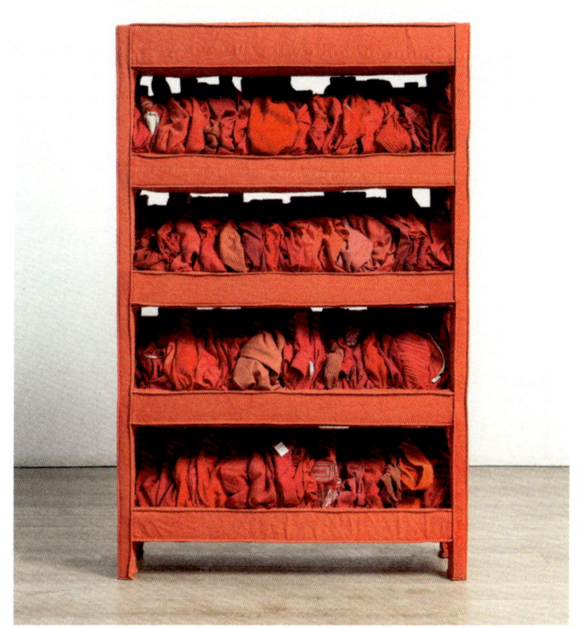

Bookshelf No. 13,
2009–13

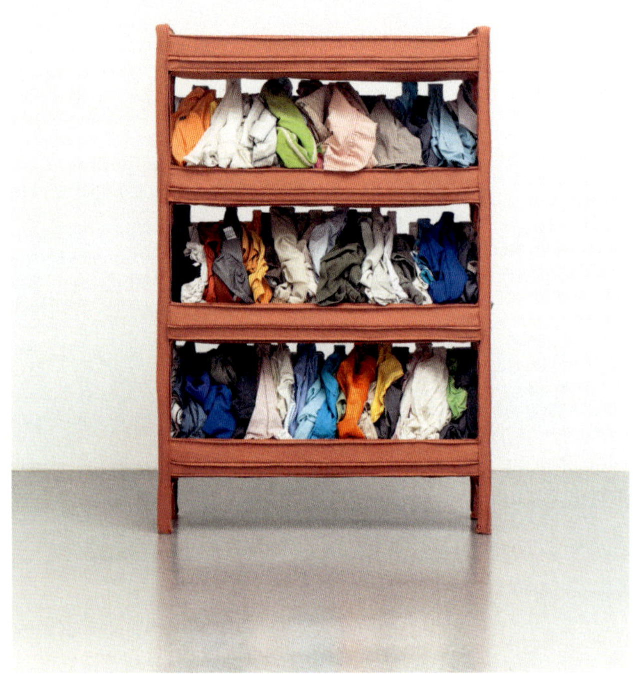

Bookshelf No. 17,
2009–13

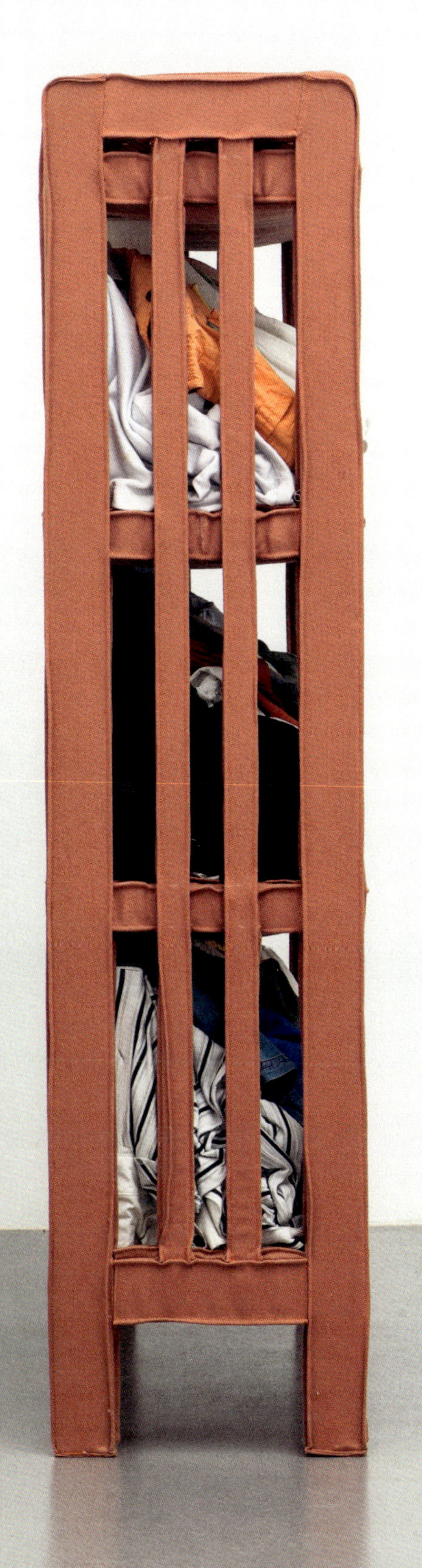

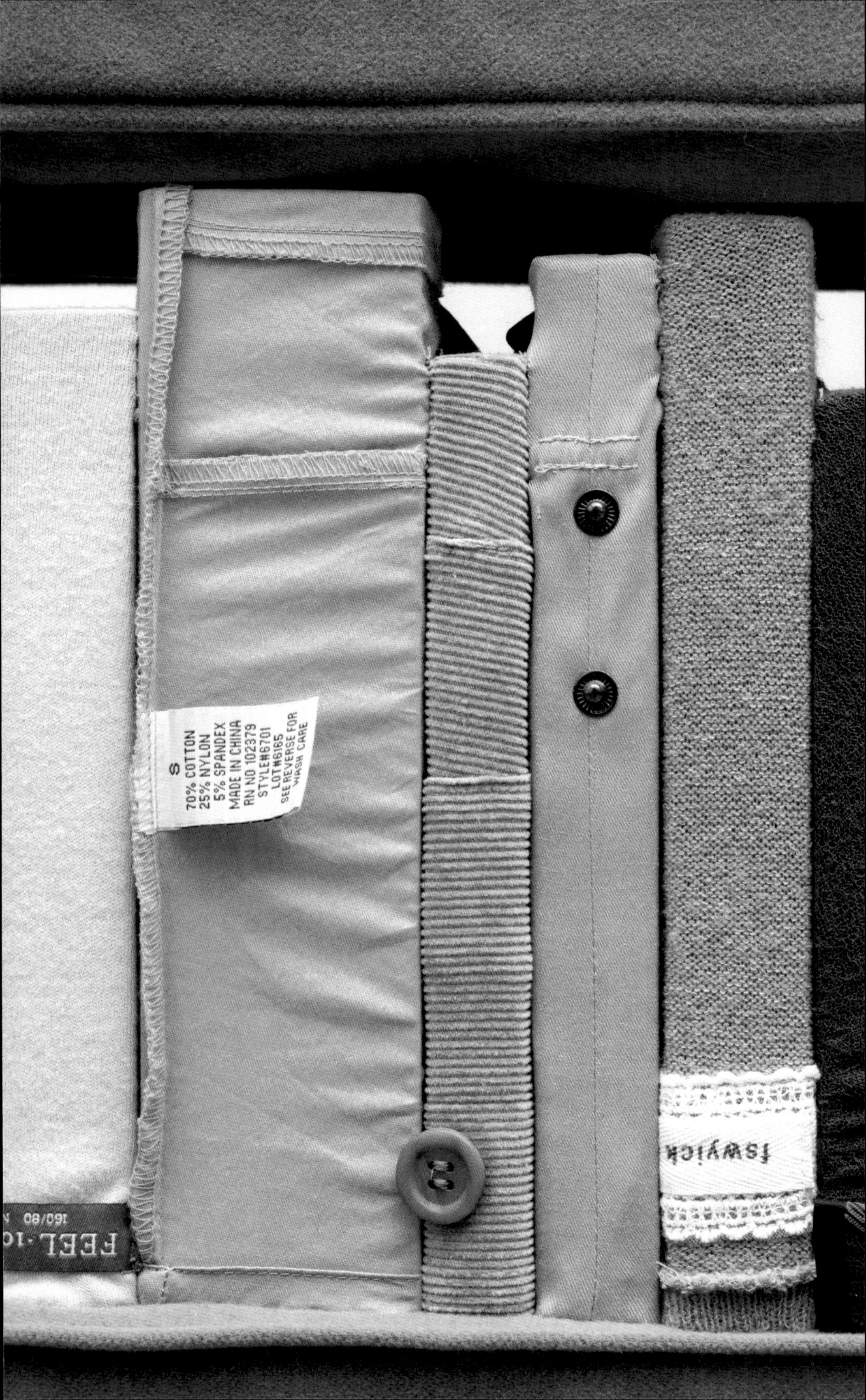

S
70% COTTON
25% NYLON
5% SPANDEX
MADE IN CHINA
RN NO 102379
STYLE#6701
LOT#6165
SEE REVERSE FOR
WASH CARE

FEEL-
160/80

Iswyich

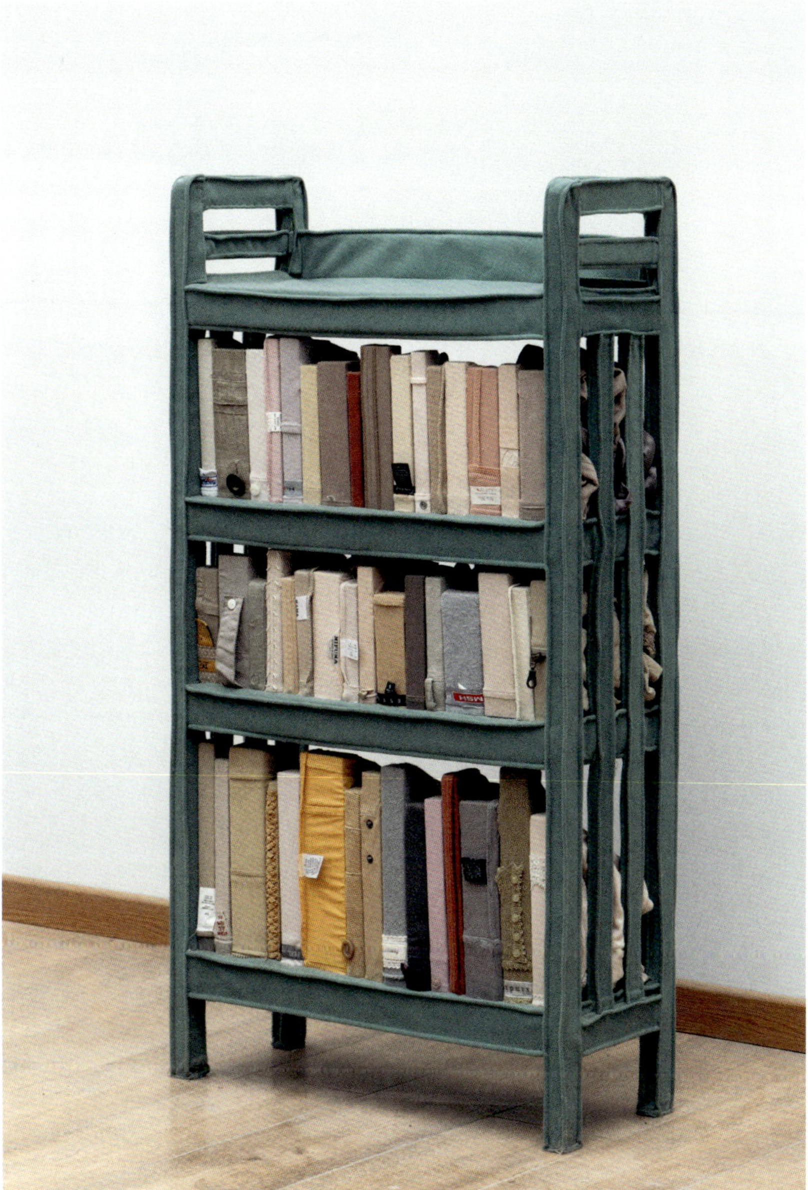

Bookshelf No. 24,
2009–13

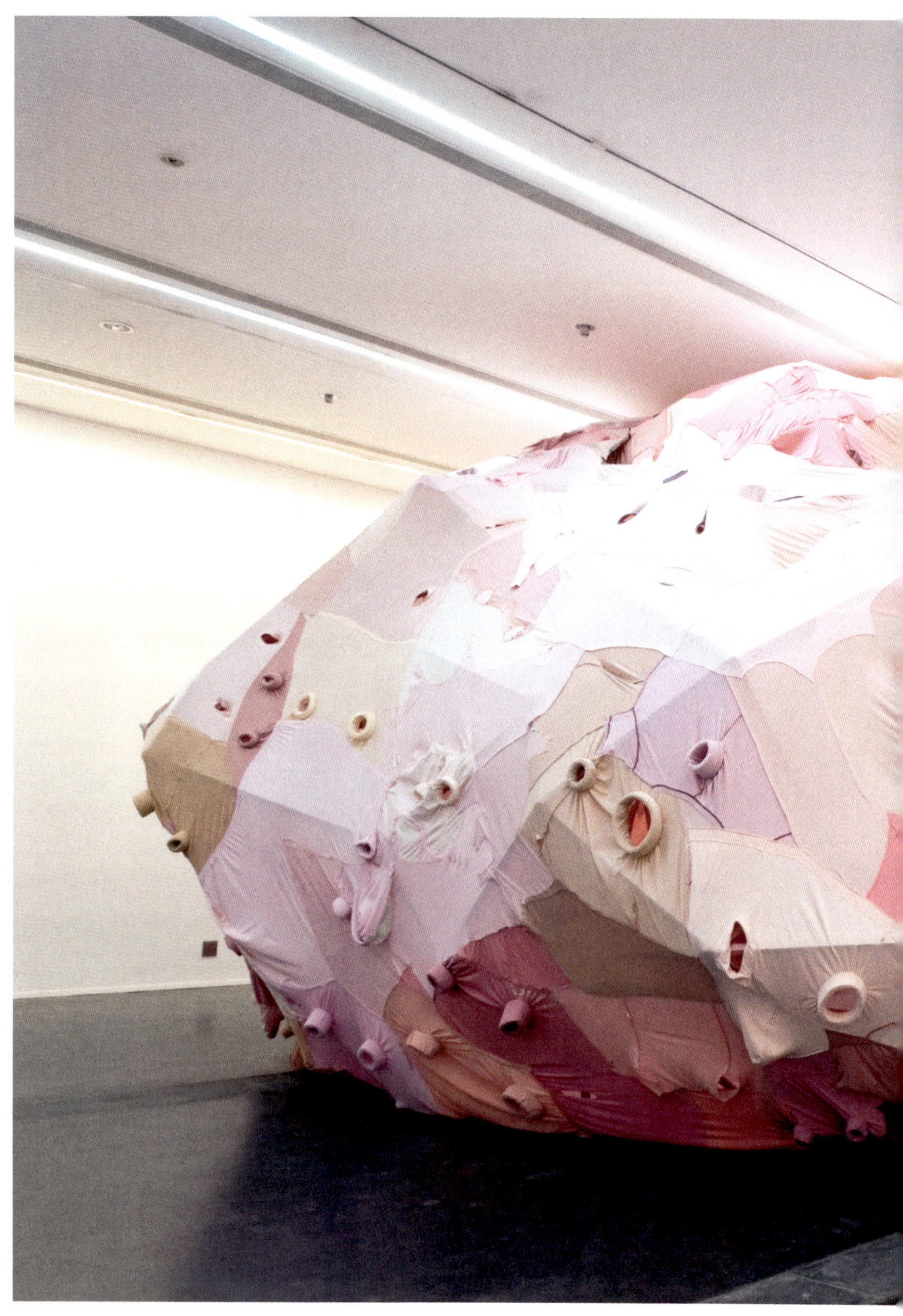

Introspective Cavity,
2008

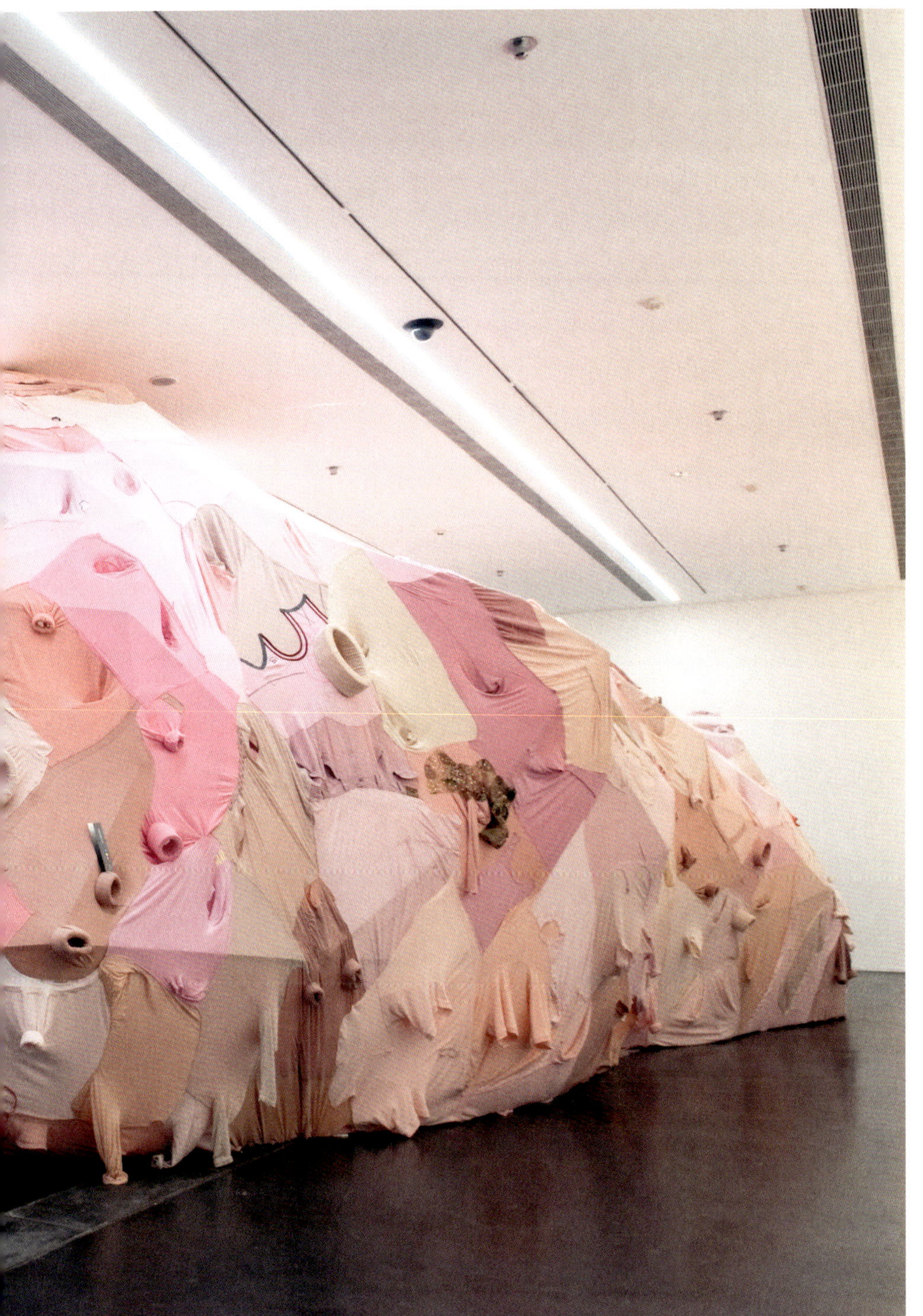

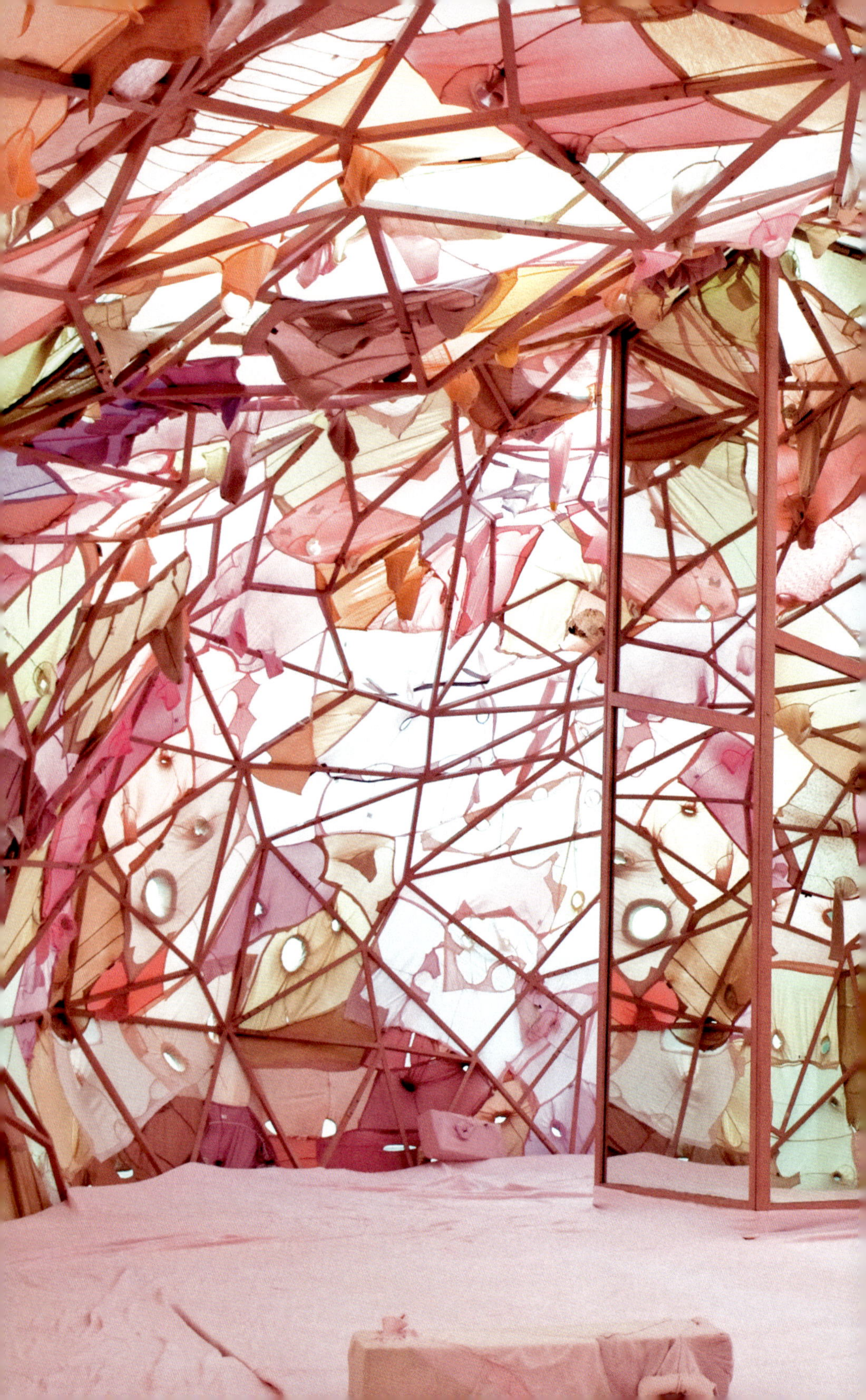

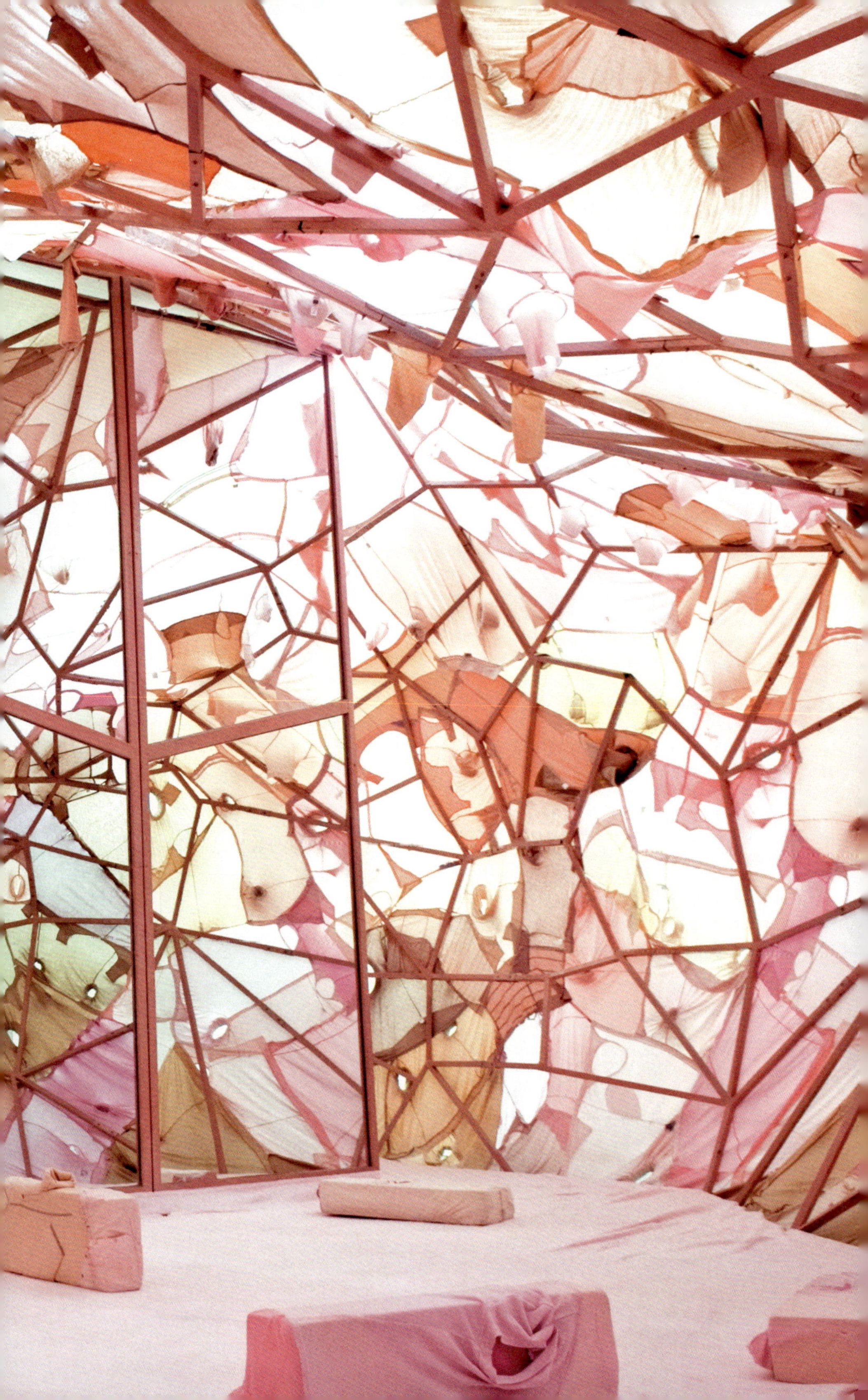

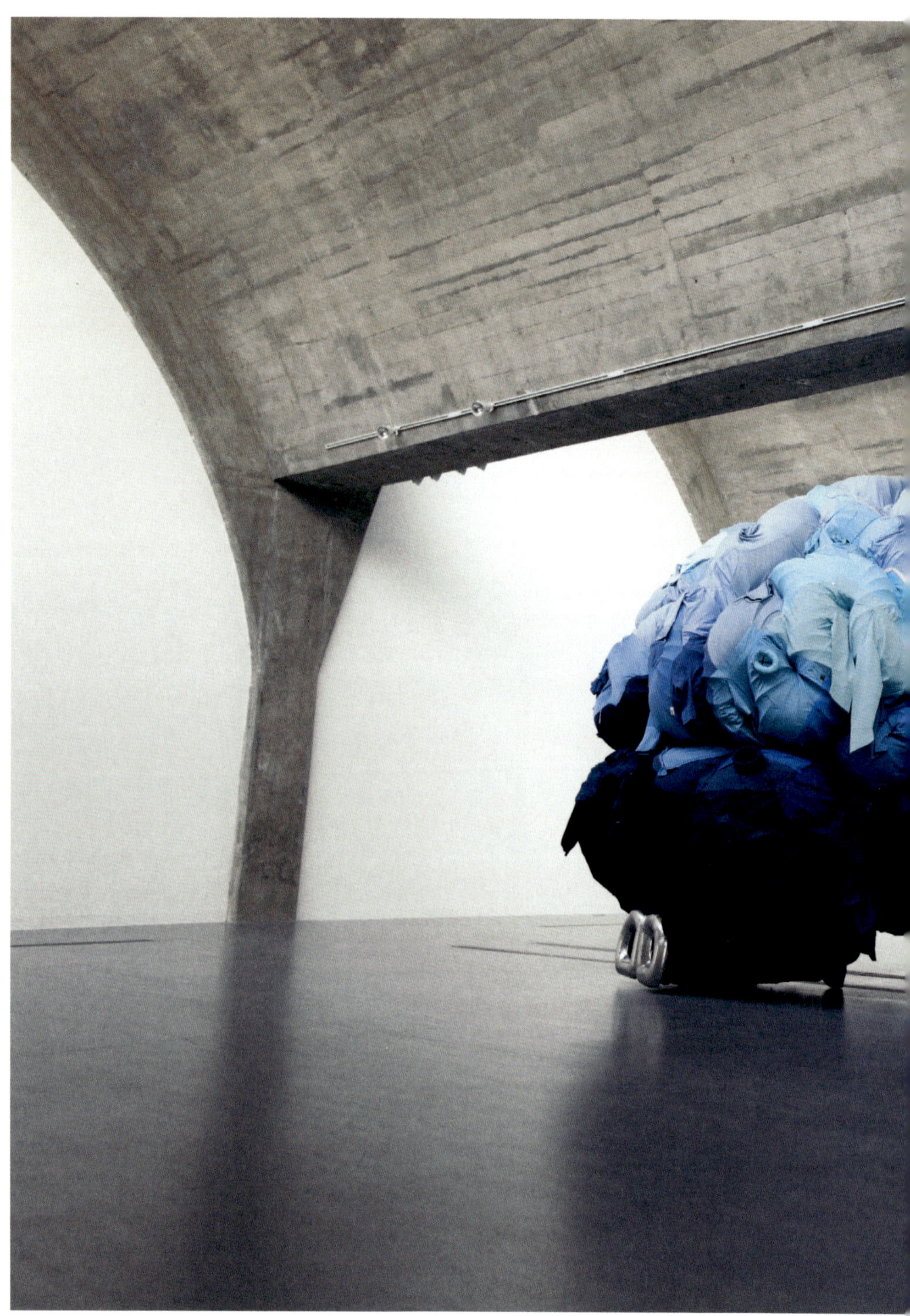

Thought,
2009

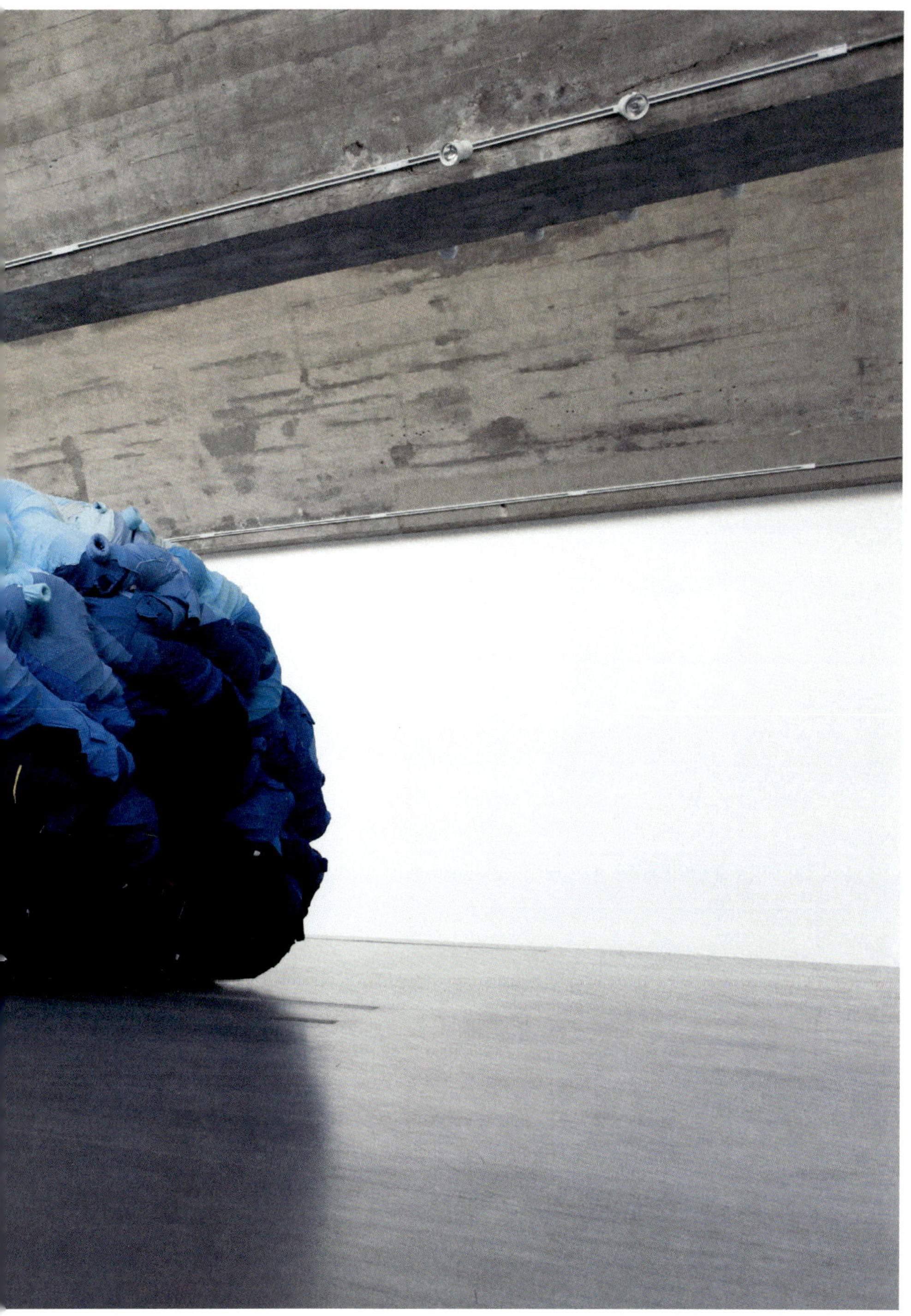

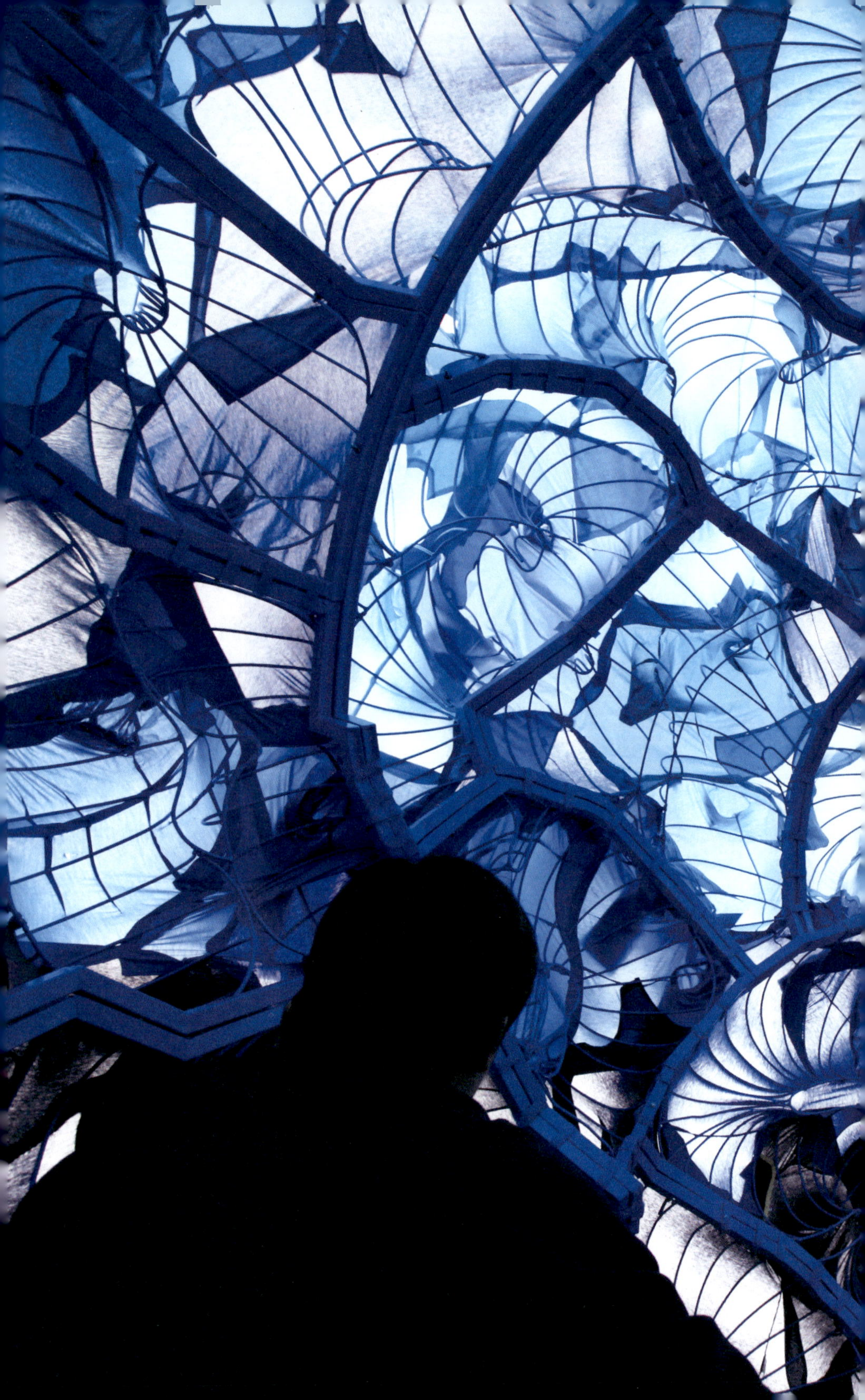

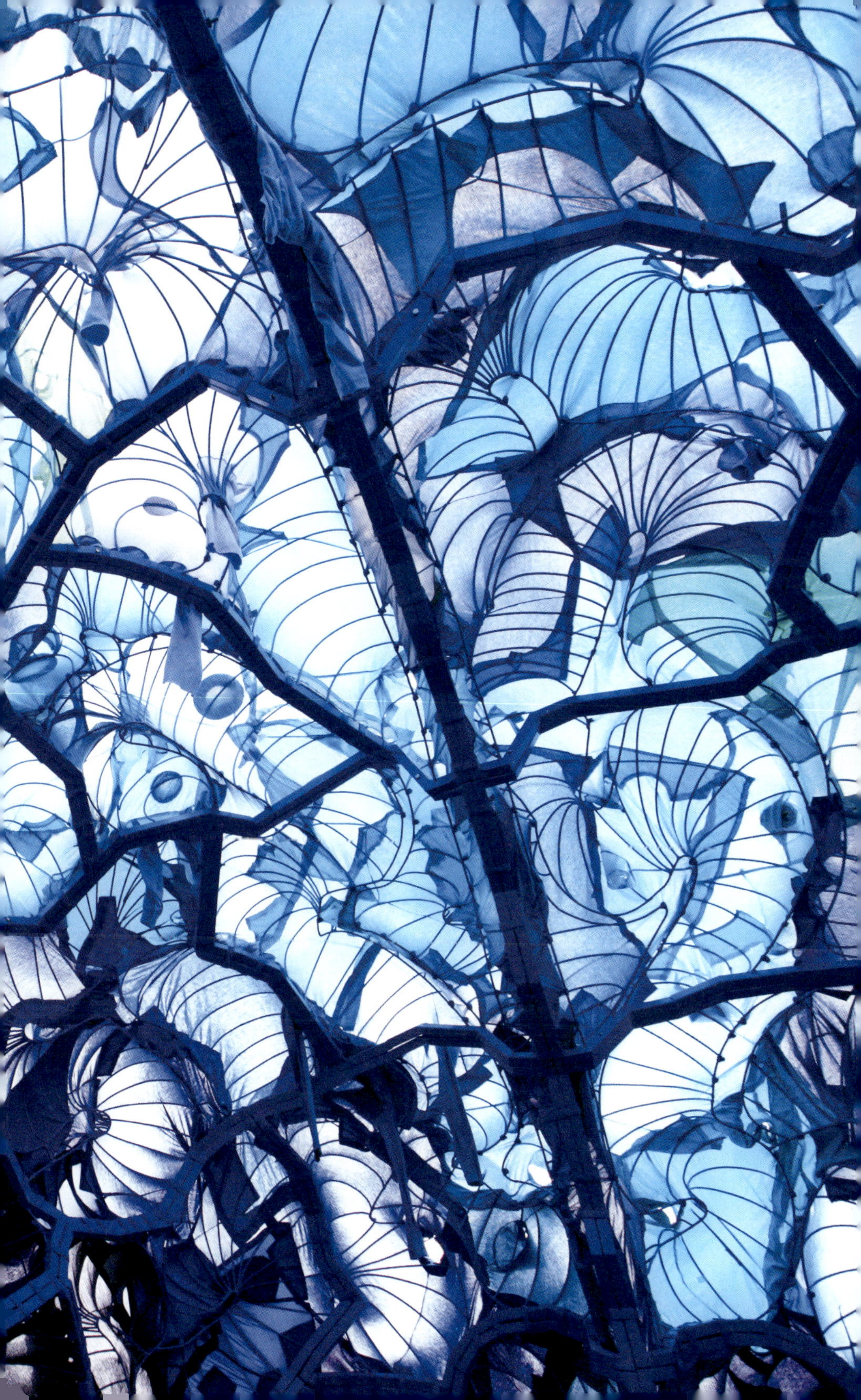

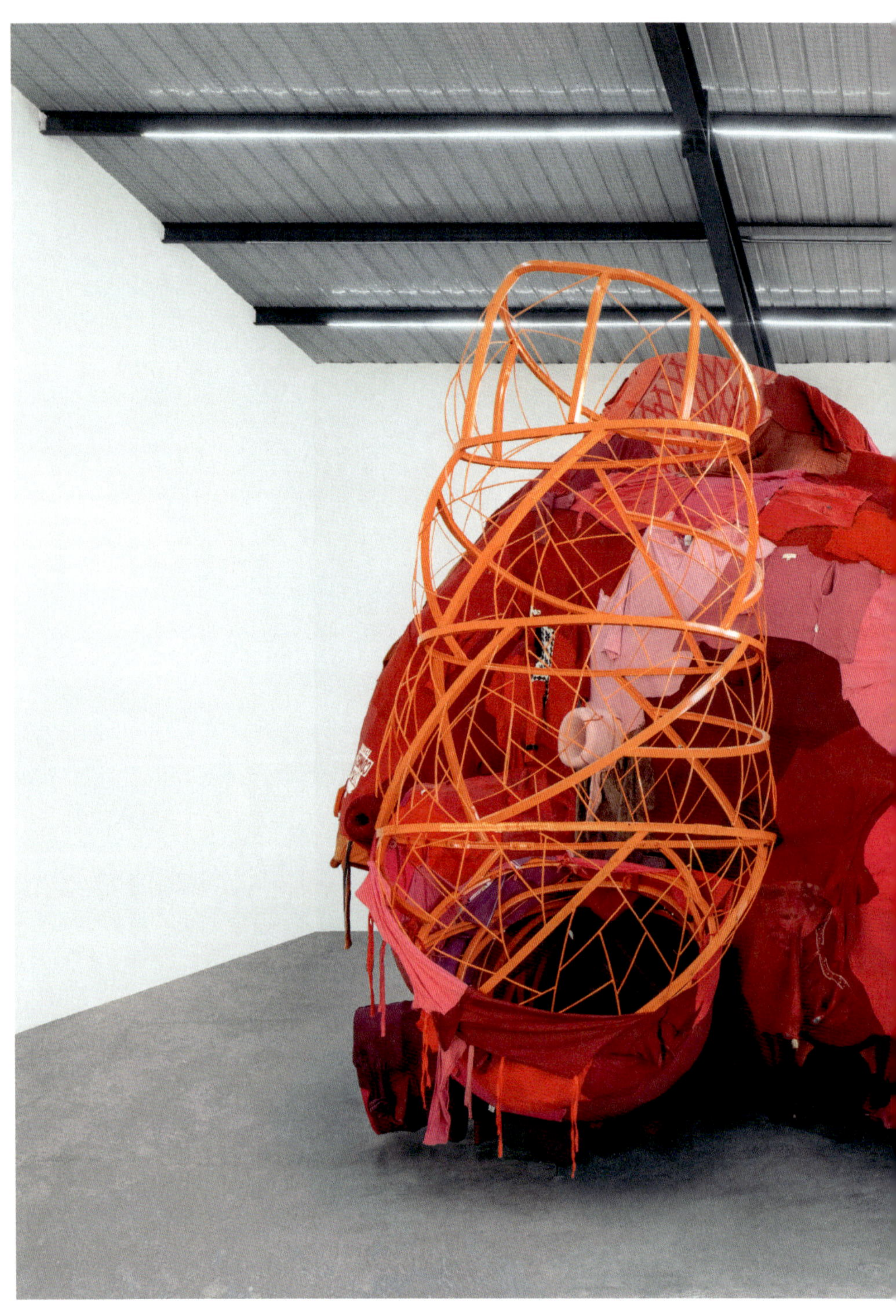

A Heart to Heart,
2025 (work in progress)

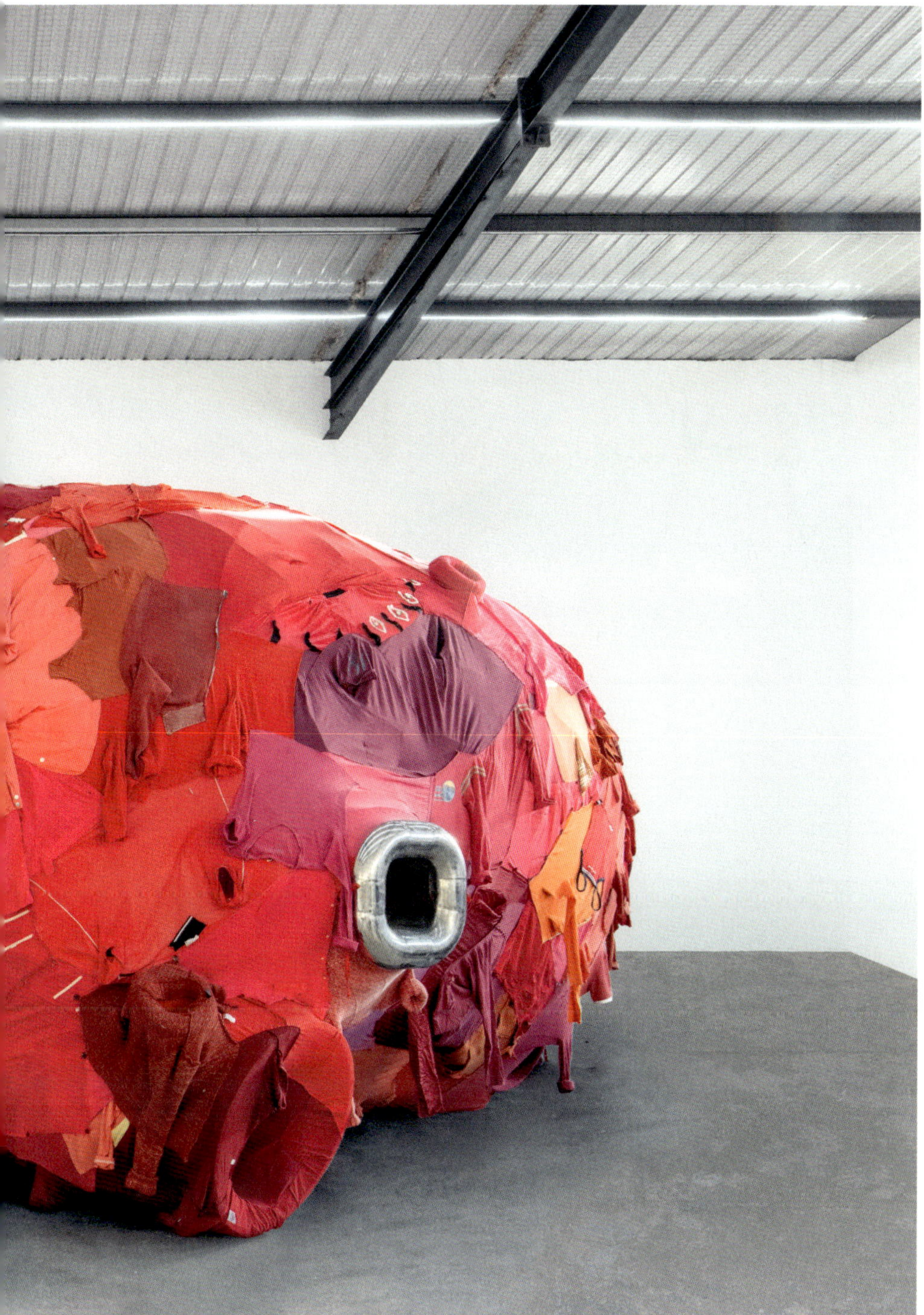

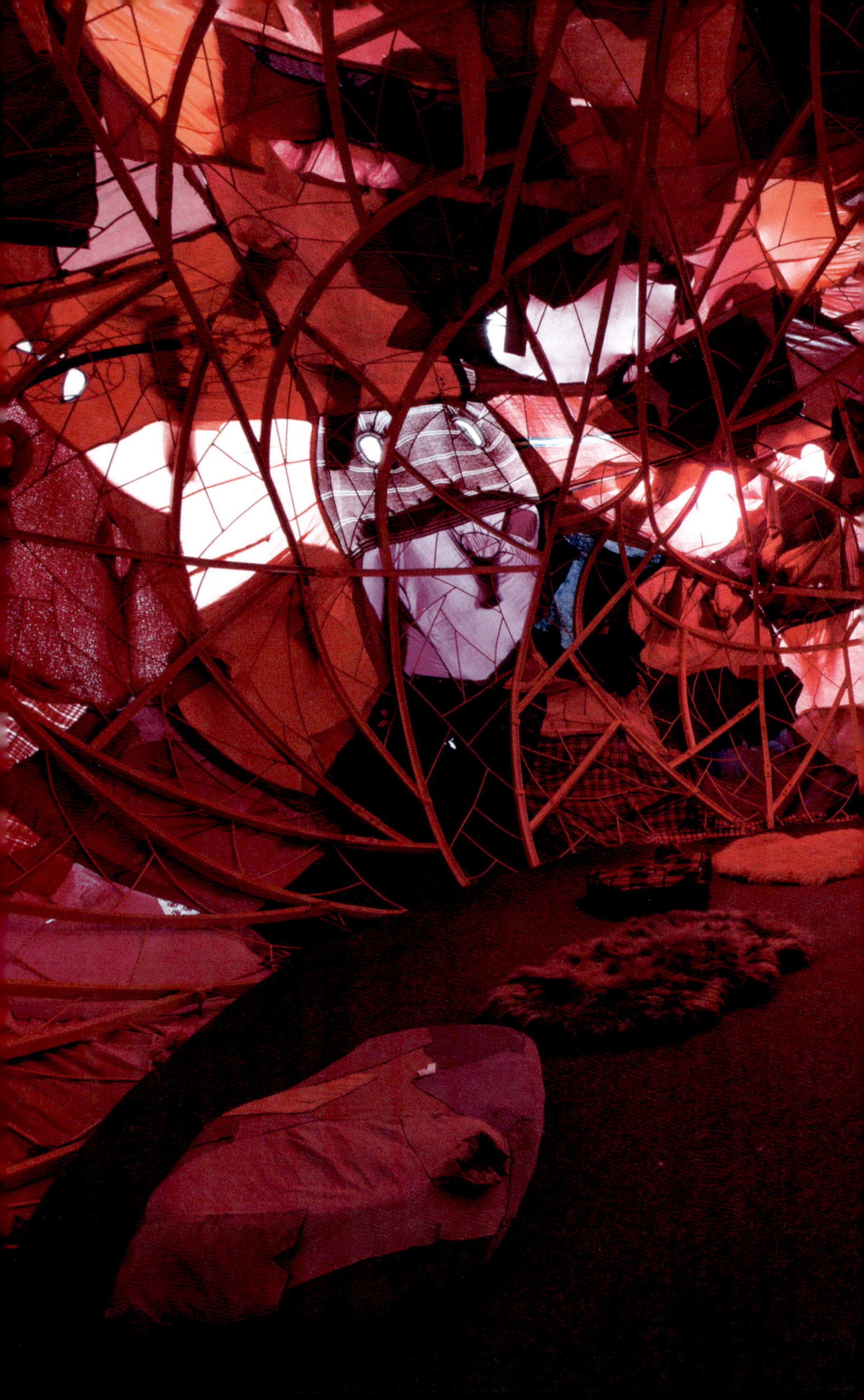

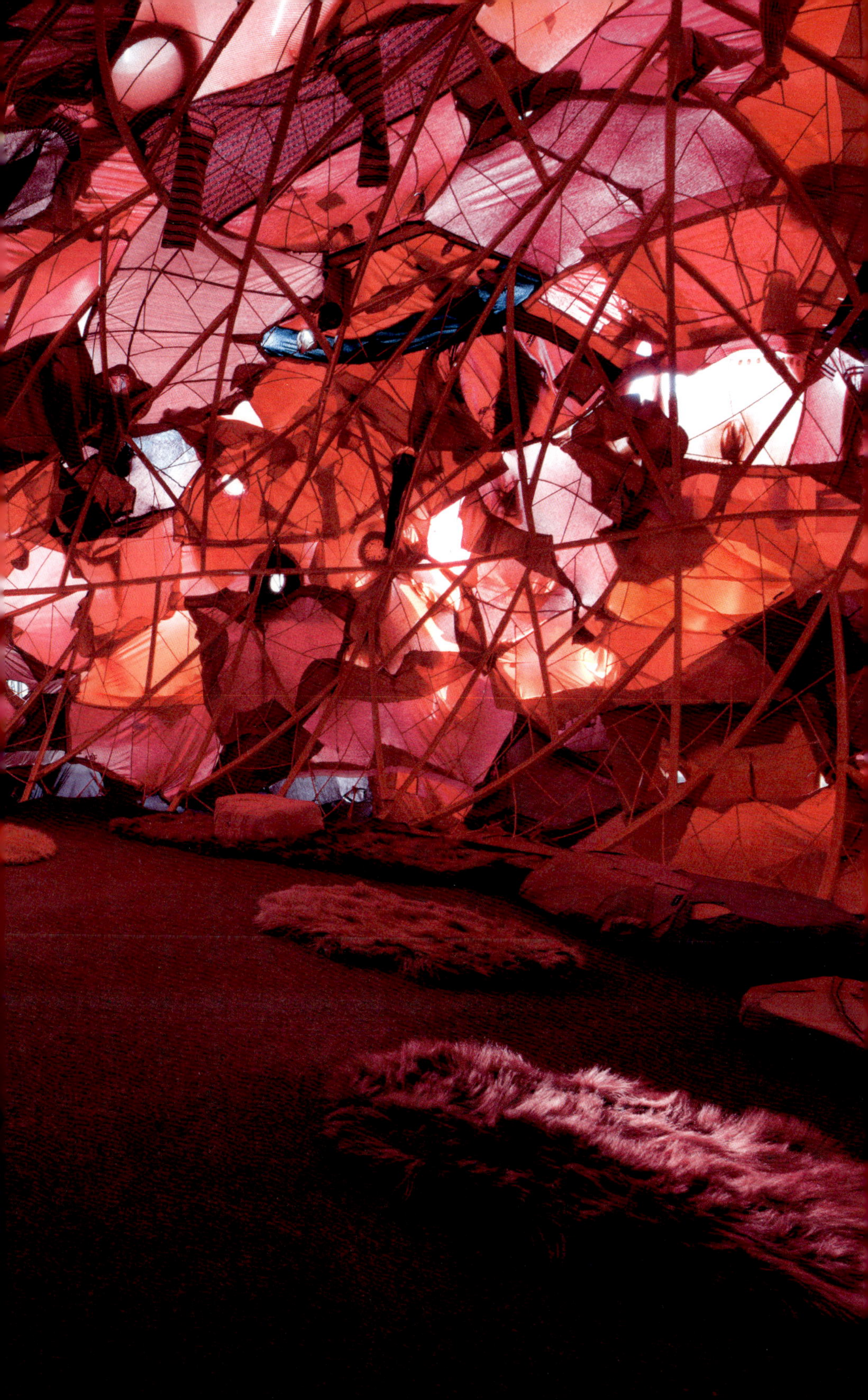

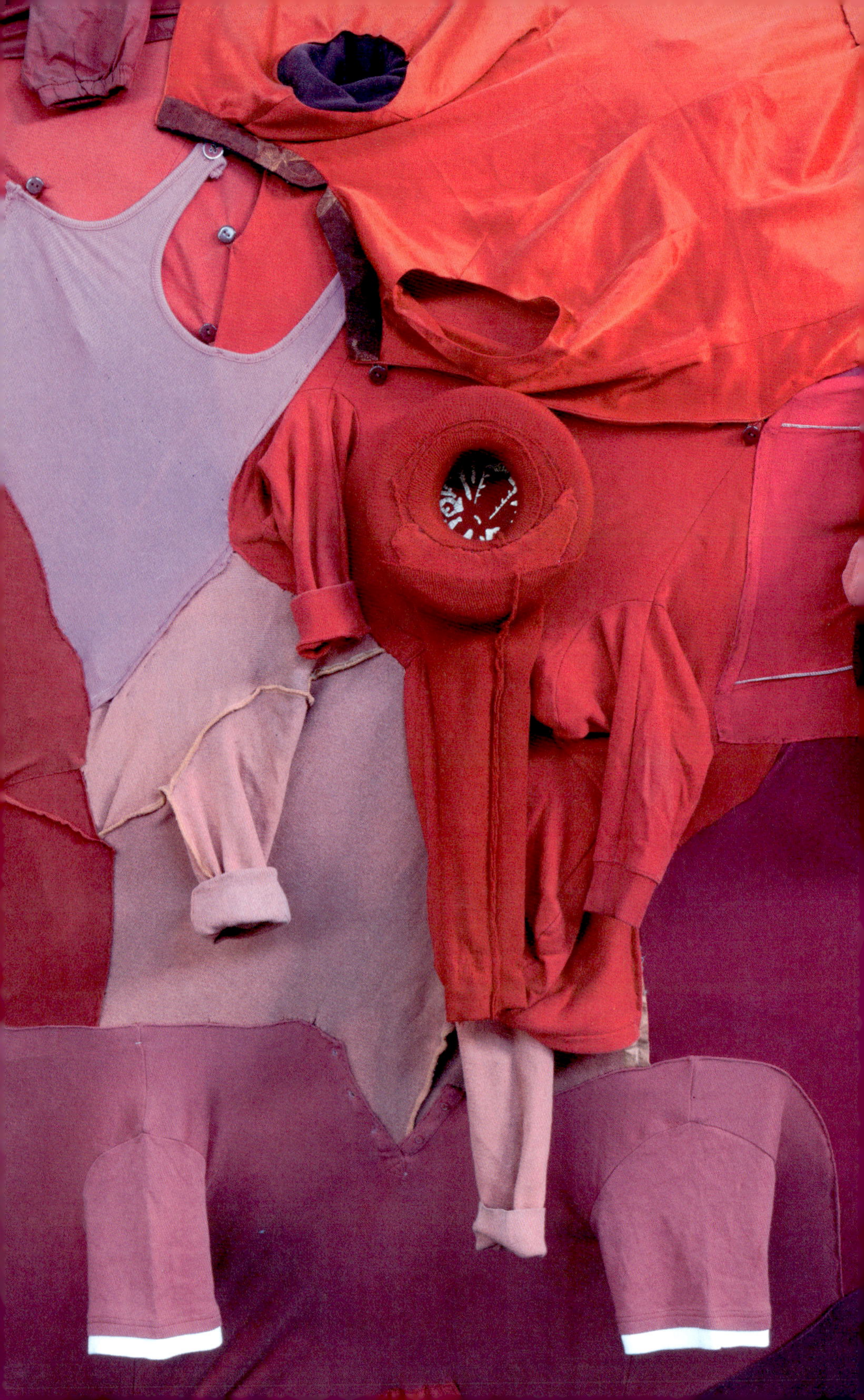

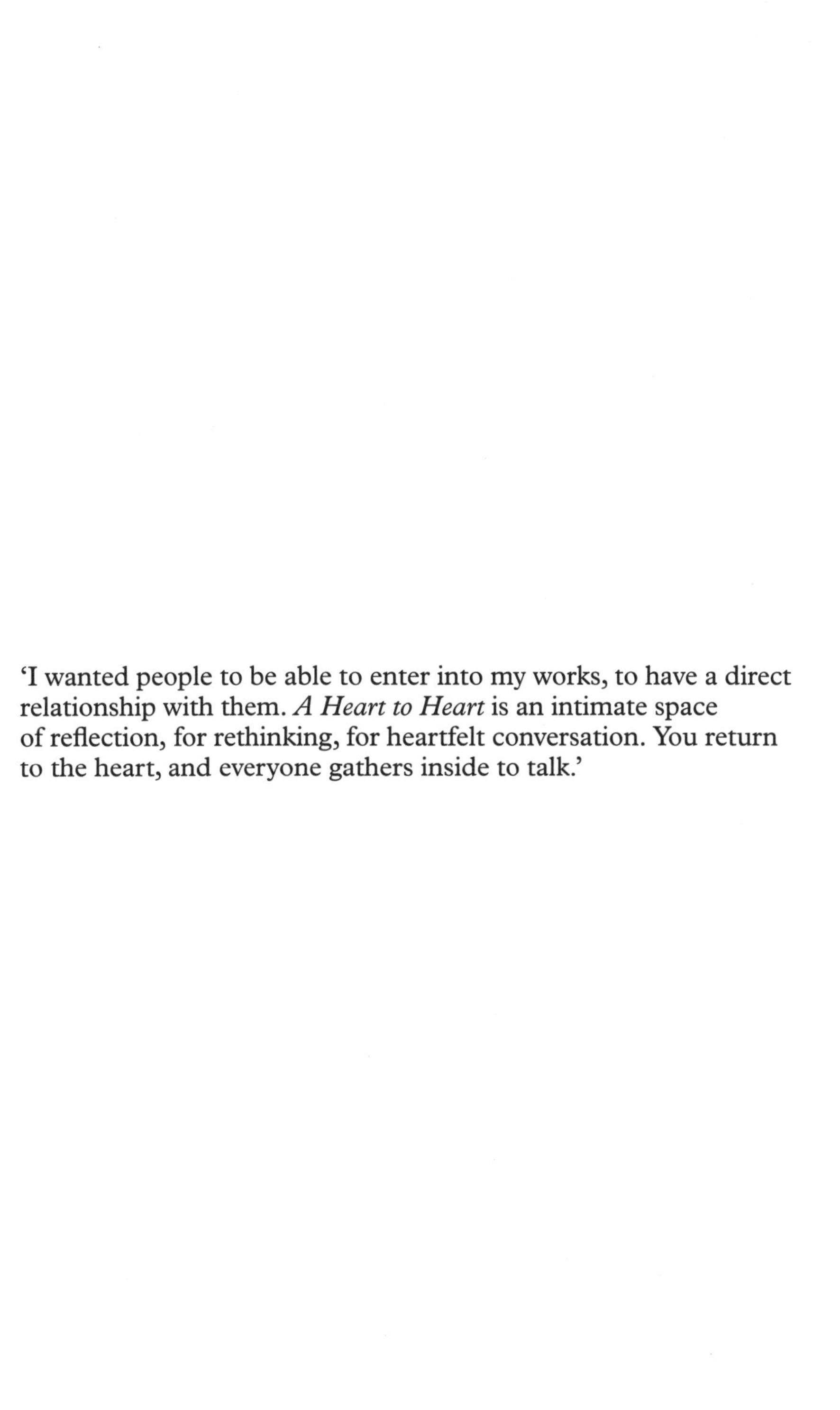

'I wanted people to be able to enter into my works, to have a direct relationship with them. *A Heart to Heart* is an intimate space of reflection, for rethinking, for heartfelt conversation. You return to the heart, and everyone gathers inside to talk.'

CHRONOLOGY

1963

- Born in Beijing, China.
- Learns sewing from her mother, who works in a clothing factory and uses leftover scraps of cloth to make and patch clothes for her children.
- Placed in the maths and science track in high school, but does not pass university entrance exam for science. After enrolling in an amateur art class, works part time at a construction site to pay for the classes needed to pass humanities tests and qualify for art academy.

1966–76

- Mao Zedong, Chairman of the Chinese Communist Party, launches the Cultural Revolution, with the aim of purging capitalist and traditional elements from Chinese society.

'We did not have the concept of an individual. All we had, and who we were, belonged to the general public or the country.'

1980s

- Rapid urbanisation in cities across China. Following the end of the Cultural Revolution increasing numbers of homes and traditional buildings are destroyed making way for new builds.

1985

- Accepted into Beijing Normal Academy, majoring in oil painting. Its conservative art programme is based on Soviet painting techniques and socialist realism. Here she meets fellow artist Song Dong.
- Attends *Robert Rauschenberg: ROCI CHINA* at the National Art Museum of China, Beijing. This exhibition is one of the catalysts of the Art New Wave movement in China.

'I didn't paint much, making just a few pictures each year. I got really tired of it, and my spirits sank even lower when I forced myself to take up a brush. Then I came into contact with this new art.'

1989

- Graduates from Beijing Normal Academy. Begins teaching painting at the middle school attached to the Central Academy of Arts and Design, a position she holds for ten years, while beginning her artistic career.

1989

- 4 June: Tiananmen Square Massacre. Hundreds of peaceful student protesters killed by government troops in Beijing.

1992

- Marries Song Dong.

1994–95

- Begins working beyond canvas, exploring installation and performance. Incorporates her own worn clothing as a creative material.

1994

- *'94 Outdoor Art*, group exhibition, multiple venues, Beijing.

1995

- Takes first flight, to Chengdu, China, for the creation of her work *Washing River* (pp. 56–57).
- *Dress Box* (p. 95) forms part of first solo exhibition *One-person Exhibition of Installations* at the Contemporary Art Museum, affiliated with the Academy of Fine Arts, Beijing. First time using clothing, which she calls 'the second skin of humans'.
- Begins photographic series *My Clothes* (pp. 96–97), ongoing until 2021.
- Installation *Cement Shoes* included in group exhibition *Displacement*, Capital Normal University Museum, Beijing.
- Stages performance *Washing River* (pp. 56-57) in Chengdu, beside the Funan River as part of the experimental art project *Keepers of the Waters*, organised by American ecofeminist Betsy Damon.

1996

- *The Ruined City*, Capital Normal University Museum, Beijing.

'Sometimes I'd see a building on my way to work and it would be gone on my way home. Cement left a deep impression on me.'

- First exhibition outside China: *7th Com-art Show of Artists from Korea, China and Japan*, group exhibition, Suwon, Korea.
- Stages two performances in Tibet: *Living Water* (pp. 58–59), part of the *2nd Keeper of the Waters* project, and *Shoes with Butter* (pp. 60–63).

1997

- *Dining Table*, Ruine Der Künste, Berlin.
- *Against the Tide*, group exhibition, The Bronx Museum of the Arts, New York.
- Included in *Another Long March: Contemporary Art Show*, Chassé Kazerne, Breda, Netherlands – the first survey in the West of Asian conceptual and installation art, presenting 18 artists from leading Chinese art centres: Beijing, Shanghai, Hangzhou and Guangzhou.
- *China City: Korea-China Fine Art Exchange*, group exhibition, multiple venues, Beijing.

1998

- *Inside Out: New Chinese Art*, group exhibition, PS.1 Contemporary Art Center, New York.
- *Half of the Sky: Contemporary Chinese Women Artists*, group exhibition, Frauenmuseum, Bonn.

'The Women's Museum in Bonn said they had to hold an exhibition of Chinese women artists, so they sent a Chinese woman artist based in Germany to visit China to search for women artists. That was how they found me.'

- The works *The Doors* (p. 11) and *Changes* included in group exhibition *Cities on the Move*, Secession, Vienna, travelling to Musée d'art Contemporain de Bordeaux; P.S.1 Contemporary Arts Center, New York; Louisiana Museum of Modern Art, Humlebaek, Denmark; Hayward Gallery, London; Rama IX Art Museum, Bangkok; Kiasma Museum of Contemporary Art, Helsinki.

1999

- *One Year Not at Home*, Künstlerhaus Schloss Balmoral, Bad Ems, Germany, with accompanying artist monograph.
- Participates in the *3rd Asia Specific Triennial of Contemporary Art*, Brisbane.
- *Transience: Chinese Art at the End of the 20th Century*, group exhibition, The Smart Museum of Art, Chicago.
- *Supermarket: Art for Sale*, group exhibition, Shanghai Square, Shanghai.

2000

- Receives the Chinese Contemporary Art Prize and the UNESCO/Aschberg Youth Scholarship.
- *At the New Century: 1979–1999 Contemporary Art of China*, group exhibition, Chengdu Contemporary Art Museum.
- *Text & Subtext: Contemporary Asian Women Artists*, group exhibition, Earl Lu Gallery at Lasalle College of the Arts, Singapore, travelling to Ivan Dougherty Gallery, Sydney; Artspace, Woolloomooloo, Australia; Museum of Far Eastern Antiquities, Stockholm; Stenersenmuseet, Oslo.

2001

- *Clothes Airplane: Made in Siemens*, Siemens Art Project, Beijing.
- *Portable City: Beijing* (p. 14), the first work in the *Portable Cities* series.
- *Living in Time: Chinese Contemporary Art Exhibition*, group exhibition, Hamburger Bahnhof, Berlin.
- Begins collaboration *The Way of Chopsticks* with husband Song Dong. This is a way to anchor family life amidst the increasing demands of the artists' international careers.

2002

- Participates in *1st Guangzhou Triennial, 2nd Fukuoka Asian Art Triennale* and *4th Gwangju Biennale*.
- Creates *Portable City: Shanghai* and *Portable Shopping Mall* (pp. 76–77).
- Prompted by the 9/11 terrorist attacks in New York and Washington she initiates an ongoing project *International Flight* creating airplanes to prompt viewers in different locales to consider the pleasures and anxieties of air travel.
- Birth of daughter with Song Dong, Song ErRui.

2003

- *Sars Times: Song Dong and Yin Xiuzhen*, Ise Foundation, New York.
- *Home and Away: Crossing Cultures on the Pacific Rim*, group exhibition, Vancouver Art Gallery, Canada.
- *Time After Time: Asia and Our Moment*, group exhibition, Yerba Buena Center for the Arts, San Francisco.
- *How Latitudes Become Forms: Art in a Global Age*, group exhibition, Walker Art Center, Minneapolis, Minnesota, travelling to Kiasma Museum for Contemporary Art, Helsinki; Contemporary Art Museum, Houston, Texas; Museo Rufino Tamayo, Mexico City; Museo de Arte Contemporáneo, Monterrey, Mexico; Art Gallery of Hamilton, Canada.

2004

- Participates in *26th São Paulo Biennale* and *14th Sydney Biennale*.

2005

- *The Wall: Reshaping Contemporary Chinese Art*, group exhibition, Albright-Knox Art Gallery, Buffalo, New York, travelling to Millenium Art Museum, Beijing.
- *On the Edge: Contemporary Chinese Artists Encounter the West*, group exhibition, Cantor Arts Center at Stanford University, California.

2006

- Creates the installation *International Airport: Terminal 1* (pp. 50–51).

'Every time I pick up my luggage it feels like carrying my home … It's like carrying your homesickness.'

- *Restroom*, Gallery at Redcat, Los Angeles.
- *Between Past and Future: New Photography and Video from China*, group exhibition, House of World Cultures, Berlin.
- *China Now*, group exhibition, Sammlung Essl, Vienna, travelling to Cobra Museum Voor Moderne Kunst, Amstelveen, Netherlands.

2007

- *Weapon* (2003) and new work *Collective Subconscious* (pp. 52–55) included in *52nd Venice Biennale*.
- *Global Feminisms*, group exhibition, Brooklyn Museum, New York.

2008

- *Yin Xiuzhen: Introspective Cavity*, Ullens Center for Contemporary Art, Beijing, marks the start of ongoing *Cavity Series* – large-scale, hollow, enterable installations of various organs.
- *All Inclusive: A Tourist World*, group exhibition, Schirn Kunsthalle, Frankfurt.
- *Unbearable Warmth* and *Flying Machine* included in *Trans Local Motion: 7th Shanghai Biennale*, Shanghai Art Museum.
- *Mahjong: Contemporary Chinese Art from the Sigg Collection*, group exhibition, Berkeley Art Museum, California, travelling to Peabody Essex Museum, Salem, Massachusetts, USA.
- *New World Order: Contemporary Installation Art and Photography from China*, group exhibition, Groninger Museum, Groninger, Netherlands.

2009

- *Sit in China*, group exhibition, Museum Angewandte Kunst, Frankfurt.
- Begins *Bookshelf* series (pp. 104–15).

2010

- *Project 92*, Museum of Modern Art, New York, features the new work *Portable City: Dunhuang* (pp. 40–41).
- *China in Four Seasons*, Govett-Brewster Art Gallery, New Plymouth. Debuted *Black Hole*.
- *Dreamlands*, group exhibition, Centre Pompidou, Paris.

2011

- Participates in *3rd Asian Art Biennial*, Taiwan and *4th Yokohama Triennale*.
- *Trans/Formation: Cities, Spaces and Times*, group exhibition, Alhóndiga, Bilbao.
- *Car Culture*, group exhibition, Zentrum für Kunst und Medien, Karlsruhe, Germany.

2012

- *Yin Xiuzhen*, Groninger Museum, Netherlands, travelling to Kunsthalle Düsseldorf. Features first European performance of *Washing River* and first showings of *Bookshelf No. 15* and *No. 16*, *Portable City: Xi'an*, *Portable City: Düsseldorf* and *Portable City: Groningen*.
- *Skyscraper: Art and Architecture Against Gravity*, group exhibition, Museum of Contemporary Art, Chicago.
- Participates in *1st Kiev International Biennale of Contemporary Art* and *9th Gwangju Biennale*.

2013

- *The Way of Chopsticks: Song Dong and Yin Xiuzhen*, Philadelphia Art Alliance. Collaboration with their daughter, Song ErRui.
- Participates in *5th Moscow Biennale of Contemporary Art*, debuting *Portable City: Moscow* and *1st Hangzhou International Fibre Art Triennial*.
- *Rewriting Landscape: Contemporary Art from China and India*, group exhibition, National Museum of Modern and Contemporary Art, Seoul.

2014

- *Yin Xiuzhen: Washing River*, Tasmania Museum and Art Gallery, Hobart.
- Participates in *1st International Biennale of Contemporary Art*, Columbia and *2nd Changwon Sculpture Biennale*, South Korea.
- *Yin Xiuzhen* published by Phaidon, only the second in their long-running series of contemporary art monographs to feature a female Asian artist.
- *Formalism*, group exhibition, Power Station of Art, Shanghai.

2015

- *Glasstress Goktika*, group exhibition, Fondazione Berengo, Venice.
- *Chinese Utopias Revisited: The Elephant*, group exhibition, Bozar, Brussels.
- *A New Dynasty – Created in China*, AROS Aarhus Kunstmuseum, Aarhus, Denmark.

2016

- *Slow Release*, Garage Museum of Contemporary Art, Moscow
- Begins *Blending Instrument* series (see p. 79).
- *Utopia and Beyond*, group exhibition, Castello Di Rivara Museum of Contemporary Art, Turin.

2017

- *Washing River*, group exhibition, Museum MACAN, Jakarta.
- *Art and China after 1989*, group exhibition, Solomon R. Guggenheim Museum, New York, travelling to San Francisco Museum of Modern Art.
- Participates in *Shenzhen & Hong Kong Bi-city Biennale of Urbanism/Architecture*, China.

2018

- *NOW: A Dialogue on Female Chinese Contemporary Artists*, group exhibition, Turner Contemporary, Margate, UK.
- *Ambush All Sides – Another Way of Intervention through Social Vision*, group exhibition, Art Museum of Sichuan Fine Arts Institute, Chongqing, China.

2019

- Begins *Wall Instrument* series.
- Participates in *May You Live in Interesting Times: 58th Venice Biennale.*
- *The Allure of Matter Material Art from China*, group exhibition, Los Angeles County Museum of Art, travelling to Smart Museum of Art, Chicago; Seattle Art Museum, Washington; Peabody Essex Museum, Salem.
- Participates in *Boundless – Hangzhou Triennial of Fiber Art*, Hangzhou, China.

2020

- *Sky Patch*, Centre for Heritage Arts and Textile, Hong Kong.
- Debuts *Ripple* series at *Harmony Power: The First Jinan International Biennale*, group exhibition, Shandong Art Museum and Jinan Art Museum.
- *"Global(e) Resistance" A Study of Contemporary Strategies of Resistance*, group exhibition, Centre Pompidou, Paris.
- *Listen to Your Eyes*, group exhibition, Museum Voorlinden, Wassenaar, Netherlands.

2021

- *Nine Tiered Pagoda: Spatial and Visual Magic*, group exhibition, Pingshan Art Museum, Shenzhen.

2022

- Participates in *The 7th Guangzhou Triennial: Symphony of All The Changes*, Guangdong Museum of Art, Guangzhou, China.
- *TRAIN. ZUG. TRENO. TREN.* group exhibition, mudac – Museum of Contemporary Design and Applied Arts, Lausanne, Switzerland.
- *Stepping Out! Female Identities in Chinese Contemporary Art*, group exhibition, Lillehammer Art Museum, Norway, travelling to Kunstforeningen GLSTRAND, Copenhagen; Museum der Moderne Salzburg, Austria.

2023

- Participates in *Time Gravity – 2023 Chengdu Biennale*, China.
- *Annealling*, Shanghai Museum of Glass.
- *Familiarly Known is Not Properly Known: Viewing in Everyday Vision*, group exhibition, Guangdong Museum of Art, Guangzhou, China.

2024

- *Piercing the Sky*, Power Station of Art, Shanghai.
- *Connecting Bodies: Asian Women Artists*, group exhibition, National Museum of Modern and Contemporary Art, Seoul.
- *Grande Ville*, group exhibition, Magasins Généraux, Paris.

2025

- *Metamorphosis: Chinese Memory and Displacement*, group exhibition, China Institute of America, New York.
- *Fluxus, by Chance*, group exhibition, West Bund Museum, Shanghai.
- *Ten/10: 10th Anniversary Special Exhibition of MOCA Yinchuan*, group exhibition, MOCA Yinchuan, China.

2026

- *Heart to Heart*, Hayward Gallery, London.

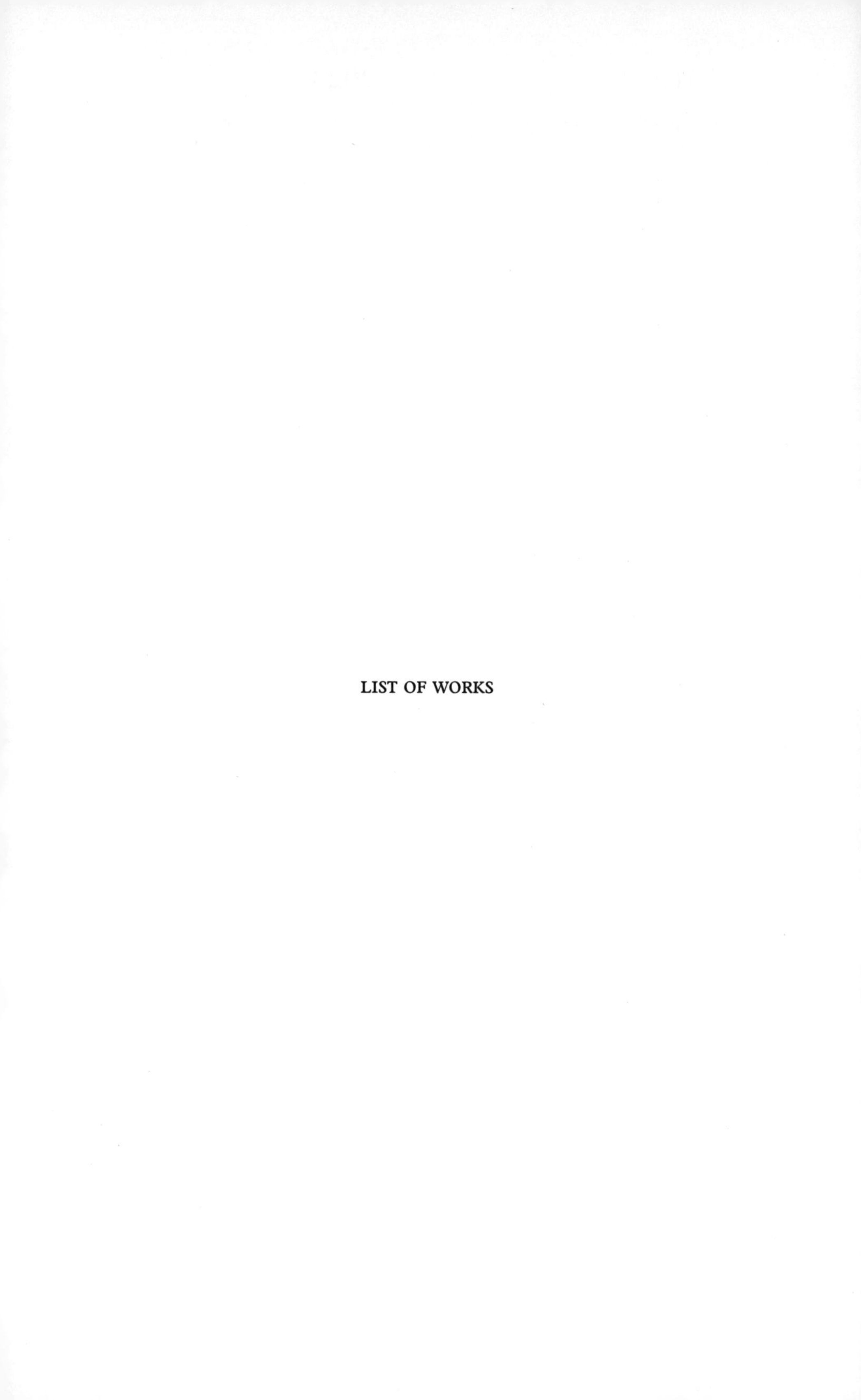

LIST OF WORKS

All works are courtesy
of the artist and Beijing
Commune unless stated
otherwise. Dimensions are
given in centimetres, height
before width and depth.

EXHIBITED WORKS
- *Dress Box*, 1995
  Wooden trunk lined
  with paper, clothes,
  cement, bronze plaque,
  and single-channel
  VHS tape transferred to
  digital video (colour,
  silent)
  Overall (open):
  72 × 67.5 × 44.5
  Overall (closed):
  38 × 67.5 × 44.5
  Duration: 21 min. 31 sec.
  M+ Sigg Collection,
  Hong Kong. By donation.
  p. 95

- *My Clothes*, 1995/2021
  32 colour photographs
  Each 53.3 × 80
  pp. 96–97

- *Washing River*, 1995
  4 colour photographs
  Each 50 × 90
  pp. 56–57

- *Washing River*, 1995
  Video
  Duration: 15 min. 35 sec.
  Betsy Damon Archive:
  Keepers of the Waters
  (Chengdu and Lhasa).
  Courtesy of Betsy Damon
  and Asia Art Archive.

- *Living Water*, 1996
  C-Print
  50 × 90
  pp. 58–59

- *Shoes with Butter*, 1996
  C-Print
  50 × 90
  pp. 60, 62–63

- *Ruined City*, 1996
  Cement powder,
  furniture, tiles
  Dimensions variable
  pp. 65–69

- *Beijing Opera*, 2001
  Digital print on synthetic
  silk canvas, stools,
  folding chairs, sound
  Dimensions variable
  pp. 70–75

- *International Flight*, 2002
  Steel frames, used clothes
  Two parts, each
  600 × 700 × 150
  pp. 48–49

- *Portable Shopping Mall*,
  2002
  Suitcase, plastic toys,
  lights, poster, acrylic sign
  Overall (open)
  100 × 63 × 160
  Overall (closed)
  60 × 40 × 50
  pp. 76–77

- *Portable City: New York*,
  2003
  Suitcase, used clothes,
  light, map, magnifying
  glass, sound
  150 × 82 × 92
  pp. 44–45

- *Portable City: Shenzhen*,
  2003
  Suitcase, used clothes,
  light, map, magnifying
  glass, sound
  143 × 97 × 74
  pp. 36–37

- *Collective Subconscious
  (Blue)*, 2007
  Minibus, stainless steel,
  used clothes, stools,
  music
  140 × 190 × 1420
  pp. 52–55

- *Bookshelf No. 1*, 2009
  Used clothes, wood
  226 × 126 × 43
  Courtesy of the artist
  and Pace Gallery
  pp. 106–07

- *Bookshelf No. 5*, 2009–13
  Used clothes, wood
  165.5 × 96 × 26
  Courtesy of Y.D.C.
  p. 107

- *Bookshelf No. 13*, 2009–13
  Used clothes, wood
  140 × 90 × 30
  Courtesy of the artist
  and Pace Gallery
  pp. 110–11

- *Bookshelf No. 17*, 2009–13
  Used clothes, wood
  127.5 × 85 × 29.5
  Courtesy of the artist
  and Pace Gallery
  pp. 112–13

- *Bookshelf No. 24*, 2009–13
  Used clothes, wood
  102 × 56 × 23
  pp. 114–115

- *Portable City: Melbourne*,
  2009
  Suitcase, used clothes,
  light, map, magnifying
  glass, sound
  153 × 87 × 80

- *Portable City: Dunhuang*,
  2010
  Suitcase, used clothes,
  light, map, magnifying
  glass, sound
  147 × 87 × 58
  pp. 40–41

- *One Sentence No. 24*, 2011
  Stainless steel, used
  clothes
  42.8 × 4.5
  p. 101

- *One Sentence No. 30*, 2011
  Stainless steel, used
  clothes
  36.8 × 4.5
  p. 100

- *One Sentence No. 31*, 2011
  Stainless steel, used
  clothes
  38.1 × 4.5
  p. 102

- *One Sentence No. 63*, 2011
  Stainless steel, used
  clothes
  28.8 × 4.5
  p. 103

137

- *Bookshelf No. 10*, 2012–13
  Used clothes, wood
  193 × 106 × 30
  Courtesy of the artist and
  Pace Gallery
  pp. 108–09, 140

- *Bookshelf for Song ErRui:
  Study Hard*, 2013
  Used clothes, wood
  130 × 100 × 30
  Courtesy of the artist and
  Song ErRui
  pp. 104–05

- *Portable City: Seoul*, 2013
  Suitcase, used clothes,
  light, map, magnifying
  glass, sound
  160 × 85 × 71
  pp. 46–47

- *Portable City: Hamburg*,
  2014
  Suitcase, used clothes,
  light, map, magnifying
  glass, sound
  128 × 81 × 91
  pp. 34–35

- *Portable City: Brussels*,
  2015
  Suitcase, used clothes,
  light, map, magnifying
  glass, sound
  150 × 86 × 66
  pp. 42–43

- *Blending Instrument
  – Knife No. 3*, 2016
  Porcelain, knife
  31 × 41 × 5.5
  pp. 80–81

- *Blending Instrument
  – Mirror No. 4*, 2017
  Porcelain, mirror
  40.5 × 30.5 × 3.5

- *Blending Instrument
  – Ruler No. 3*, 2017
  Porcelain, ruler
  90 × 40 × 3.5
  p. 79

- *Wall Instrument No. 17*,
  2018–19
  Porcelain, used clothes
  98 × 98 × 6
  Courtesy of Y.D.C.
  pp. 86–87

- *Wall Instrument No. 19*,
  2018–19
  Porcelain, used clothes
  92 × 92 × 11
  pp. 86, 87, 142

- *Wall Instrument
  – The Surging Waves
  Chronicles Vol. 7*, 2021–22
  Porcelain, used clothes
  98 × 90 × 11
  pp. 84–85

- *Ripple Stress Series I
  – No. 10*, 2021–23
  Glass, fruits
  83 × 82 × 14
  pp. 88–91

- *Ripple Stress Series I
  – No. 11*, 2021–23
  Glass, fruits
  105 × 105 × 17
  pp. 92–93, 139

- *Skin of Oblivion*, 2024–25
  Porcelain, used clothes
  123.5 × 96 × 8
  pp. 82–83

- *A Heart to Heart*, 2025
  Steel frames, used clothes
  760 × 800 × 395
  pp. 124–28

- *International Airport:
  Terminal 2*, 2025
  Used clothes, wood,
  airport trolleys, bench
  Dimensions variable

- *Portable City: London*,
  2025
  Suitcase, used clothes,
  light, map, magnifying
  glass, sound
  152 × 98 × 78
  pp. 38–39

ADDITIONAL WORKS
- *The Doors*, 1995
  72 photographs,
  36 wooden blocks
  9 × 13 × 5 each
  p. 11

- *Tree Harp*, 1995
  Photograph
  120 × 180
  p. 11

- *Portable City: Beijing*
  Suitcase, used clothes,
  light, map, magnifying
  glass, sound
  2001
  148 × 88 × 30
  p. 14

- *International Airport:
  Terminal 1*, 2006
  Used clothes, wood,
  airport trolleys, barriers
  Dimensions variable
  pp. 50–51

- *Introspective Cavity*, 2008
  Steel frames, used
  clothes, mirrors
  1500 × 900 × 435
  pp. 116–19

- *Thought*, 2009
  Steel frames, used clothes
  340 × 510 × 370
  pp. 120–23

PHOTOGRAPHIC CREDITS
All works of art
© Yin Xiuzhen
All images courtesy of the
artist and Beijing Commune

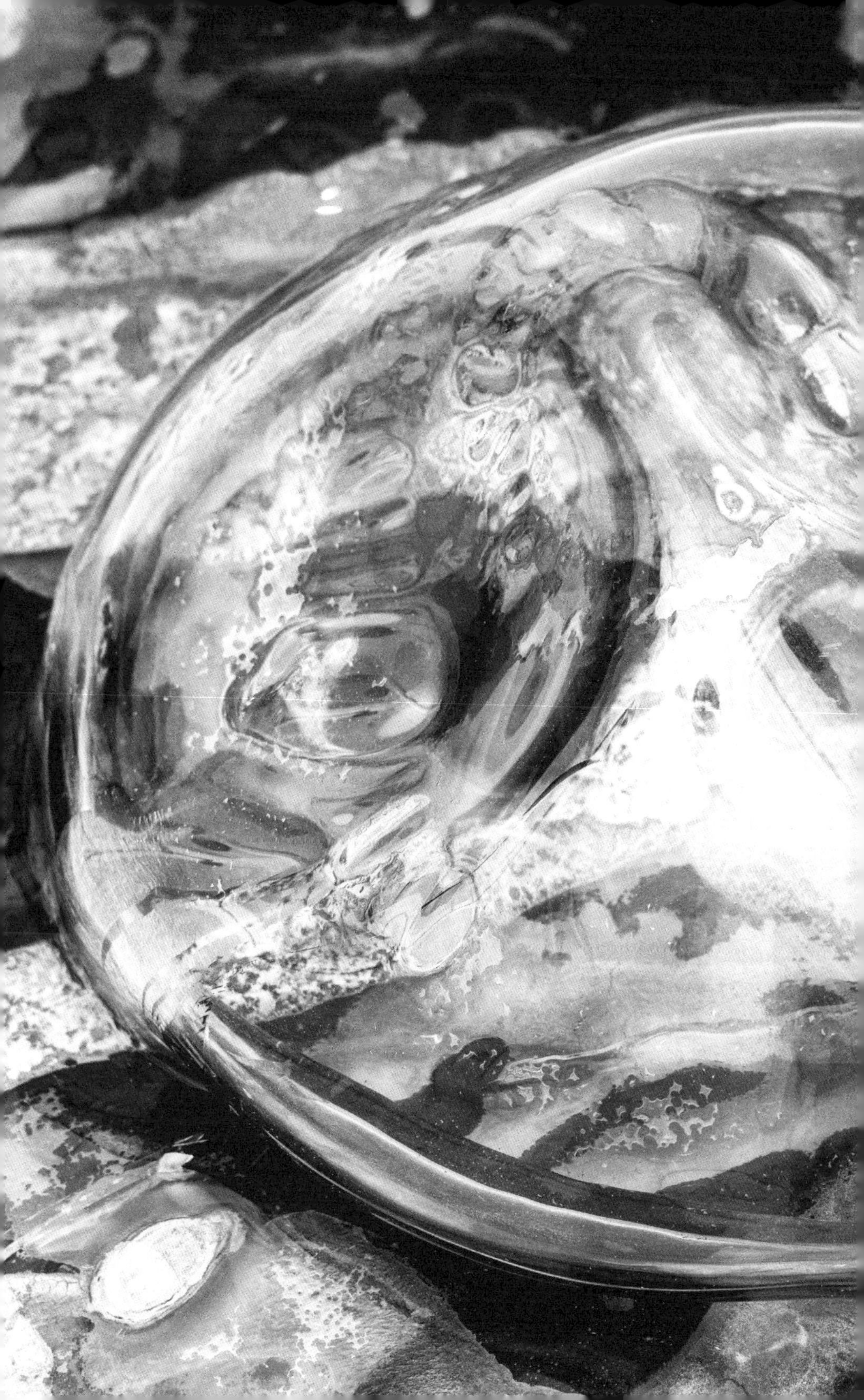

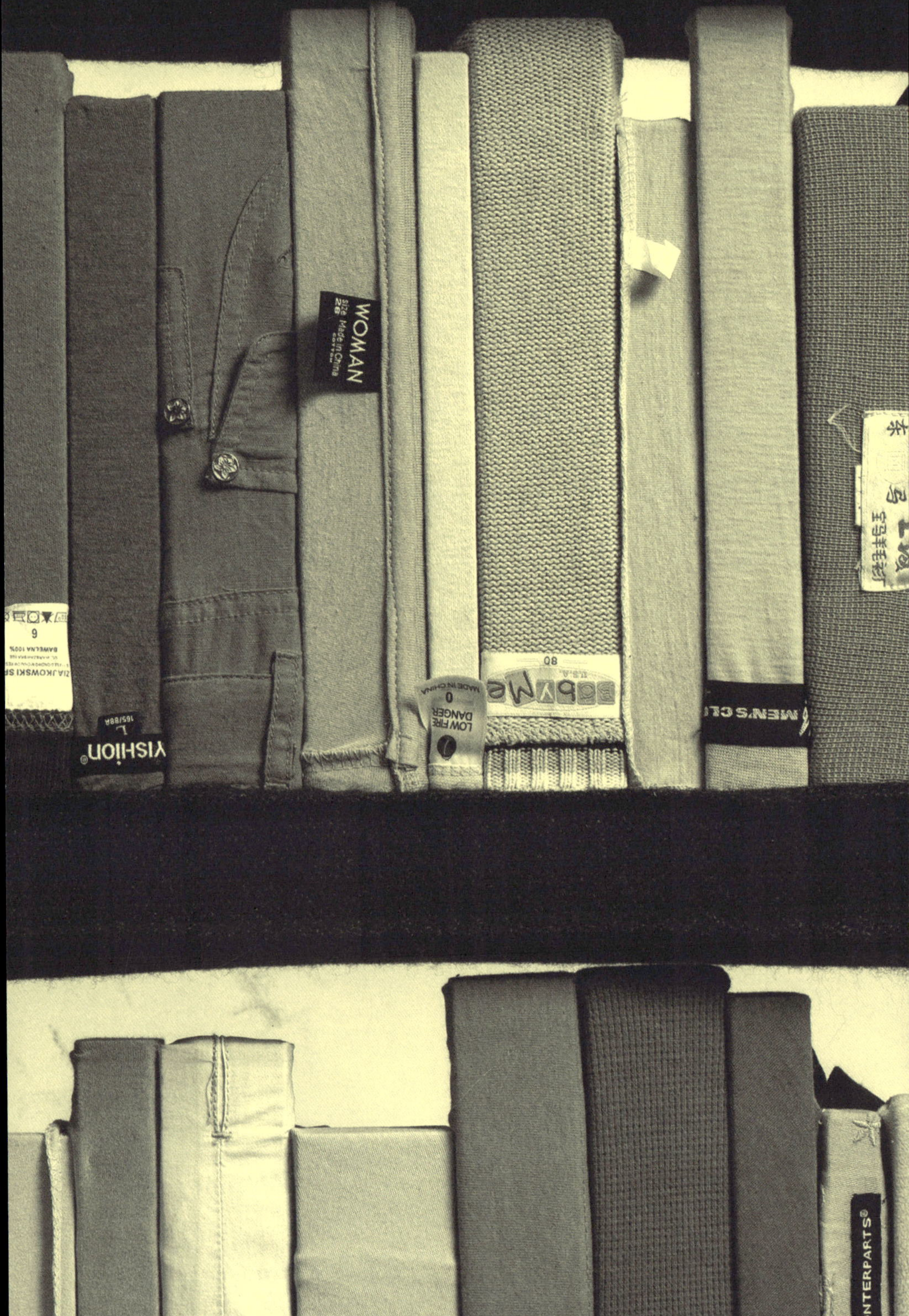

WOMAN
size 26
Made in China
YISHION
LOW FIRE
DANGER
MADE IN CHINA
MEN'S CL
COUNTERPARTS

ACKNOWLEDGEMENTS

Yin Xiuzhen: Heart to Heart was realised with generous support provided by the Huo Family Foundation. We are also grateful for key support from Beijing Commune, Eleanor and Francis Shen, and Max and Monique Burger and the TOY family.

LENDERS TO THE EXHIBITION
- Betsy Damon Archive: Keepers of the Waters (Chengdu and Lhasa). Courtesy of Betsy Damon and Asia Art Archive
- M+ Sigg Collection, Hong Kong. By donation
- Pace Gallery
- Y.D.C.
- Yin Xiuzhen and Beijing Commune
- Yin Xiuzhen and Song ErRui

EXHIBITION CREDITS

Yung Ma,
   Senior Curator
Hannah Martin and Thomas Sutton,
   Assistant Curator
Felix Choong,
   Curatorial Assistant
Archie Bell,
   Installation Manager
Vivienne Joncourt
and Sophie Ridsdale-Smith,
   Registrars
Mary Richards,
   Publisher
Juliane Heynert,
   Senior Installation Manager
Matt Arthurs and Philip Gardner,
   Hayward Installation Technicians
Ben Allchurch, Andy Craig,
Isabel Ferreira, Tom Matthews,
Adam Mc Gowan and Joe Richards,
   Freelance Installation Technicians
Kate Sullivan,
   Deputy Director, Visual Arts
Alison Maun,
   Indemnity Coordinator
Ellen Duffy,
   Administration and Events Coordinator
Maria Peña,
   Visual Arts Administrator
Marcia Ceppo,
   Operations and Logistics Manager
Jules Denton,
   Operations Administrator
Nancy Bryan,
   Librarian
Leonie Warner,
   Senior Visitor Experience Manager
Kate Ford, Jack Rooney
and Malini Stevenson,
   Duty Managers

Zijing Rie Ye,
   Seamstress
Jennifer Ubenyi,
   Curatorial Intern
Fatima Sheriff,
   Bring Out Potential Placement

We are grateful to all our collaborators across Southbank Centre, without whom this exhibition would not have been possible. In particular, we would like to acknowledge the contributions of our colleagues in Southbank Centre's Creative Learning, Design, Development, Digital, Health and Safety, Marketing, Press and Retail teams.

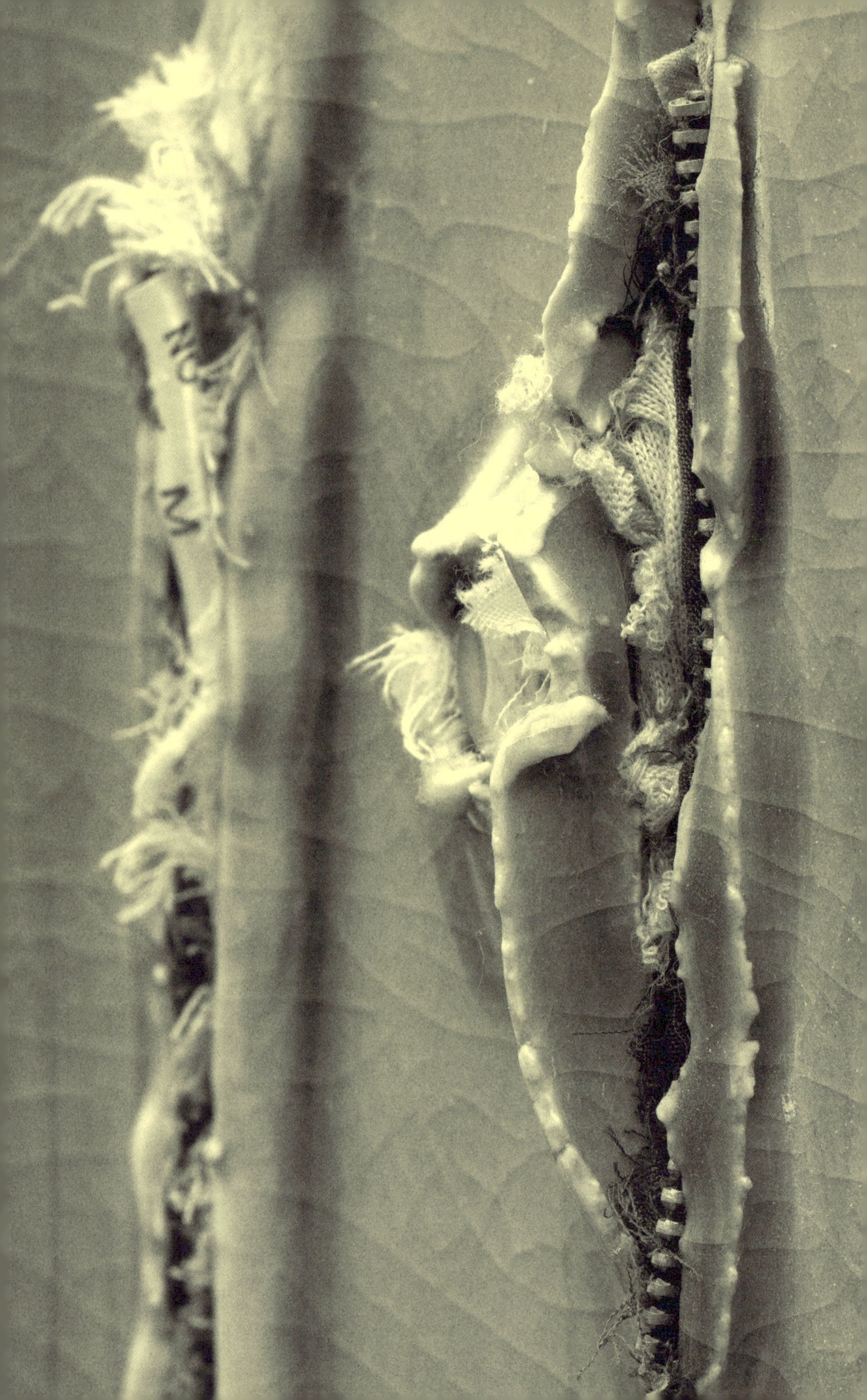

Published on the occasion of the exhibition
Yin Xiuzhen: Heart to Heart
Hayward Gallery, London
17 February – 3 May 2026

Curated by
    Yung Ma
Assistant Curator
    Hannah Martin and Thomas Sutton
Curatorial Assistant
    Felix Choong

Yin Xiuzhen: Heart to Heart was realised
with generous support provided by
the Huo Family Foundation. We are also
grateful for key support from Beijing
Commune, Eleanor and Francis Shen,
and Max and Monique Burger and the
TOY family.

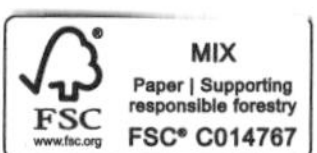

Published in 2026 by
    Hayward Gallery Publishing
    Southbank Centre
    Belvedere Road
    London SE1 8XX
    www.southbankcentre.co.uk

Hayward Publisher
    Mary Richards
Catalogue designed by
    In the shade of a tree

Printed in Belgium on paper from
sustainable forests

A catalogue record for this book is available
from the British Library

ISBN 978-1-85332-386-7

143

This catalogue is not intended to be used
for authentication or related purposes.
The Southbank Board Limited accepts no
liability for any errors or omissions that
the catalogue may inadvertently contain.

Distributed in North, Central
and South America by
    ARTBOOK | D.A.P.
    75 Broad Street, Suite 630
    New York, NY 10004
    tel: +1 212 627 1999
    www.artbook.com

Distributed in the rest of the world by
    Thames & Hudson Ltd
    6–24 Britannia St
    London WC1X 9JD
    www.thamesandhudson.com

INTERART S.A.R.L. (GPSR)
    19 rue Charles Auray
    93500 Pantin
    Paris, France
    http://www.interart.fr/
    productsafety@thameshudson.co.uk

Cover
Collective Subconscious (Blue), 2007
(detail)

Notes on Contributors
LYDIA YEE is a freelance curator and
writer. She was formerly Chief
Curator at the Whitechapel Gallery and
Curator at the Barbican Art Gallery,
where she organised numerous critically
acclaimed exhibitions of modern
and contemporary art.

YUNG MA is Senior Curator at the
Hayward Gallery, London. Before
joining the Hayward, he held key
curatorial positions at institutions
including the Centre Pompidou
in Paris, where he was Curator in
the Contemporary and Prospective
Creation Department, and the
M+ Museum in Hong Kong, where
he was Curator of Visual Art.

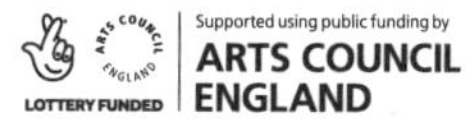

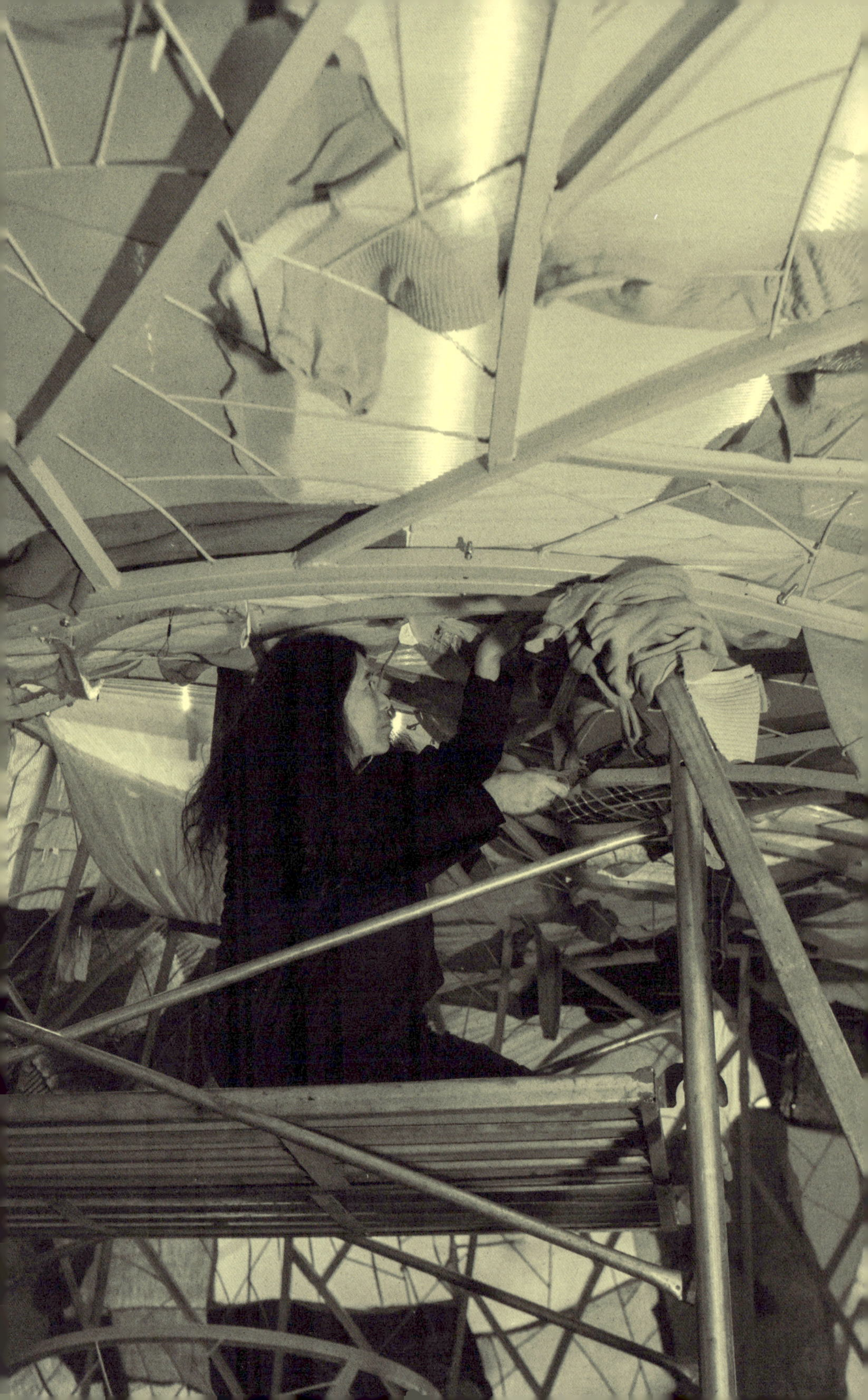

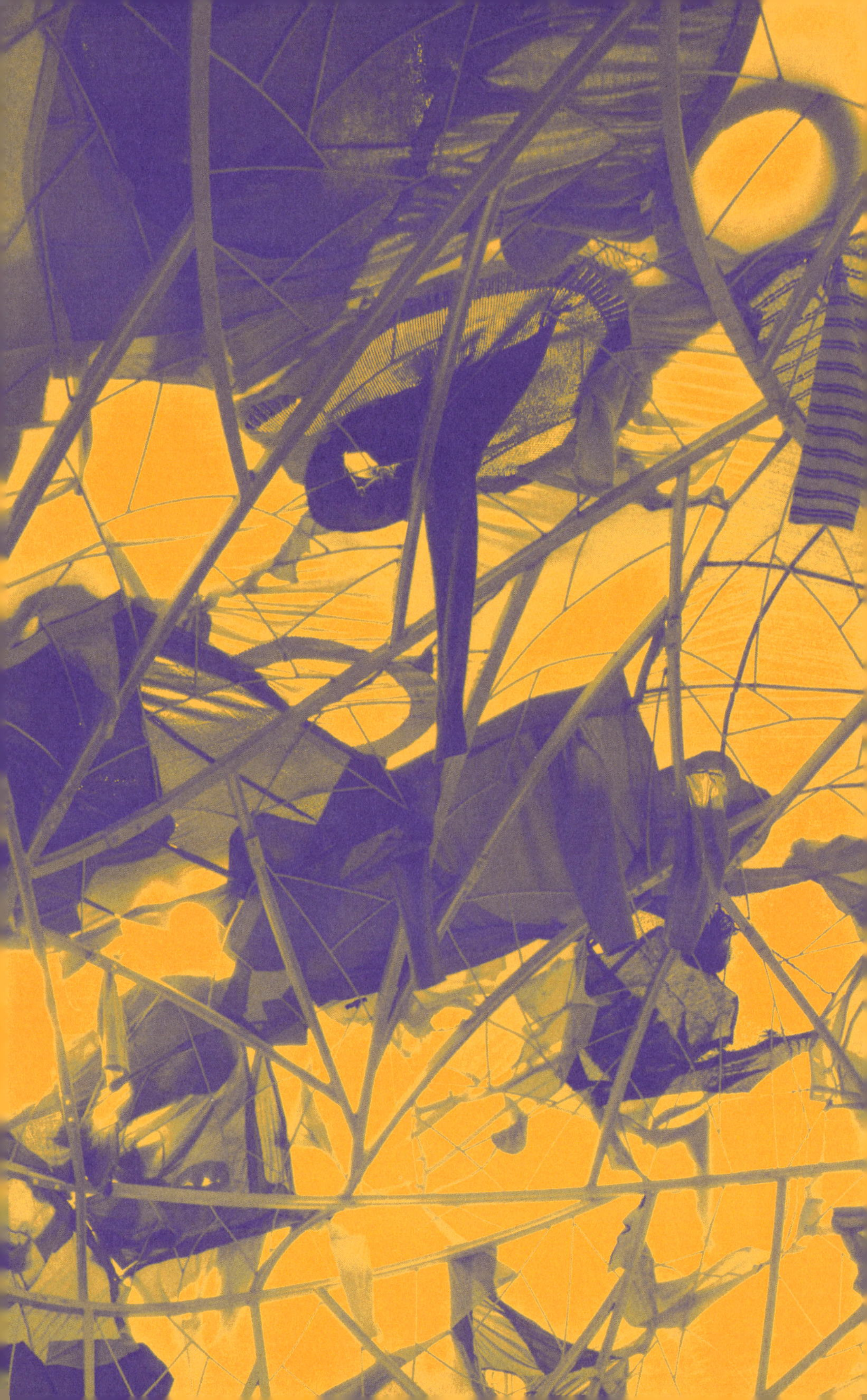